RALLYING

21 YEARS OF WORLD CHAMPIONSHIPS

RALLYING

21 YEARS OF WORLD CHAMPIONSHIPS

DAVID AND AMANDA CAMPBELL

Introduction by COLIN McRAE

Weidenfeld & Nicolson, London

The authors would particularly like to thank the following for all their help and encouragement. Chris and Jo Forster, Sue Winwood, Chrissie Chorley, Rick Smith, Colin Wilson, Andy Pope, Mike Greasley, Bob (Mate) McCaffery, Adam at Colin Taylor Productions, Hugh Bishop, everyone at *Motoring News*, Michèle Arron, Melvyn Powell and Chris Huntley at Prodrive who between them coralled Colin McRae into a corner. And not least all the drivers across the world who have thrilled, amused, exasperated and confounded us, especially Britain's first World Champion (one day, we hope), Colin McRae.

First published in 1995 by
George Weidenfeld & Nicolson Ltd
Orion House
5 Upper St Martin's Lane
London WC2H 9EA

A product of FORSTER Books
Designed by Bob Bickerton

British Library Cataloguing-in-Publication Ltd
A catalogue record for this book is available from the British Library

ISBN 0-297-83527-0

Printed in Italy

Contents

*Previous page:
Attilio Bettega –
the Italian hero
who became a
victim of Corsican
roads.*

Introduction

Welcome to the history of the World Rally Championship and I'm really happy to contribute to this authoritative work about the sport. Although I now consider myself a championship regular, browsing through the book highlights the huge impact drivers such as Hannu Mikkola, Walter Röhrl and Ari Vatanen have made on the sport. Contemporaries such as Juha Kankkunen, Didier Auriol and Carlos Sainz are all world champions and regular winners; clearly my ambition is to achieve that level of performance.

Even in my relatively short world championship career I am sure people are now remembering my rallies for the right reasons, and occasions like the 1000 Lakes in 1992 can be put down to the 'learning curve'. I finished 1994 on a high, winning the RAC Rally after several years of frustration on my home event. The general public and the media must have been wondering whether Roger Clark's victories were sacred! The atmosphere in Chester that Wednesday afternoon was magic. It was an unforgettable day, as was the day of my victory in New Zealand in 1993 – I had arrived. That event had people reaching for the record books, as it was Subaru's and my own first victory in the championship, and there was Roger Clark's name again – he was the last Briton to win a rally at this level. I am glad to see it is all recorded in this book and you can read how I did it twice in New Zealand, once in Britain and nearly did it in Sweden.

How 'I' did it, should read how 'we' did it. Derek Ringer has seen all the highs and lows of the McRae world championship experience and has not complained yet! Prodrive, who run the 555 Subaru World Rally Team, and Subaru must also share the credit for what has been achieved. They gave me the opportunity to compete at this level and have given great guidance, sticking with me when others could easily have cried enough. The best possible way to repay these supporters, my family and the rally fans I have met around the world is to take that elusive first title by a British driver. It is a realistic goal but there is no short cut to gaining experience and it is pretty competitive at the sharp end with rallies being won by seconds after nearly 500 kilometres (310 miles).

Many great drivers have graced the stages since 1973 and the rally car is as dynamic as it's ever been in any era of the sport. Enjoy reading about the inspirational performances since the beginning of the series in what I believe is the most challenging of motor sports.

COLIN McRAE

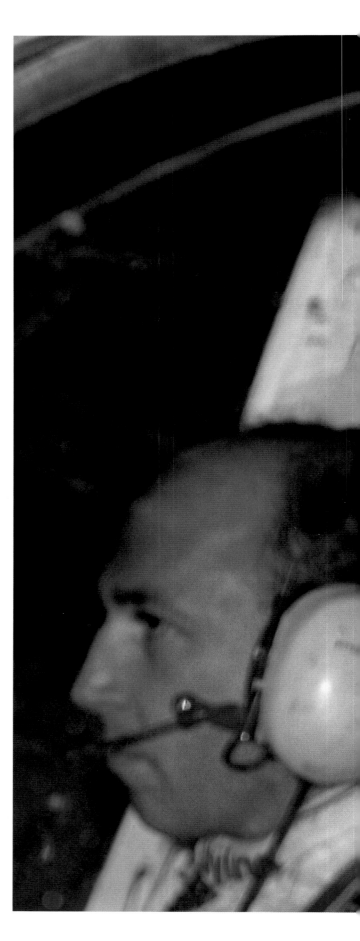

*Colin McRae,
Britain's hope for
the world title.*

Left: Colin McRae
at the wheel of his
Subaru.

Following page:
One of the most
successful rally
drivers to date,
Juha Kankkunen
hurtles through the
dramatic Swedish
countryside in his
powerful Peugeot
205 T16.

1

Prologue

Rallying as it is today – a multi-million pound sport, high technology, fierce battles over TV rights, sponsorship and highly paid drivers.

Collectively, jaws around the bar fell to the floor. The juke-box blaring out 'Mustang Sally' seemed to stop as the mechnics dancing on the tables froze in disbelief. 'Yeah, it's true,' slurred a journalist, slightly the worse for wear. 'I have it on good authority that Carlos Sainz is on £2 million a year. More than that Damon Hill – twice as much!' Colin McRae, the golden boy who was just in the throes of celebrating his third Rally of New Zealand win, rolled his eyes. 'Aye, he's doin' alright.'

Hardly a blip. The music wound up again, and the celebrations resumed.

That small moment of time in Auckland in July 1995 told you practically everything you ever needed to know about world championship rallying as it is today. Yes, the traditional celebrations after each rally are still as boisterous and good-humoured as ever. Normally, in a hotel bar the public can wander in and join the fun with the superstars who have just finished the event. No form of sport is as accessible, or as much fun!

But rallying in the nineties is a serious game. The budgets are huge – £50 million or more per team – the risks are great, and the commercial interests are frightening.

The battle for commercial advantage is almost as fraught as that on the special stages. Teams of PR people crash out information, herd journalists from one place to another, and fight for attention from radio and TV crews in an effort to score more publicity for their sponsors.

There is as much talk about market segments, demographic profiles and column inches as tyre choice, power outputs and drive shafts.

By far the biggest battle of 1994 was not that between Carlos Sainz and Didier Auriol as they vied for the World Drivers' Championship. Rather it was that between the owners of TV rights, the FIA and the teams themselves over how best to get more television coverage for their commercial backers.

Still, without the big budgets of 555, Castrol, Toyota, Marlboro, Subaru, Repsol, Mitsubishi, Ford and Mobil, who would pay for all this fun?

For thankfully, that's what rallying is still all about, commercial benefits or not, and there's nothing like a rally to pull the crowds.

'Did y'know, Colin is one of Britain's highest paid sportsmen?' came a cry after the Carlos bombshell. McRae rolled his eyes again – his round!

Previous page: Carlos Sainz, seen here on the Tour de Corse, one of the fastest rallies in the world, is world champion- ship rallying's highest paid driver at over £2 million – more than many Formula One drivers.

The media circus hits town. Capturing audience attention through television has become the Holy Grail of the money men.

2

The Early Days

The sixties was a magical decade, not just for the people with lots of hair who liked wearing plastic boots, but also for rallying. The sport represented all the freedoms that the decade espoused.

Rallying's party started a long time before the Commission Sportive Internationale decided to mould its disparate rounds into a world championship in 1973.

Indeed, most of the early challengers for those championship honours were already scarred from earlier battles.

The sixties was a magical decade, not just for people with lots of hair who liked wearing long plastic boots, but also for rallying. The sport represented all the freedoms that the decade espoused. It was the decade of the Flying Finns and the even more Flying Minis, the little red car that epitomized the sixties both on and off the roads.

Classic rally combinations were at their peak: Erik Carlsson in a succession of Saabs, Pat Moss in the big Austin Healey and then a Saab, Tom Trana and Gunnar Andersson in Volvos, Harry Kallstrom in the Lancia Fulvia and of course Timo Mäkinen, Rauno Aaltonen and Paddy Hopkirk in Mini Coopers.

There was the tortoise of Saab and the hare of BMC's Mini Cooper. The former had been winning for years, and would carry on winning into the eighties with Stig Blomqvist and the 99 Turbo (albeit on just the one occasion), the latter a young whippersnapper of a car that sped onto the rally scene and won events as diverse as the 1000 Lakes, Acropolis and Monte Carlo rallies, before being retired from world championship duty at the end of 1968.

Stuart Turner joined BMC and introduced a professionalism to the servicing and practising and a wiliness that belied his youth and lack of managerial experience – when he joined BMC it was straight from the Verglas desk at *Motoring News* and he was just 27!

Nonetheless, he introduced the use of racing tyres on tarmac, ice-notes for rallies such as Monte Carlo and the most ruthless interpretation of rallying directives the sport had ever seen, although he always appeared to stay just on the right side of the fence. Most importantly, he introduced the first of the Flying Finns to a British car, signing Rauno Aaltonen and Timo Mäkinen in an unprecedented step which brought momentous success. Aaltonen was something of a coup, *Motoring News* observing him at work: 'All the time Rauno was co-ordinating brake, accelerator, clutch and gear-lever as deftly as Sandy Macpherson plays his theatre organ.' Thirty years on, the name of Macpherson and his organ might cause a few blank looks but even then Aaltonen was a legend.

Although the Saab would later be capable of 170 bhp in 96 V4 form, in the sixties the 96 had a maximum output of 80 bhp, the 1275cc Cooper S could manage 100 bhp – peanuts these days, but remarkable for just 3 metres (10 feet) of car back in 1964.

Not everyone was a fan of the flying box, notable amongst the less enthusiastic being the French organizers of the Monte Carlo Rally in 1966. Everyone tells the tale, to the extent that it has now reached the proportion of rally legend, but it is so archetypical of both the intransigence of the organizers at the Monte Carlo Rally and the resourcefulness of Turner that an opportunity to retell in précis form shouldn't be missed.

Entered in Group One for the first time, which amongst other regulations restricted the engine size, the whole of the French sporting press and the organizers were horror-struck to find that even in neutered form the ghastly British boxes were once again trouncing all-comers on their rally. When at the rally finish, Minis took the first three places with Roger Clark in fourth spot in a Lotus Cortina, you could almost hear the outpouring of

Gallic apoplexy – they must be cheating, after all, how else would they have been quicker than the mighty Porsche or our gallant Citroens uphill?

Never ones to worry about the opinion of the rest of the world, the good folk at the AC de Monaco, stripped the Minis. That they could find nothing illegal – for instance the Group Two engine they were convinced they would find in the Group One car – left them undaunted and then, aha! The lights! BMC and Ford had fitted a halogen bulb in their headlights – how dare they!

That was it, an excuse to disqualify all the cars down to the Citroen of Pauli Toivonen. In 1966 the incident was outrageous, taken up by every British newspaper and sparking off huge anti–French feeling. In retrospect, although nothing quite as scandalous has happened since, the Monte Carlo Rally has continued to tread its own path to a lesser and greater degree. The use of riot police to quell angry competitors in 1973 was a further instance, and Michele Mouton's crash when a stage was closed earlier than scheduled another ...

Homologation was a bit of a grey area at that time, with all sorts of brass–necked shenanigans going across the teams, but it all boiled down to the fact that there was really no method in place in those days of verifying production numbers, and so a car might appear with all the correct papers intact but preceding the roll of the production line by some weeks! Under these conditions, often some weird and wonderful devices appeared on rally cars, in the case of post-1964 Minis a very useful little valve which counteracted the very undesirable – in a rally – effects of hydrolastic suspension!

If the performances of the Cooper Ss on the stages broke new ground, so did the method of servicing the little cars – by rolling them on their sides – but on more than one occasion a Mini left the service area looking a little more battered than it had when it arrived!

The exploits of the drivers were not to be outdone by tales of the cars. Notable was Erik Carlsson, a big chap who found his Saab was going nowhere when it became entrenched in clinging African mud on the 1964 Safari Rally, the only course of action being to roll it over and over until it was clear!

By the sixties rallying had changed from a preserve of the amateur to a more serious undertaking as manufacturers began to realize the marketing implications of their rally successes. The Scandinavians were professionals, wage packets became heavier and heavier as the top drivers found themselves in demand from the top teams of the day: BMC, Saab, Ford, Rootes and later Lancia.

Practice for rallies began to take on a modern shape, with stages undertaken not just once or twice when the drivers were passing but for weeks in advance, crews making their own pace-notes to suit each car's performance and service halts becoming ever more organized and well-manned, with a greater and greater choice of tyres available – 12 in all for the 1968 Monte Carlo Rally.

While the first victory for the Cooper was the 1961 Tulip Rally just eight months after it was first homologated, and the Cooper S took the touring category of the 1963 Tour de France, the most successful period for the Mini spanned 1964 to 1967, when it took 24 major international victories including three wins on the 1000 Lakes with Timo Mäkinen and an Acropolis win for Paddy Hopkirk – a remarkable achievement considering the rough stages and the Mini's lack of ground clearance.

Saab and BMC battled for joint honours, with the Austin Healey at the opposite end of the BMC scale being as big and heavy and grand as the Mini was small, light and unassuming. Pat Moss took it to victory on the demanding 4830 kilometre (3000 mile) Liege Rally of 1960, Rauno Aaltonen in 1964.

The sixties was still the preserve of front-wheel drive, front-engined machinery, the Saab and Mini having the early and mid years almost all their own way until along came Lancia's Fulvia. First launched as a saloon in 1963, it was not an immediate success, too big and underpowered at 1100cc producing around 58 bhp. A 1300cc coupé followed in 1965, followed by the HF versions at 100+ bhp. The Mini Cooper S was still the car to beat, and although by 1968 it was reaching its sell-by date, Lancia found it a hard nut to crack, although Ove Andersson came within a hair's breadth of beating Rauno Aaltonen in the 1967 Monte Carlo Rally, losing by just 13 seconds. It wasn't until the final year

of the decade that the Fulvia became a winner, with first the 1.3 HF and subsequently the 1.6 coming good. For Cesare Fiorio it was just as well. In 1969 he had signed practically every top driver available in order to make his car victorious, and even in the sixties that represented a considerable investment in terms of wages to secure the services of Ove Andersson, Tony Fall, Simo Lampinen, Sandro Munari, Pat Moss, Hannu Mikkola and Harry Kallstrom.

It was Tony Fall who captured the first Fulvia laurels, winning in Portugal, but the wild-looking Harry Kallstrom who really got the best from it, winning the RAC Rally, San Remo, Spain and a curious but arduous marathon event at the Nürburgring which lasted for 84 hours. The latter, Kallstrom didn't achieve on his own, even the Swedish Fulvia master needing help from Tony Fall and Sergio Barbasio. Kallstrom became European champion and the Fulvia had inherited the crown from the Mini Cooper S to take into the next decade.

Sweden's Harry Kallstrom gave the Lancia Fulvia six world-class wins.

Following page: Jean-Pierre Nicolas on his way to clinching the first World Championship for Renault Alpine in 1973.

3

The Golden Era

Ford Escorts, Renault Alpines and Lancias – the top cars of the day that are still remembered as the all-time great rally machines.

Growing up in France in the late sixties and early seventies was an ideal kindergarten for future rally stars. Is it any wonder that Didier Auriol and François Delecour were spawned from that age?

The Renault Alpine was all-conquering and its quartet of daring drivers Jean-Pierre Nicolas, Jean-Luc Therier, Bernard Darniche and Jean-Claude Andruet must have seemed like four dashing musketeers. Between the four drivers, they gave the Alpine A110 35 victories in world, European and French championship events, winning the International Championship for Makes in 1971 and again in the inaugural year of the world championship in 1973.

The rear-engined Alpine with its lightweight plastic body had an extremely good power to weight ratio, and with the weight firmly settled onto its driven wheels, only a Porsche could touch it as it went shooting up the alpine roads of Monte Carlo, Corsica or Austria. Coming down the other side was a different story however, with nothing more difficult to control downhill, especially if it was wet or icy.

Its championship-winning years were split when Lancia snatched a third possible title in 1972, out from under the nose of Alpine. The Fulvia, successful in 1300cc specification in the late sixties found its full potential once the 1600 engine had been developed and homologated. It was also the first car to boast a full sponsorship deal, competing in 1972 and beyond in the now familiar red and white of Marlboro. In rallying terms, it was a real coup, the first full commercial tie-in with an outside backer, and it set a precedent for the million-pound deals that bankroll the sport today. The Fulvia straddled the transition years between the sixties and seventies; in rallying terms a time when sporting coupès were supplanted by out and out racers and although it was still winning when the Renault Alpine was launched it looked at least a decade behind the design of the sexy French sportster.

The Italian car marked the last great successes for a front-engined, front-wheel-drive configuration, still capable of fine victories in 1972, notably in Monte Carlo, Sicily and Morocco, before being rendered obsolete by first the arrival of the Alpine and subsequently the arrival of Lancia's own successor, the Stratos.

The anarchic Monte Carlo of 1973, the first round of the first world championship proper, was the scene of Alpine domination, the first all-French victory since 1961, taking the top three places – Jean-Claude Andruet co-driven by 'Biche' (Michele Petit) winning, Ove Andersson with Jean Todt second, and Jean-Pierre Nicolas and Michel Vial in third place; then came the lonely Escort of Hannu Mikkola winning the touring car category in front of a further two Renault Alpines. As far as heralding in the new championship series, the event was an utter disaster with armed police called in to quell a riot by disgruntled competitors who had been excluded. The alarming situation arose on Burzet, the third of the common run's special stages. The stage had been blocked by snow several days prior to the rally, and despite the fact that no new snow had fallen, the wind was so strong the road couldn't be cleared. Crews waiting for the common run to start heard about the problem via ice-note crews who hadn't been able to get through and so it was assumed the rally would be re-routed, a simple option, since the stage looped back onto the road.

Leaving Monte Carlo crews believed that since they hadn't been informed of a re-route, the conditions on the Burzet stage must have changed for the better. Not so. A snow plough that had been sent in found that as soon as

Nicolas took third place in the 1973 Monte Carlo, the first round ever of a World Rally Championship. Renault Alpines took an historic 1–2–3 with Andruet leading home Andersson and Nicolas.

it had cleared a path through the stage, the wind was blowing snow back onto the road. Fifty crews managed to get through before a Capri spun and wedged itself between two snowbanks. The start marshals kept sending crews in, creating an horrific blockage.

The AC de Monaco decided that no extra time allowance would be announced and so all crews bottle-necked behind the Capri were officially excluded on the grounds that firstly they had failed to complete the stage and secondly they were OTL. This exclusion order covered almost 150 crews, many of whom had spent a fortune travelling to Monte Carlo in order to compete. There was uproar when the crews banded together and decided that if they weren't to be allowed to finish the rally, no-one would. They reasoned that while the thoughts of 150 private crews might be ignored, 50 teams including works crews would be more noticeable by their absence.

They decided to block the road into Digne and hold the crews until everyone was over their maximum lateness. Somehow the organizers got wind of the plan and alerted the police who sent vanloads of gendarmes down to stop everyone but surviving crews from getting through to the Digne road. The blockade was already in place by the time the police arrived and the works crews were forced to use their imagination to circumvent the problem. Timo Mäkinen led the way. He ran at the blockade in his Escort, veering off up a steep bank at the last moment, passing the massed lines of protesters.

Rauno Aaltonen took another approach, getting out of his car and walking around. Returning to his Datsun the Finn revved his engine, climbed a bank, burst through a hedge, rattled across a field and over a ditch to crash

through a hedge clear of both police and protesters. Like a scene from *Carry on Rallying* this route was adopted by other crews who found themselves having to dodge cars from the blockade who were determined to chase them into retreat.

Gerry Phillips writing in *Motoring News* about the incident happened upon a great story: 'A pair of women competitors were furious when they were prevented from continuing by police ... one of them decided to stand up to the pistol-waving gendarmes when the barricade was lifted to let another woman in a 2CV through. The woman driver stood in front of the car refusing to let it move until she was allowed to follow. Police started to threaten

Opposite: Jean-Pierre Nicolas, one of the greats of the early seventies. This page: Shekhar Mehta (top) jumps to victory in his Datsun 240Z on the Safari Rally in 1973. A young Markku Alèn (bottom) gets his career under way in an Escort on the 1973 RAC Rally.

and she shouted, "Don't you dare touch me." The other crews backed her up to a man and advanced themselves.' Wisely the police let her through.

The second round of the new circuit was almost as controversial as the Swedish Rally had banned the use of studs – essential for grip on the tractionless snow and ice typically found on the rally.

Known as the KAK Rally, the stud ban was made on safety grounds and the toll the metal was taking on the roads. At the time between 600–800 studs per tyre were not unusual for a fast stage. Without studs, the recce – always a lengthy business – became downright laborious, one crew taking 30 minutes to get away from the start line in the prevalent icy conditons.

Luckily there was snow for the rally – better than ice –

but even so spectators converged at every stage start to give the competitors a push start. It also brought out the ingenuity of tyre makers, with Pirelli making a special rubber hedgehog of a tyre covered in prickles; it was by all accounts fairly ineffective, but a nice idea nonetheless.

Portugal had been included in the series for the first time, and after two almost farcical rounds, it was a relief to have a rally not ruined by ill-considered organizational intervention. Alpine scooped a one-two with Therier and Nicolas respectively. The Renault Alpines were not present at the Safari Rally, as they were considered too fragile, and Datsun won an event, the first of five Safari wins for Shekhar Mehta. Further wins that year for the French marque included Morocco ('the toughest test yet of how far a car can be driven'), Acropolis, San Remo and Corsica.

Opposite: Hannu Mikkola flies high on his way to victory in the 1000 Lakes Rally.

Below: Ove Andersson, driver and creator of Toyota Team Europe.

The only other combination to manage more than a solitary rally win that year was Timo Mäkinen in the Escort RS1600 who won in Finland and the RAC. The latter rally almost proved too popular with over 400 applications received for 250 places. The thought these days of running 250 cars on a rally is bad enough, but most modern organizers would weep at the prospect of half that number willing to pay to enter their rallies!

The first world championship had been won – warts and all – in resounding manner by Renault Alpine.

No sooner had the world championship laurels been settled around the Dieppe team than the omnipotent OPEC countries rudely intruded on rallying's world by holding the non-oil-producing world to ransom, restricting the supply of oil and hiking the price per barrel up to record levels.

Petrol coupons were introduced – although never used – in the UK in an effort to cut petrol consumption and the route of the 1973 RAC Rally had been cut by 10% as a rationing measure, but *Motoring News* at that time had some rousing words on the subject: 'If anyone tells you during the rally that it is anti-social and ought to be stopped, don't forget to tell them that if the airlines cancelled just one transatlantic jumbo jet, just one, the equivalent fuel saved would run the whole of the RAC Rally, service cars and all,' it advised.

Shortly after the RAC, all rallies in the UK were banned. The effect worldwide varied from country to country but a big casualty of the situation was Toyota which not only cancelled its rally programme but froze team manager Ove Andersson's budget.

Only eight from a previous thirteen world championship rallies were run in 1974, the first of the year being the TAP Rally of Portugal. Fiat chose the event to debut its 124 Abarth and it took the top three places. Lele (Rafaelle) Pinto was the winning driver, with Ninni Russo, the future manager of Lancia co-driving Alcide Paganelli into second place and a young Finnish combination by name of Alèn and Kivimaki in third spot! The 1000 Lakes that year brought the Ford competitions department out of the cupboard where it had been organizing table-top rally championships across the country in order to keep busy during the fuel crisis. The top two were Hannu Mikkola and John Davenport and Timo Mäkinen and Henry Liddon, both in Escort RS1600s. What, you wonder, would they have done differently if they could have seen then what the future held?

The San Remo Rally was the setting for the introduction of the most significant rally car of the seventies, the Lancia Stratos, just five days after its homologation. The Italian reply to all that unacceptable success the other side of the Alps, the Stratos was a mid-engined wonder car, that became the yardstick against which other cars would be judged.

There had been a temple to motor sport in Turin since 1949, a self-contained motor sports facility dedicated to the optimum development of rally and circuit racers, but they had never had a project like the Stratos ...

A Ferrari Dino engine, 2.4 litres of transversely mounted V6 power, was the starting point for this first of all supercars, encased in a glass-fibre shell in the distinctive arrowhead. To begin with, the car was capable of producing over 250 bhp – not much more than the best of the saloon cars, the Escort. However, its larger capacity meant that it always had much more power at low revs than its rivals and that was allied to better suspension, with single-seater-style double wishbones all round, when most top rally cars had live axles that would have been familiar to the intrepid men who started racing in the 19th century. The mid-engine gave it excellent traction and the steel chassis was deceptively tough: whereas the Alpines never looked like winning the Safari, the Stratos might easily have done so and they came second and third at the first attempt, in 1975. Bad luck, rather than unsuitability, prevented the car from winning either the Safari or the Acropolis.

On tarmac, the Stratos was in its element. Lancia could be quite certain of winning the Monte (then as now, a tarmac rally with a bit of snow thrown in, rather than a true winter event like the Swedish), on home ground at San Remo and in Corsica. The mid-engined machines swept the top three places on the 1976 Monte and the top four at San Remo. Such successes not only scared off the opposition, but laid the basis for three successive world titles, from 1974 to 1976. Its dominance meant that Lancia could afford to pick and choose events and the Turin team never even bothered with the 1000 Lakes.

It wasn't the perfect car: the wheelbase was as short as a Mini's and that made it twitchy on slippery surfaces, although none other than Miki Biasion, a brilliant Lancia driver from a later era, reckoned that the Stratos' lack of understeer gave it better handling than its Group B successor, the 037. Nevertheless, while Björn Waldegård

won the 1975 Swedish, the world championship team was embarrassingly drubbed by the works Saabs a year later in fresh snow and the steeply raked windscreen always created distracting reflections at night, which was a particular drawback on a rally with a secret route, like the RAC.

But the Stratos' abiding weakness was political, not mechanical. By the end of 1976, a 24-valve works car gave 275 bhp and was capable of winning almost anywhere in the world. The snag was the badge on the bonnet. Fiat – Lancia's owner – had swallowed its 1974 defeat at the hands of its subsidiary with good grace, stepping out of the limelight to replace the 124 Spider sports car with the boxy 131 Abarth saloon. Now that the 131 was ready, Fiat badly wanted to be world champion and it had no compunction about nobbling the Stratos to improve its chances. The most charismatic car of its age was still winning world championship rallies as late as 1981, despite minimal development and the loss of the 24-valve head when the rules changed at the end of 1977. It won 17 world championship rallies and might easily have triumphed in twice as many. Although it loomed menacingly over uglier, less capable opponents for the rest of the decade, marketing considerations turned the late seventies into a battle of the saloons.

Below: Timo Mäkinen won the RAC in 1975 in the new Mk2 Escort.

4

Calm Before the Storm

The Lancia Stratos banished by Fiat Group, the late seventies and early eighties were the preserve of super saloons such as Fiat's 131, the Ford Escort and the Opel Ascona 400.

Once Sandro Munari had completed his Monte Carlo hat trick, the works Lancias were rarely seen in 1977, although the Italian won the inaugural FIA Cup for Drivers, a poorly publicized forerunner to the World Championship for Drivers. Instead, Fiat launched an assault of unprecedented ferocity on world rallying.

The 131 was good, but by no means the best car of its type. In its favour, it had adjustable, independent suspension front and rear, 38 centimetre (15 inch) wheels with big brakes, lightweight plastic body panels and a bomb-proof, non-synchromesh gearbox. The drawback was the twin-cam, 2 litre engine. Outwardly similar to the Escort's, its long stroke meant that it never gave the same power, even though Fiat went to the trouble of developing fuel injection at a time when even the mighty Stratos usually made do with carburettors. At best, a 131 gave 235 bhp. To beat a 250 bhp Escort that weighed much the same, Fiat had to make the most of every advantage going and, in winning the world championship three times, it proved the old adage that topline drivers and teamwork are as important to success in rallying as the car itself.

Fiat's foremost driver in 1977 was without doubt Markku Alèn. The winner of 19 world championship rallies by 1989, the lanky, fiery-tempered Finn possessed a staggering turn of speed on any surface. He had already beaten Hannu Mikkola in a straight fight in 124s and won the 1976 1000 Lakes, even though his 131 ran on three cylinders for much of the rally. He was ably supported by the likes of Maurizio Verini (the 1975 European champion), Fulvio Bacchelli, Timo Salonen, Simo Lampinen, Andruet, Darniche – even Timo Mäkinen. By the end of 1977, Fiat had succeeded in prising Walter Röhrl away from Opel and it was rumoured that it was prepared to sign up drivers not to drive for Ford in a no-holds-barred effort to win the title.

After the successes of the early seventies, Ford had stayed largely at home when the Mark 1 Escort gave way to the mechanically similar Mark 2. Given the awesome superiority of the Stratos, this was merely prudent: while Ford could be fairly sure of winning the RAC Rally,

taking the British event every year from 1972 to 1979, visits to the Monte, Morocco and the 1000 Lakes in 1976 failed to produce a victory. Disgusted with Italian politics, Waldegård had joined the team for the 1976 RAC, thereby depriving Lancia of a near-certain victory, but Ford relied very heavily on the gentlemanly Swede until Mikkola returned from Toyota for 1978.

Ford emerged from 1977 with considerable credit, winning the Safari, the RAC and the Acropolis (all through Waldegård) and the 1000 Lakes thanks to Kyösti Hämäläinen, a dedicated Finn who drove the entire route from memory and never made an impact anywhere else, but the Fiat was undeniably superior on tarmac, and the team was prepared to throw cars and money at the world championship in seemingly limitless quantities. Victory in Portugal, New Zealand, San Remo, Canada, and Corsica deservedly gave the Italians the world title.

They did even better in 1978, Röhrl and Alèn taking four straight victories in mid-season, while Darniche completed the Corsican hat trick begun in 1975 in a private Stratos. Yet Ford had narrowed the gap: only a last-minute puncture gave Alèn a clear victory in Portugal after a breathtaking struggle with Mikkola. The 5–2 scoreline did Ford less than justice and it came as no great surprise that Fiat decided to take a 'rest' in 1979. Sure enough despite the occasional presence of Darniche and a Stratos with a surreptitious degree of works backing, Waldegård and Mikkola ruled the roost. Ford even went to the lengths of producing a special tarmac Escort, with a fuel-injected engine producing an alleged 270 bhp, 28 centimetre (11 inch) wide rear wheels, and altered weight distribution by moving the engine back in the chassis. It didn't win, as another of those infamous Monte scandals enabled Darniche to pip Waldegård by just six seconds after a dramatic final night in which the Frenchman made up six minutes; it was a bravura performance, but Waldegård would have won if a rock hadn't mysteriously found its way onto the road and cost him a minute at the crucial stage. That was almost Ford's only disappointment in 1979, as it took its only manufacturers' crown and

(with a little help from Mercedes), Waldegård became the first World Rally Champion.

There were occasional successes for Saab, but the 99 in 16-valve and then Turbo form was an unwieldy device, and the problems of feeding over 250 bhp through the front wheels alone were considered insuperable. Instead, manufacturers generally adopted the Escort pattern: front engines, with special 16-valve heads rarely seen then on shopping cars, pumped 250 bhp to the rear wheels of compact saloons like the Talbot Sunbeam (which used the Lotus Elite's engine), the Vauxhall Chevette, the Datsun Violet and the Toyota Celica. British Leyland ran a limited programme for the TR7, although it was more

successful in V8 form, in spite of limited development.

Aside from Datsun's domination of the Safari, an event on which it crushed Mercedes, the Japanese were no more than bit players, scoring on reliability rather than speed. Mehta could be counted upon to win the Safari, while Salonen was exceptionally quick on the classic roads of New Zealand, but the fact that the team regularly finished in the top three in the world championship was proof that most manufacturers picked and chose events without much regard to status, not a sign of an impending Japanese breakthrough. Toyota's continued presence owed more to Andersson's persistence than a burning desire to win the world title.

Mercedes characteristically picked a novel route, elbowing its way into the party with 5 litre 450 and 500SLCs with an unheard-of 300 bhp, automatic gearboxes, computer simulation and the kind of budget that a Third World country could only dream of, yet it failed to win anything more significant than the weakest round of the world championship in the Ivory Coast and, having made some of the sport's most talented drivers a good deal richer, it tiptoed away at the end of 1980.

The ultimate variation on the theme came from Opel: knowing that the Kadett would become front-wheel drive, team boss Tony Fall (a former works driver for BMC,

Lancia and Datsun) chose the bigger Ascona. Borrowing a leaf from Talbot's and Vauxhall's book, he went for a bigger capacity, getting 2.4 litres by using the Rekord's diesel cylinder block. It gave the car a small but useful power advantage. The Ascona 400 won the 1980 Swedish in Anders Kullang's hands and the 1983 Safari with Ari Vatanen, before giving way to the lighter, more powerful Manta. Opel was a powerful, slickly presented team, with drivers like Röhrl, Vatanen and the superbly gifted Henri Toivonen, and backing from Rothmans, but it was all too late: time had run out for the rear-wheel-drive hot rods. Fiat had swept to its third title in 1980 once Ford withdrew, Röhrl becoming drivers' champion, while David Sutton's private Escort team battled with the resourceful Talbot squad in 1981, Vatanen winning the drivers' title for the former, while Des O'Dell's men took the manufacturers' crown home to Coventry.

By then, family cars were no longer rear-wheel drive. Ford had pulled out, because the Mark 3 Escort – Britain's best seller for so many years – was front-wheel drive. Manufacturers wanted rules that suited the cars they sold, or gave them a free hand to do something else. The early eighties were therefore the calm before the storm. Much greater freedom from Group B regulations (which required only 200 road cars) and the impending arrival of the Quattro would change rallying for good. Overnight, the Escort, the Sunbeam, even the Manta 400 would be turned into museum pieces – as much use as Spitfires in the jet age.

Opposite: The greatest of them all? Henri Toivonen blasts to victory on the 1980 RAC Rally.

This page: Stig Blomqvist persisted with Saab to good effect such as on the 1978 RAC (below). Meanwhile Mercedes (bottom) put a great deal of money and effort into African events.

5

Birth of a Legend

THE AUDI QUATTRO
In the beginning there was Audi.

*'It is the most terrifyingly
effective way of covering loose
surface at speed ever devised
by man.'*

*Motoring News,
in-car with Hannu Mikkola, 1981*

Like Charles Atlas walking onto a beach full of pigeon-chested weeds, the Audi Quattro burst into rallying in 1981. With its stocky, four-square frame it kicked sand in the face of all other manufacturers instantly making two-wheel drive seem inadequate. Not only did it introduce four-wheel drive into the world championship, but turbo power as well.

Launched as a road car at the Geneva Motor Show in 1980, the A1 Quattro made its world championship debut on the 1981 Monte Carlo Rally. Although the Audi team had wanted Walter Röhrl, the German was already engrossed in talks with Mercedes, subsequently signing for them, and so Audi's team for that inaugural year was Hannu Mikkola and Michele Mouton.

As a car representing the future of rallying, and every high-tech innovation available, it is hard to remember that this thoroughbred was actually sired by something of a carthorse, a lightweight military vehicle, produced under the Volkswagen banner, and named the Iltis. Walter Treser, the senior project manager who had raced and rallied himself, thought there was more potential in the 5-cylinder longitudinal engine than as a base for the multi-purpose jeep and put it forward as a plan for a production car. He also thought the company might dismiss the idea out of hand so the whole unit was installed into an Audi 80 which then gave the Audi chairman a demonstration of its capabilities. He was suitably impressed and the project got the go-ahead with the results on show for all to see in Geneva. For Audi, the car would hopefully promote a younger image, and capitalize on the sporting sales link missing from its marketing strategy.

Hannu Mikkola was persuaded to take on the role as test driver for 1980, with an option to take on the world championship programme planned for 1981. Even from its earliest days the Quattro showed it was capable of handling like the tank it resembled, Mikkola recalling in *Rallycourse* of 1981: 'I had to allow a metre either side for safety when I was really going like hell.'

Its first world championship event was the 1981 Monte Carlo Rally where two Quattros were entered, one for Mikkola, one for Mouton, fresh from Fiat. It was not a dream start. While Mouton's car didn't last from Paris to Monaco, Mikkola needed only the first six stages of the rally to build up a lead of almost six minutes. Rival team managers, prior to the event so sceptical of the workability of the Quattro, despite its victory on the non-championship Janner Rally, looked distinctly ill at ease. Their discomfort was to be short-lived on this occasion, as on the seventh stage Mikkola's foot missed the brake sending the big Audi off the road. Whatever the final result, in this case victory for Renault with its debutante 5 Turbo, rallying had seen the first glimpse of the awesome domination the Quattro would be capable of.

Sweden was next, and only a one-car entry from Audi, for Mikkola on the specialist snow event. Conversely, on an event run in such slippery conditions, four-wheel drive was not a huge advantage as all cars were permitted to use big traction-giving studs on their tyres. Victory for the Audi was important; it was so radical all eyes were noting its every stage time, its every corner, its every start. An early world championship win was crucial to give confidence to the team that was still very new to rallying. Mikkola took the Quattro back to the Karlstad finish a little over two minutes in front of Ari Vatanen's Escort; the Audi's innings had got a good solid start.

Mikkola has been dubbed an unlucky driver, but his retirements in Portugal and Corsica had more to do with the Audi engine's shortcomings than any third party fate.

Previous page: The mighty Quattro launched itself on the rally world in the early eighties.

Opposite: The Quattro was not best suited to tarmac, but in the absence of decent opposition Hannu Mikkola was able to build a massive lead in the 1981 Monte Carlo before, ironically, sliding off on snow.

The Acropolis Rally was a total disaster from the Audi viewpoint when halfway through the event Mikkola, leading comfortably over rough stages tailor-made for the Quattro, was disqualified along with Mouton who had led the rally after the first stage, and Franz Wittman for alleged illegalities in the cars' cooling systems. The heat in Greece was always going to be a problem for the Quattros, which from the earliest days in testing had shown a tendency to overheat, and so a special cooling system had been devised to overcome any problem. The cars had been scrutineered and passed at the start, but a further technical inspection, halfway through the event, had deemed the cooling devices to be illegal, and the cars were not allowed to restart. The fact that they were sent home on the spot was unusual, the accepted course of action would be to allow the cars to continue and then, depending on the result of findings, they would be disqualified or not. Audi appealed against the disqualification, unsuccessfully, and as a direct result of the incident, the team manager Walter Treser left the team to be replaced by Roland Gumpert who had worked on the Iltis some years before.

If reliability was becoming a thorn in the German team's side, it was making Mikkola old overnight. Leading in Finland, Mikkola picked up over four minutes of road penalties after mechanics couldn't repair his engine within the specified time. For Mikkola, who had set fastest times on 29 out of 48 special stages, third place was hardly just reward.

San Remo gave the Quattro its second championship win, in the hands of Michele Mouton, a marvellous moment giving her her first world rally success, and the first victory to a woman driver. It was a good team victory, particularly after the stresses of Greece and the disappointment in Finland.

In what time was available between rallies and recces the Audi engineers were at work trying to lessen the mechanical failures dogging the team, as well as embarking on a steep learning curve of each rally in the world championship series itself. While other manufacturers like Ford, Opel and Lancia could call on years of experience in setting up cars for the individual vagaries of each particular event, it was all new to Audi.

The hard work paid off on the final round of the 1981 season when the Ingolstadt team celebrated its most emphatic win of the year, Mikkola trouncing opposition including Blomqvist, Vatanen, Toivonen, Waldegård and Alèn, by over 11 minutes. It was quite simply a whitewash, despite Mikkola rolling his Quattro early in the event. Mouton was third until a relatively minor off put her out of the event agonizingly close to a good finish on her first visit to the RAC.

By 1982 Audi had lost the element of surprise it had enjoyed the previous year. However, it had also lost some of the engine problems and much of the excess weight it had struggled with in 1981, and was set to enjoy its most successful year, winning seven out of 11 rallies it entered and walking away with the manufacturers' trophy – a just reward for its courage in blazing a new trail through rallying. It was still beset by mechanical problems, most

On events like the RAC Rally (opposite), where traction was at a premium, the big Quattro had little trouble in bringing the likes of Stig Blomqvist victory. Likewise, on snowy events such as the Swedish (below), Rörhl found the machine a joy to drive.

crucially for Michele Mouton in New Zealand when she was leading in a rally that could have given her valuable points in her battle against Walter Röhrl, but most consistently for her team-mate. Mikkola had a wretched year with his Quattro breaking on no less than five consecutive rallies covering a four-month period. There was no common weakness, just a niggling run of misfortune. Nonetheless there were victories for Mouton in Portugal, Greece and Brazil and for Mikkola on the 1000 Lakes and the RAC rallies. Its form on dry tarmac still remained below average, and despite what detractors of Mouton might say, the Quattro, with its longitudinal engine sited over the front wheels to make it very nose-heavy, was not an easy drive, particularly on twisting stages.

These two weaknesses were exactly the points of attack Lancia relied on when planning its 1983 campaign with the 037. On an uphill gravel stage the two-wheel-drive super-turbocharged car wouldn't have a chance, but on every other stage its superior handling and throttle response would put it on an equal basis if not give it the advantage.

Lancia, not Audi, took the world championship manufacturers' title in 1983, calling on years of streetwise rally knowledge the team used every ounce of wile to squeeze this last championship out of a two-wheel-drive car. The resource of Abarth exaggerated the inexperience of Ingolstadt which was flatly outflanked. It was a hard lesson to learn, but illustrated that there was more to winning championships than coming up with the best car.

By 1984, Peugeot would be ready to unveil its T16 rally special, which prompted Audi's engineer Jorg Bensinger to comment: 'Audi has used a production car to demonstrate the superiority of four-wheel drive in motor sport. Now that our competitors are increasingly using out-and-out racing cars with four-wheel drive, we must also think about whether a basically different concept may promise more success.'

The Quattro Sport, the shorter more powerful Audi, ultimately capable of producing more than 500 bhp from its 20-valve engine, had even greater handling problems – due to its shorter length – than its predecessor, prompting Walter Röhrl to label it 'dangerous' after an accident on the 1984 San Remo Rally. Its debut, on Corsica 1984, had been overshadowed by the more immediate impact of the T16. Audi, it seemed, was watching the initiative slip away.

The Sport was not the way to win the advantage back for Ingolstadt. Röhrl was vocal in his criticism of the car (prompting one team manager to say he always felt relieved when Röhrl was driving for someone else because then he knew his car was safe from criticism) and the team ran the old Quattro A2s in parallel. It was usually the latter that were the more successful. It wasn't until the Ivory Coast that the Sport finished a rally, winning the event to give Stig Blomqvist the driver's championship and Audi the double of titles.

The Sport Evolution 2 showed that the Ingolstadt engineers hadn't totally lost their inventiveness. A large wing on the rear of the car, and spoiler on the front, created useful downforce, even at 100 kph (62 mph), giving the car handling much improved on any of the previous Audis. Coupled with the most powerful engine in the sport and some overdue weight redistribution towards the rear of the car, Audi had a winner. The problem was that all the manufacturers who had been caught on the hop back in January of 1981 had now had time to produce their own challengers. Audi's reign was over.

The Super Quattros, such as this bewinged Sport 2 driven by Röhrl on San Remo in 1985, spawned the Supercars that emerged in this period from Peugeot, Lancia, Ford and Austin Rover. Unlike these specials, however, no amount of wings and power could overcome the fact that even the most outrageous Quattros were still based on production models.

6

Champions

BJÖRN WALDEGÅRD

*Previous page:
Despite their
charisma, it took
more than a great
driver to win a
championship.
Here Ari Vatanen
(left) is pictured
with Björn
Waldergård (far
right) together
with two other
'greats' from
Ford: ace
mechanic Mick
Jones (middle
right) and
manager at Ford,
John Taylor.*

Björn Waldegård became the first ever official World Drivers' Champion in 1979, after a season-long duel with Hannu Mikkola. It was also to be a year of contrasts, beginning with a rock mysteriously appearing on the penultimate stage of the Monte Carlo Rally as Waldegård headed Frenchman Bernard Darniche, and ending with a second place on the Bandama Rally, last event of the season in that year, to take the inaugural title by just one point.

Seventeen years earlier, he had made his competition debut in a 1200 VW Beetle, winning his first event, the Gastabudstrofen Rally two years later. Like so many future drivers, he had actually started off co-driving before discovering he was a lot quicker than the first-choice driver. The driver in question was Lars Helmer and they simply swapped seats and continued their partnership until 1972 when Helmer left to pursue his business interests and Waldegård installed Hans Thorsezelius as his co-driver! In contrast to Blomqvist, Trana and Andersson, fellow Swedes who all started rallying in Saabs, Waldegård became something of a Beetle wizard, occasionally swapping to a Mini Cooper. Scania Vabis, the Swedish VW and Porsche importers, gave him a Beetle for Swedish

*Björn Waldegård
blasts through the
rocky Acropolis
Rally in 1979
(above) and
celebrates victory
after the event in
traditional
champagne style
(opposite). That
victory was
decisive in
handing him the
first ever world
championship
crown for drivers.*

national rallies, and then in 1965 he drove a Porsche 911 2.0. In 1968 he took the first of his three consecutive Swedish Rally wins for Porsche as well as the Monte Carlo in 1969 and 1970. He also made his debut in world sports-car racing in 1970 finishing fifth in the Targa Florio in a Porsche 908. He gave Porsche six outright victories in the period from Sweden 1968 to Austria 1970, managing to extract the optimum performance from the rear-engined car.

Porsche began to lose interest in its rally programme and the 911 Waldegård took to second place on the 1971 RAC Rally was his own entry. Between 1972 and 1975 he freelanced for various manufacturers, including Citroen, Volkswagen, Fiat, Toyota and Opel, before joining Lancia in 1975 alongside Sandro Munari in the Stratos.

A Swede alongside an Italian in an Italian team. If from the outside the equation didn't appear tipped in his

favour, from the inside it was even worse, with team manager Cesare Fiorio insisting on team orders in favour of the Italian once too often. It was a shame that politics clouded the issue because the combination of Waldegård and the Stratos was the best of both worlds: a driver as good on asphalt as on gravel, and a car that was simply unsurpassed at the time.

Waldegård, after his mixture of drives, quickly adapted to the Italian car, and won with it on his first outing, the Swedish. A Swede winning in Sweden was permissible. However, in San Remo, the home event for both the Lancia team and Munari, Fiorio had other ideas and when the Swede was ordered to delay starting the last special stage of the 1976 event by four seconds to improve Munari's chances, he showed what he thought by beating his colleague and winning the event by four seconds. Fiorio later explained that he felt it was unfair that either driver should win the event so he had decided that the last stage would be a 'race within a race'.

Ford was only too happy to sign him as a replacement for the retiring Timo Mäkinen, but Lancia huffily cancelled Waldegård's RAC entry. In stepped Ford with a hastily prepared third Escort, and the last laugh was on Waldegård as he took third place completing a Ford sweep.

The Swedish and Safari Rallies are at opposite ends of the rally scale, the former a snow event, the latter a marathon test of mud, dust and stamina. Waldegård won his home event five times in his 25-year world championship career, and became something of a specialist on African events, winning the Safari on four occasions and the Ivory Coast, three times. His mastery of Africa did nothing for his team manager's nerves however, Ford's Peter Ashcroft recalling an occasion *en route* to Waldegård's 1977 victory when his Escort became bogged down in a mud hole. The local inhabitants, used to the rally supplementing their annual income, waited for just these moments to earn some 'push money'. All the Ford crews knew that sooner or later they would need the help of these locals and were allocated a bag of loot for just such an occasion. Waldegård contacted Ashcroft. 'Give them the money then, Björn,' urged Ashcroft, anxious that his star driver was not about to lose certain victory for the sake of a few shillings. But Waldegård wasn't happy. Why should he hand over money to these opportunists when he might be able to free the car himself? Minutes ticked by, and Ashcroft in the communications plane above could see Munari was beginning to catch up, 'Give them the money,' he insisted, but Björn wasn't budging, it was only when an agitated Ashcroft yelled down the radio to threaten his driver, that Waldegård decided enough was enough. Throwing the money to the locals who quickly freed the Escort from its muddy prison, Waldegård sped off over the horizon, leaving Ashcroft to witness Munari landing in the self-same hole!

1977 was a good year for Waldegård, winning the Acropolis and RAC rallies, the latter from Hannu Mikkola; the two top drivers at the time shared countless battles but in true sporting spirit.

In 1978 Ford had the dream team of Waldegård, Mikkola and Vatanen with Roger Clark on selected events. Ashcroft recalls, 'There was such a fantastic team spirit then. Björn would radio back after a stage, "I was on the wrong tyres, tell Hannu."'

Their mutual respect was apparent, and it added to the achievement Waldegård felt in winning the 1979 championship as he told *Motoring News* at the time: 'That was the best thing about the championship ... It was such a close fight with Hannu all year. Every time it was hard to win, but to try and do this and beat Mikkola – one who could always have a chance of winning – that is good. Then it is satisfying to win that title because I had to work to win by one point.'

In the team that was set to take the manufacturers' title, the question in 1979 was really would it be Waldegård or Mikkola? The two team-mates were so evenly matched, but Waldegård held the drivers' lead from Sweden until the season's finish, despite outright victories on only two events, as opposed to Mikkola's four. The two rivals were both in Mercedes for the decider. The big taxi-like 450 SLCs simply too big for the majority of world championship events, but strong and reliable, ideal for Africa!

Despite so much at stake, sportsmanship prevailed between the two contenders. Mikkola came across a fallen tree – a common hazard on the rally – and radioed back to warn his colleagues. Mikkola won the rally, but Waldegård the championship, but already it was time to seek another programme as Ford, having won the manufacturers' title, decided to make a hasty exit from rallying.

Despite the drivers' title, it was all downhill in career terms for Waldegård. A mixture of drives in 1980 for Fiat and Mercedes gave him a full programme of nine rallies, but only one victory, this time one better on the Ivory Coast.

In 1981 he began his long association with Toyota, but had a frustrating year as the Celica shook off development problems with its transmission.

Given the opportunity to drive one of the Michelotto Ferrari 308GTB 4-valves in San Remo he took it, and set some competitive times before the engine overheated a little before the mid-way point.

With Toyota he continued to build on his reputation as an African master, combining speed with the mechanical sympathy and instinct for car preservation necessary to suceed in Africa.

In total he drove 11 different makes of car in various world championship events, taking his last victory in 1990, when he won the Safari Rally for Toyota with its Celica GT4. It was a bittersweet moment however, as Waldegård learned during the event that after ten years with the Cologne team, his contract was not to be renewed for 1991; after victory however, TTE President Ove Andersson must have had a change of heart regarding his compatriot Swede, for Waldegård popped up again in Kenya the following season, finishing fourth.

WALTER RÖHRL

From bishop's secretary to World Rally Champion isn't a conventional career path, but Walter Röhrl did his best to break as many conventions in rallying as possible.

The tall, sombre German, almost detached from the passion and activity around him on a rally, became world champion twice, the first driver to achieve a double of titles, winning in 1980 with Fiat and in 1982 with Opel.

It is easy to parcel him up as an archetypal Bavarian. A techno-pilot. But often he gave his best performances when he was stung into action, such as Brazil in 1982 against his arch rival, Michele Mouton. He said later of his drive that it was madness, that he pushed his Opel and himself way over the limits of what he would consider calculated risk, but there was no doubt on that occasion his ego overruled his head at the thought of being beaten by Mouton in a battle he so evidently wanted to win.

Despite his many years in the sport and the – at times grudging – respect he commanded from managers and colleagues alike, Röhrl was always an oddball. His level of fitness, his professionalism, his dour demeanour and his detached assessment of cars and rallies all served to set him apart from his less cerebral colleagues in the sport.

His team-mates speak highly of his team spirit, Stig Blomqvist recalling the service point in San Remo the year he (Blomqvist) was trying to win the world championship. Only one set of tyres was available, and without being asked Röhrl drove away on his old rubber.

For managers however, his outspoken – some would say arrogant – manner often gave problems, none more so than Tony Fall, manager of the Rothmans-Opel team for whom Röhrl drove and became world champion in 1982. The snag with Röhrl came in that he believed he was doing his best job for sponsors driving the cars fast and winning rallies for the Rothmans team; what he felt was outside his brief were the innumerable publicity opportunities. He would conveniently forget to wear correct team gear for photo-calls or simply not show at Rothmans functions. Added to his distaste for a public relations role was his disenchantment at driving a car with which he had to take silly risks to have a chance of beating Audi. Oh, and there were certain rallies, namely the 'secret' RAC, which he did not like and did not want to contest.

All the elements were building to a pressure point which boiled over on the eve of the 1982 RAC Rally when Röhrl was a no-show at the official Rothmans party. Tony Fall had had enough and sacked his German star before the rally had started.

These days better remembered for his great drives for Audi, Röhrl was a master of old-fashioned two-wheel drive, too, for Fiat (below) and Opel.

Whatever you thought of the person, his ability to step into a car and win was outstanding.

With a brother who had been killed in a motoring accident, Röhrl was sensitive to the feelings of his parents and his first rally excursions were rather furtive. At the start of his career he drove four different cars, a Fiat 850 Coupé, BMW, Alfa and Porsche, in four different rallies. None of the cars managed to finish a rally, but he was sufficiently quick to attract the attention of Ford Germany, who approached him with a drive, and for 1971 and 1972 he drove a works Capri from Cologne, winning on his fifth event, the Wiesbaden Rally.

But still he did not enjoy the support of his family, to the extent that he seriously considered giving up. A short break made him realize he needed to rally and he rejoined Ford Germany, driving the Capri 2600RS again, setting good times against first-class opposition on the Olympia Rally and winning the German Baltic Rally.

Opel smelt talent and offered him a better programme than Ford, and in the Ascona that year he won three European rallies, following it up in becoming European champion in 1974. The following year he moved up a league, winning his first world championship rally, the Acropolis, in the Ascona.

The Opel Kadett which replaced the Ascona didn't have the former model's strength, and its lack of reliability frustrated Röhrl to such an extent that he went and bought his own Porsche to rally. His anger was understandable; from eight starts the Kadett finished only one rally. It was not the sort of record Röhrl wanted to extend.

He joined Abarth and the 131 for the 1977 Rideau Lakes Rally in Canada, staying with the team on this first of two occasions, until the end of 1980, the year he first became world champion. He was bemused by the politics at Fiat, at the Italian parochialism, reflected in his attitude towards driving in the same team as Sandro Munari, Cesare Fiorio's protégé and favourite son. 'I would say to Fiat that if Sandro is driving one time more, don't call me: I would never go anywhere if Sandro was driving,' he told Martin Holmes in *World Rallying*.

The 1980 season began with a tremendous victory for both Röhrl and the team, the first of four he would take, in Monte Carlo. Portugal followed, and an extraordinary incident in which a Fiat service barge almost wiped out its own leader in a road accident! Fortunately the damage wasn't serious enough to cause any loss of time and Röhrl took an orchestrated first place after Fiorio had ordered a charging Markku Alèn to stop challenging the leader and settle for second place.

Röhrl had always expressed a wish to return to a German manufacturer and prior to his contract with Fiat had arranged to drive for Mercedes on the Safari Rally. However, Fiat would not allow this and so Röhrl's time for driving one of his country's own products would have to wait.

Meanwhile, back in 1980, Röhrl and Alèn's Fiats experienced transmission problems on the rough Acropolis, giving Röhrl only a fourth-place finish, but sufficient to maintain his drivers' championship lead from veteran Anders Kullang. A victory on the inaugural world championship rally of Argentina – the Rally Codasur Ultra Movil YPF to be absolutely correct – against Mercedes gave him another maximum score, and an insight into the pulling power of circuit racers. As a one-off for the Argentine event, Grand Prix hero Carlos Reutemann had been drafted in, driving a fourth Fiat, and

such was the huge interest in the driver, the Argentine army was used to keep crowds under control at service areas! His third place was celebrated more than Röhrl's victory.

There was no 1000 Lakes for the German, the job being left to team-mate and Finnish master Markku Alèn who took his first victory of the year; but a steady second place in New Zealand behind an emergent Timo Salonen was already making the tall figure odds-on favourite for the title, despite his car increasingly showing its age against stronger opposition.

The San Remo Rally of 1980 was a difficult one for Fiat inasmuch as the Abarth factory called a strike five days before the rally was due to start, impounding the cars. Nothing daunted, Fiorio came up with cars for each of his drivers. Röhrl had an unfinished car in tarmac spec, Alèn a finished but old car in tarmac spec, and for Italian Attilo Bettega there was a car in gravel trim! The rally started with four tarmac stages, followed by 31 loose with the final 14 stages on tarmac. Vatanen was leading with only a few of the gravel stages remaining. It then began to rain, softening the stages and giving Röhrl more confidence to drive faster in his delicate car. He took the lead on the 33rd stage and kept it to the end to give himself a 50-plus lead over Vatanen for the championship, and Fiat a 30-point advantage over Ford.

Corsica was where he wrapped it up, second place on an event where Vatanen and Mikkola were absent giving him enough points to take the title. 'In 1980,' he said later in an interview with Steve Fellows for *Rallycourse*, 'I had shown everyone I was the best ... OK, everybody knows I am the fastest, now I have to show them that I am also a very clever driver.'

He had to wait rather longer than anticipated to show the world his tactical strengths after making a bad decision to sign for Mercedes. It was very much a decision of his heart, he had wanted to drive for the Germans ever since his career started. They gave him a five-year contract. 'It was everything special for me. It was fantastic to be a Mercedes driver.' Unfortunately for Röhrl the euphoria was to be short-lived as shortly before the 1981 season was due to begin, the manufacturer in an extraordinary volte-face pulled the plug on its rally programme. Having turned down Audi, who had promptly signed Michele Mouton, there was nowhere for him to go and so for the first time the reigning world champion had no car or team with which to defend his title.

For 1982 he had his choice of team, but decided to plump for another spell with Opel under Mr Fall. It wasn't the start of a beautiful relationship but he still managed to win the world championship from Mouton and Audi in a year which had looked like belonging to four-wheel drive. The battle for the title in 1982 is detailed under Mouton's heading, but the German certainly didn't win any friends amongst the female fraternity for his misogynistic views. It was, however, a gritty and determined performance by the double champion who simply refused to accede to Mouton and the Audi's loose surface advantage.

It was a short but not so sweet return to Opel, ending in acrimony, but to Röhrl, already a Lancia driver again for 1983, it was water off a duck's back. The Italians were impatient to get him into the 037 Rally and he was impatient to make it work.

Röhrl was only interested in being associated with a car capable of winning, and after the Rothmans-bias of Opel he found a safe haven in the self-contained unit that was Lancia.

It was a dream start when Röhrl and Geistdorfer won their third consecutive Monte Carlo Rally, beating Audi on a dry event. After the victory it was only natural that he would be dubbed 'The Montemeister' by the specialist press, taking first an Abarth 131, then an Ascona 400 and finally the 037 to wins on the event. The fact that he equalled Sandro Munari's four wins the following year in a Quattro made his record on the event all the more impressive and demonstrated his knack of winning performance from a variety of cars.

A 'bonus' win over the hot ante-post Audi favourites in Greece when the German team struck trouble, Röhrl inheriting Hannu Mikkola's long-held lead after the Finn's Quattro was forced out by mechanical trouble, and victory in New Zealand at the expense of Michele Mouton, whose Audi broke after leading for 20 of the 33 stages, gave him runner-up spot to Mikkola in the drivers' championship and helped his team to take a surprise championship title from Germany.

In 1984 he finally joined Audi, his experience and nous undoubtedly helping Ingolstadt to win the makes' title. He wielded great influence with the management in Ingolstadt, often dictating which rallies he would and would not compete on, and consequently what his team-mates would – or wouldn't – do. If colleagues resented this favourable treatment, he seemed to care little, preferring to spend time at home with his family, skiing or riding his bike.

The Sport Quattro had the mechanical failures but not the success of its forerunner the Quattro, and Röhrl, unlike team-mate Blomqvist who gave the car its only world championship victory, could not turn the car into a winner. He did however manage to lead for the majority of the Rally of Portugal before its transmission broke, underlying Röhrl's opinion that the design of the Sport was inherently flawed, a thought he didn't always ensure remained private.

When he won in San Remo in 1985 with the Second Evolution Quattro it was a pleasant surprise even to Röhrl. The team had carried out extensive – but not particularly encouraging – testing to try and solve the conundrum of the Sport's handling, but the handling had improved and allowed Röhrl an optimistic view of the future with Audi.

In Portugal the following year, Röhrl was amongst the leading protagonists insisting on a withdrawal from the event after the deaths of spectators. Indeed he went further, backing Audi's total withdrawal from Group B rallying, and not returning to world championship events until Group A had been announced, by which time he was behind the wheel of the Audi 200 Quattro.

Never shirking controversy throughout his career, Röhrl seemed to get worse as time went on, memorably on the 1987 Safari Rally, his penultimate appearance in the world championship degenerating into a childish tantrum, spoiling a rare Audi 200 1–2, when he refused to shake hands with the rally organizer after condemning the event and saying he would rather sweep streets for a living than drive in Kenya again.

Disillusioned by rallying, he opted for early retirement. His parting shot to the sport that had earned him his living was to condemn it as being environmentally unfriendly, before riding off into the Bavarian sunset on his push-bike.

TIMO SALONEN

Timo Salonen, cigarette in one hand, drink in another, laughing over a joke. A tendency to carry excess weight, heavy spectacles and a stubborn refusal to always toe the line, could lull the observer into believing the Finn's easy-going image would be reflected in his driving. Not quite. While it's true that towards the end of his career he certainly didn't have the motivation of earlier years and his best performances certainly weren't with Mazda or Mitsubishi, in 1985, the year he became champion, and 1986 he was capable of a blinding turn of speed that belied his appearance.

The son of a garage owner from Riihimäki in Finland, Salonen waited until he was seven before driving wrecks borrowed from his father's garage, progressing when he was 12 onto an Austin Mini Cooper which he used to drive over frozen lakes. His early love of cars had been inspired by watching Timo Mäkinen in an Austin Healey 3000. For most of his career he was partnered by Seppo Harjanne, a boyhood friend. Together they would race around lakes or on private ground, Salonen still not old enough to hold a full driving licence. Then in his twilight years at Mazda he took Voitto Silander.

At 19 he was able to compete on his first rally in a road-going Datsun 1600 SSS, and by his second event was a winner. Financing his own sport, a big accident which wrote off his rally car made him put on hold any plans for a future in rallying. He was running his own Mazda dealership and was content to concentrate on business matters. Just as he was ready to give up on the sport, the local Datsun importer offered him a Violet to contest the 1000 Lakes in: he was sixth. Between 1977 and 1978 he joined Fiat, taking his first world championship victory on the 1977 Criterium Molson du Quebec Rally in a 131 Abarth, and finishing runner-up on both the 1000 Lakes and Swedish Rallies in 1977. Fiat had given him only a sprinkling of international events and so when Nissan's offer of a world championship programme came in, he jumped at the chance. His association with the team lasted six years, spanning the 160J, Silvia 8-valve, Violet, Silvia 16-valve and finally the 240-RS. The world championship experience with the team was priceless but he admitted in a later interview that it was sometimes difficult to compete in a car not capable of outright victory: 'It starts to be quite worrying driving with Nissan, because you start rally and know with good luck you are only just top ten,' he told Mike Greasley in *Rallycourse*. Nonetheless he still managed victory in both New Zealand in 1980 and the Ivory Coast the following year.

When Jean Todt was looking for a partner for Ari Vatanen in his 1985 squad, Salonen was not his immediate choice, but his consistency and good finishing record brought his name to the fore and Salonen was a Peugeot player.

Everyone expected Salonen to play the supporting role to the 1981 world champion but the game plan changed a little. At first the two Finns found themselves treading on each other's toes; Vatanen detesting smoking and Salonen lighting up after each stage. A suggested ban in the PTS motor-home was soon overturned and the two came to agree to differ. The service crew made the most of their drivers' opposing viewpoints and made two service boards, one with a picture of a pint of milk on for Vatanen, the

Salonen gets the Fiat 131 into swing in Canada in 1977.

other with a drawing of a cigarette to show Timo where he should go!

Salonen watched his team-mate win a historic Monte Carlo Rally, the first by a Finn for 18 years. For his part, his first competitive outing in the T16 gave him a respectable third slot, albeit off the pace of Röhrl and Vatanen. He had told Todt prior to the start that he would not be driving for a win. Sweden was another third-place finish, but by Portugal it was obvious that Salonen had got the measure of the car and he won his third world championship event, his first for his new team. Despite his new-found confidence, the Finn had to wait until the Acropolis for his next victory, but it was an emphatic one and with the retirement of his team-mate Vatanen, he pulled out an 18-point world championship lead. Declaring that he didn't like travelling to New Zealand in the middle of the northern hemisphere's summer months did nothing to quell Salonen's speed, and he took his second Antipodean victory in five years. Argentina was next, another maximum score, and it seemed Salonen could scoop the title on his home ground.

A fitting backdrop to the world titles was anticipated. Salonen had never won the 1000 Lakes, the Holy Grail for rally-Finns, and was facing Markku Alèn and Henri Toivonen in Lancias in addition to Stig Blomqvist and Hannu Mikkola in Quattro Sports. However, as his rivals experienced problems instead of battling for the title, Salonen found he just had to avoid doing anything daft to win the rally by over a minute and wrap up both the drivers' and manufacturers' title with three rallies to go.

Having won the world title, Salonen was upset to find that his performance on the first round of the 1986 season was criticized by the hugely partisan French press. He had made a crucial bad tyre choice in Monte Carlo – an easy mistake to make on the always changing alpine stages – going out on wets on a stage that had dried, and allowing Henri Toivonen to take eight seconds a mile from him. Realizing that Toivonen had beaten him, Salonen decided it was better to have a safe second place in the bag than go for a first which he didn't think he could get and risk

the car. Todt was beside himself with anger as the times came in and the French press attacked him as lacking motivation. Salonen waited until Sweden to reply.

He didn't win the Swedish Rally, but he returned times that blitzed not just the opposition but those historically set by multiple-winner Stig Blomqvist. A win was out of the question when oil leaked onto the hot engine and started a fire.

A famous story attaches itself to Salonen and the Rally of Argentina that year. Arriving at the airport, Timo discovered that there was no first-class seat available for him, and while his team-mates were quite happy to travel Economy, Salonen refused point blank, insisting on waiting a day for the first available first-class route – despite the time loss *and* the fact it was a less direct route.

His history-making RAC win in 1986, the last ever on the rally for a Group B car, very nearly didn't happen. Indeed, if Salonen and Vatanen had had their way it certainly wouldn't have happened. With Juha Kankkunen heading for the world title, Salonen had little appetite for a long, probably wet and definitely cold Britain in November. Vatanen on the other hand was keen to return to competition after his Argentine accident. Todt put his foot down and Salonen won the rally.

At the end of Group B he joined Mazda, who seemed to have a competitive Group A car in its 4x4 323. Its 1600 engine struggled to keep on terms with its 2-litre rivals, and it was obvious that Salonen was becoming downhearted by trying to coax winning performances from the car. He did manage success in Sweden, but it seemed the fire had gone. After three lacklustre years in the underpowered car he joined Mitsubishi in 1991, with his first event in the Galant, the Monte Carlo. Always ready to have a joke, even at his own expense, he'd turned in a couple of stage times that seemed slower than expected. 'Was there a problem with the car?' asked a journalist. 'No, the car is too slow, but it's a problem with the driver. The car is too heavy because I carry my wallet in the boot with me!' smiled a contented Timo.

ARI VATANEN

*Ari Vatanen
always has time
for his fans.*

Even back in 1985 it was fairly evident that being tossed out of a tumbling T16 at around 220 kph (136 mph) would have a drastically detrimental effect on one's health. For Ari Vatanen, it was very nearly the ultimate accident, doctors attending him immediately after the crash in Argentina giving little hope for his survival.

That he lived bore testimony to his mental and physical strength. That he recovered fitness completely to compete again is part of the reason why at the age of 43

he attracts veritable hordes of fans wherever he competes.

The public, whether in Finland, the UK, or France where he now lives, have awarded him superstar status, and he does his best to keep his public happy.

His wild and exuberant driving style, and untamed speed – even now – make him a crowd pleaser, and his off-stage charisma is undeniable. The downside of his driving style was, travelling so fast and in such a committed manner, if he made a mistake it usually ended his rally, and more often than not, the car. Despite this, the Vatanen package of lightning speed and irresistible charm has made team managers overlook the cost in rebuilds ...

He first caught the attention of a Finnish sponsor after he'd beaten Hannu Mikkola on a round of the Finnish National Championship, the Nortti Rally in 1974. It was a close-fought event, with Vatanen edging out the hero of that year's 1000 Lakes Rally, Hannu Mikkola in a works car, by a short neck. The following year with help from the same Finnish oil company, Vatanen was fast making a name for himself and undertook both the Welsh and Scottish rallies that year in an Opel. It gave Ford boss Stuart Turner the chance to see for himself this precocious talent that had set the Anglo-Finnish grapevine rustling, and he saw enough to offer Vatanen a seat in his 1975

RAC team, as number three to Roger Clark and Timo Mäkinen.

His co-driver was Peter Bryant, and the new combination was in fourth place after the first day of just two stages. After the overnight halt, Vatanen entered the fourth stage of the long event. In his biography *Every Second Counts* he recalls travelling at around 177 kph (110 mph) when the car was launched into the trees after hitting a dip on the stage, ripping the sumpguard off. Bryant ended up in hospital, treated for shock, and the young Vatanen was convinced it was the end of his hopes of a professional rally future. He couldn't bring himself to face Turner, who finally caught up with him after two days. The meeting was short and to the point. Vatanen was to join the team for 1976.

In a Ford Escort RS2000 he won the Tour of Britain, and in an Escort RS1800 the Welsh and Manx rallies in 1976, enough to win the British championship for Ford. The following year, with an expanded programme, he won the Arctic and Scottish rallies, also in an RS1800.

In 1978 he scored his first world championship points, coming fifth in Sweden, an unlucky result when an electrical problem stopped him from giving Ford a podium sweep. Two further outings saw retirements and then on that year's RAC Rally the crew missed a control and brought disqualification for themselves.

1979 was the first of the Rothmans Escort years and Vatanen had a new co-driver, David Richards. He began to hit top form, form that would last six years, but still that elusive first world championship round win would not happen for the tall blond. The nearest he came was his home event when he was second to Markku Alèn *en-route* to his hat trick of Finnish victories. The private David Sutton Ford very nearly caught the works Fiat of Alèn but ultimately the experience of the older Finn won through and he beat the youngster by over a minute and a half.

1980 saw the same team, the same car, but by the Acropolis of that year Vatanen had at last taken his first world championship scalp. It had taken him 26 world championship rally starts.

1981 was destined to be Vatanen's year. Despite the appearance of a German car with a fancy line in all-wheel drive, it was the year that he was crowned world champion. But possibly any other manager bar David Sutton would have sacked him halfway through the season for throwing his Escort off the road once too often.

At the start of the season there was no hint as to the momentous victory that would end the year. Vatanen's Escort was forced out of Monte Carlo with engine trouble. Sweden was better, second to Mikkola who was giving the four-wheel-drive Quattro its inaugural win. Then, after trailing Mikkola for three days in Portugal, the Quattro's engine failed and Vatanen was left with a six-minute lead over Markku Alèn. It lasted only one further stage. Losing concentration on an unchallenging part of the stage, Vatanen neatly planted his Escort between two trees. He was devastated, having tossed away the opportunity to take the lead in the drivers' championship; Richards was furious, having orchestrated the sponsorship deal and pushed Vatanen's name forward as the driver to secure. For Vatanen, Portugal was a lonely place.

The Acropolis Rally was the next planned outing for the Sutton team, and Vatanen could only watch as the Audis disappeared into the distance. Then at halfway, the German team were excluded for illegal modifications.

Opposite: There were many lows as well as highs for Vatanen, and one of the lows must have been trying to drag the abortive Ford Fiesta project car around the 1979 Monte Carlo Rally. Next year would be a better year!

Vatanen once again found himself given an unexpected lead and he kept it to take maximum points, and at last the congratulations of his sponsors.

Long-time leader in the drivers' championship was Frenchman Guy Frequelin co-driven by Jean Todt in a Talbot Sunbeam.

Vatanen's championship standings weren't improved after travelling to Argentina, where testing was shortened when customs held the car up and the driver was then ill. Once the rally was under way, the Escort developed brake problems. After delays which left the crew almost on maximum lateness, the early leader crashed out in the thick dust of a slower competitor. As he reported in *Every Second Counts*: 'I was both ashamed and annoyed. It really wasn't necessary to come halfway around the world to roll a car, I could do that very well in England, in fact I often had.' Wins 1, accidents 2.

The next South American start was far more successful: in Brazil, the Vatanen/Richards combo chalked up its third win, and the season began to look as if it might yield a little more fruit.

As a backdrop to Vatanen's world championship year was his national service, a year of military training which all Finns must fulfil. Having put the training off until now, as well as contesting rallies he also had to arrange time off for them once his allocation of leave had been used up. Special permission was granted for him to practise and compete on the 1000 Lakes, a rally on which he had been beaten by Markku Alèn the previous three occasions. On the fastest rally of the calendar, Vatanen took his second world championship win in less than a month.

He could have wrapped the title up in San Remo, but it wasn't to be.

In second place, 20 seconds behind Michele Mouton in her Quattro, the Finn decided to risk the valuable 15 points he almost had in the bag for a further five and San Remo victory. It was a bad gamble. Taking a corner too close, he clipped a wall, puncturing a tyre and damaging the steering. He dropped from second to a finish of seventh, but was incorrigible: 'I was feeling very depressed when I crossed the finishing line, but it didn't last long. David Sutton and I agreed that we would probably always decide the same way – to win after pulling out all the stops is really sweet so it's worth a try!' Is it any wonder that he was every young driver's hero?

So, passports and visas had to be arranged for the trip back to Africa.

It wasn't a holiday. Early on, a local lorry was travelling too fast, on the wrong side of the road, and the Rothmans' Escort was badly damaged. Ari recalled: 'I've had plenty of accidents in my life but never one that smelt so bad. The lorry was full of some strange things that must have been some kind of fish!'

They had to crawl 640 kilometres (400 miles) in the badly damaged car to reach the first service point – only to learn that the mechanics didn't have a spare clutch plate. There was no alternative but to replace the broken clutch plate and limp on for the rest of the 2250 kilometre (1400 mile) rally. Two points for ninth place were added to Vatanen's total, working out at tens of thousands of pounds per point.

The 1981 title rested on the outcome of the RAC Rally. At the start of the event Guy Frequelin had 89 points, Vatanen 81. Just one big accident and it would all be over for Ari.

Once Frequelin went out on the 53rd of 65 stages it was a matter of Vatanen driving sensibly within his

cushion in second place, nine and a half minutes behind leader Mikkola, but almost two minutes in front of Mouton and then Blomqvist when the French driver's Audi hit transmission trouble. Ask any driver what the most difficult conditions to drive under are and he'll normally reply when you're trying to keep order – not flat out to risk an accident, nor too slow to be caught or lose concentration. It was a tough test for the driver and the team, but as Vatanen finished second, the first to congratulate the new world champion was fellow Finn Hannu Mikkola.

To his fans, it wasn't the fact that Vatanen had become champion that drew the crowds, it was his style of driving, which in the rear-wheel-drive Escorts was as flamboyant and reckless and glorious as the flight of Icarus. Of course there would be a moment when he flew too close to the sun, but unlike his tragic Greek counterpart, Vatanen lived to tell the tale. That day in Argentina was still some years away, as the Finn became the toast of the world.

Ford had not only stopped development of the Escort, by 1983 it had cancelled its RS1700T programme with the arrival of Audi's four-wheel-drive power. Vatanen was momentarily left high and dry until Tony Fall stepped in and signed the Finn for Opel shortly before the 1982 RAC Rally (on which he crashed). In the twilight of its career Vatanen managed to pull off an astonishing Safari win in the two-wheel-drive Ascona 400, on its last works appearance before being replaced by the Manta.

By 1984 Ari was a Peugeot driver, a relationship begun when Jean Todt was co-driving for Vatanen's rival for the world championship, Guy Frequelin. They had formed a mutual respect then, and Todt had pursued Vatanen as only one of four drivers that he thought would bring success to his T16.

The car was given its debut in Corsica in 1984, and a more spectacular debut Vatanen could not have imagined. The first half of the rally was a dream, and then came a nightmare. When leading the French round of the world championship, in a French car, by two minutes, Vatanen started to brake on water and was helpless to prevent the car from crashing off the road down a steep Corsican mountain. The impact from the crash had ripped Vatanen's helmet from his head but fortunately the only physical damage was a chipped shoulder blade and he was back competing on the Acropolis Rally. By Finland he gave the French manufacturer its first win for the T16, starting an incredible run of five successive wins from five starts, which culminated in his 1985 Monte Carlo win.

There have been outstanding drives in rallying history, and Vatanen's Monte Carlo win would make it on to all but the toughest person's top three moments.

Jean Todt, Peugeot Talbot Sport's director, had announced before the rally's start that his team would win the world championship that year. Since Vatanen had never won the Monte Carlo, the pressure was on both him and team-mate Timo Salonen to win from season start, particularly against a confident Walter Röhrl, winner on the Monte on the last three occasions and this time appearing in an Audi Sport Quattro.

Starting the second stage 19 seconds ahead of his rivals, Vatanen noticed that the crowds were particularly heavy on the entrance of the stage. Towards the end of the 24 kilometre (15 mile) test, he took the car wide on a narrow lane lined with spectators. Both crew members saw people everywhere, one taking a direct hit from the Peugeot, smashing the windscreen. It was every driver's worst nightmare and something observers had been

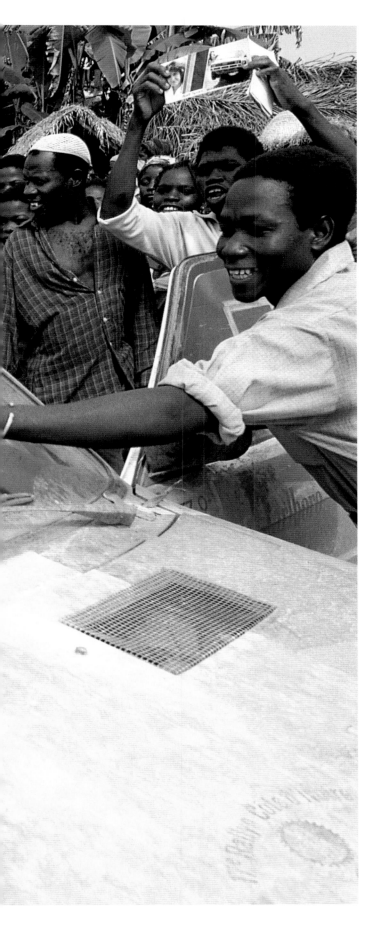

warning about especially in Monte Carlo, Portugal and San Remo. Fortunately, the most serious injury was a broken leg but it had been a traumatic experience for both Vatanen and Harryman.

Röhrl's Sport he decried as 'unmanageable' and coupled with an uncharacteristically bad tyre choice by the German, gradually Vatanen was able to overhaul him in tricky conditions in which he considers that he turned in 'one of the best drives of my career'. The time control at Gap was just one of many time controls on the event but his co-driver made sure that it is one he is never likely to forget.

Delayed at the start of the previous stage by four minutes, Terry Harryman had forgotten to add in the extra time in calculating the minute they should enter the Gap time control. The penalty for early arrival on the rally was two minutes for every actual minute early and Harryman had booked in four minutes early. From a handsome lead of four minutes the crew was behind by an equal amount. Poor Harryman was stricken; one of the sport's best, he was helpless to undo the error.

With 394 kilometres (245 miles) left of competitive special stages Vatanen had over four and a half minutes to make up. It averaged out at 1.5 seconds a mile over Röhrl over stages that the German had made his own on his last four visits.

It all came down to tyre choice; important on all rallies, crucial in Monte Carlo where success and failure depend on choosing correctly for stages which can go from ice through slush then dry tarmac on the same test.

The stage in question was the Col St Raphael, a 37 kilometre (23 mile) test, with – as usual – conflicting advice as to the most suitable tyres. The start of the stage was devoid of snow. Slicks would give the fastest time on a surface with no snow, but would be hopeless if snow was a problem. Röhrl decided first, and opted for slicks. Vatanen went for studs. There was snow on an uphill section and even with four-wheel drive Röhrl was slipping and unable to find grip. Vatanen passed the German on the stage and took the lead. It was an incredible moment for the Finn and an even more incredible final few stages as Harryman redeemed himself, ensuring his driver didn't lose concentration. It was the first time Peugeot had won in Monte Carlo for 53 years and Vatanen was a hero of France. It must have looked odds-on for a second world championship title for Vatanen, especially after winning in Sweden, but a run of mechanical failures and another accident in Corsica meant the honour went to his team-mate Timo Salonen. Ari took second place in New Zealand and then came Argentina.

Harryman and Vatanen had recced well for the rally, practising each stage at least three times. Indeed they had gone over the stage where they were eventually to have their giant accident on a fourth occasion. There was a small dip on the stage, but between recce and the rally, a great deal of rain had fallen, turning the small dip into a fairly deep hollow. The T16 hit the dip flat out and began its nose dive, which then flipped the car over and over again down the road and eventually into the undergrowth. Vatanen's seat had broken and he was tossed around as the car rolled. Harryman's stayed put, but when the Peugeot helicopter eventually located the car and crew it seemed unlikely that Vatanen would survive. He was given 3 litres of blood before transferring to hospital in Cordoba.

Doctors believe that the Finn's high level of fitness and general good health enabled him to pull through the fractured cervical vertebra, crushed rib cage and eight broken ribs, punctured lung, damaged lumbar vertebrae, and smashed left ankle and knee. Days after the accident,

Michele Mouton pulls in for a quick wash and change on the 1985 Ivory Coast Rally.

doctors were still noncommittal, and there remained the possibility of brain damage. It was ten days after the crash before they were confident that he would survive with no permanent damage, but the 1981 world champion was in hospital until October.

The accident had a profound effect on Ari, nonetheless. Long after he left hospital, he suffered from debilitating depression throughout most of 1986 and a delusion that he had contracted AIDS during one of the many blood transfusions he had received. It was, he recalls, the most testing time of his life, and a time when his wife Rita even had to hide the telephone from him to prevent him talking to reporters and giving them his obituary – so convinced was he that he was going to die of AIDS. Working with his doctor, he managed to push the black cloud behind him and started testing with Peugeot for the Paris–Dakar.

It was the start of a new era for Peugeot as well as for Vatanen. While he had been recuperating, his colleague Henri Toivonen had been killed and Group B banned. Peugeot no longer had an interest in rallying as such and so decided to contest desert raids. Thus his comeback in the T16 would be on the 1987 Paris–Dakar, one of the most physically demanding events of the motor sports year crossing a ridiculous 12,850 kilometres (8000 miles) of desert and rough terrain. Yet he won it. There have been more prolific winners and more stylish drivers, but as far as many are concerned Vatanen is in a class of his own.

While he found success in rally raids, and contested one-offs for Peugeot like the Pikes Peak Hillclimb, Vatanen was still anxious to return to world championship rallying, and did so on the 1987 Safari Rally in a Subaru. He finished tenth in Africa and followed it by a return to the 1000 Lakes, with a Ford Cosworth where he turned in a performance that showed all the aggression, speed and impetuosity of old had survived the Argentine experience, and although it was an orchestrated second place – Stig Blomqvist was ordered to stop challenging his team-mate when in third place – it was nonetheless a necessary result for the Finn to notch up.

Despite his Finnish performance, Vatanen had trouble getting a full programme. Time hadn't waited for him while he convalesced, and drivers outnumbered seats in the early days of Group A – boom time for rallying it was not. He joined Andrew Cowan's Mitsubishi in 1988 just in time for the RAC Rally, but car, driver and team never really gelled and failed to find the pace in the Galant that team-mate Kenneth Eriksson could.

Subaru was next, the team run by his world championship-winning partner David Richards, but again although from 11 starts there were just two retirements through accidents, that elusive post-accident win failed to materialize, despite second places on the RAC in 1992 and 1000 Lakes and Rally of Australia the following year.

In 1994 he rejoined Ford on a selected event basis, still wanting to tuck a final win under his belt, proving to his detractors that he lost none of his skill in Argentina – or is it proving to himself?

MICHELE MOUTON

To a sport which had already seen the likes of Pat Moss and Anne Hall, rallying's welcome to Michele Mouton should have been infinitely more gracious than it

was. 'How does it feel to be getting beaten by a woman?' a journalist asked Björn Waldegård in 1982 as Mouton led the Rally of New Zealand. 'I'm not being beaten by a woman, I'm being beaten by a car,' growled the Swede.

Into a world where women had been cast to provide the er, lurve interest and tea, Mouton arrived with a total disregard for whom she beat, just so long as she beat them, an attitude which her fellow Frenchmen found hard to digest. Indeed, after taking the French ladies' title in 1974, she dominated Group Three in the series the following year to such an extent that her beaten rivals refused to accept her victories were won fair and square. They were silenced when, after her group win in Corsica that year, scrutineers stripped the engine on her Renault Alpine only to declare it totally legal.

Try and disregard it as she might, in a sport where men and women could be seen to compete on equal terms, the girl from Grasse was regarded as a novelty, and on every single one of the 50 world championship rounds that she started she carried the unwanted baggage that no other competitor had to take. Before each rally, journalists would seek her out for the 'Woman in a Man's World' feature. She would be on television, radio, a PR person's delight in a sport so steeped with testosterone. While other drivers could enjoy an uninterrupted recce, Mouton would often have to sacrifice practice for some publicity function. Once the rally had begun, there was no more competitive driver than Mouton. Indeed, her infamous feud with future fellow-Audi driver Walter Röhrl stemmed largely from her failure to understand any driver competing for anything less than outright victory. Wins were her goal, not points, and she couldn't hide her scorn for those who didn't have the same raw aggression. Tactics, as far as she was concerned, were something your rivals worried about.

From a teenager slipping from her parents' home to 'borrow' the family car to the first woman driver to win a world championship round, and come within an ace of taking the 1982 drivers' crown, Mouton didn't know what a rally was until a boyfriend took her to Corsica at the age of 22.

Up until then she had been happy to race herself on her journey to and from work, from her home in Grasse, trying each day to better her time in the Renault 4 she drove. After Corsica she started co-driving for friends but, as was the common pattern for drivers, soon got itchy feet and jumped sides to get behind the steering wheel.

In 1974, encouraged by her father, she took part in her first international event, the Tour de France. It was not a great success, as she finished her rally with a much damaged Alpine A110 struggling to the end of a stage after crashing against a bridge. Nothing daunted, on that year's Corsica Rally she made her debut in the world championship and finished 12th.

In 1975 she dominated Group Three in the French championship, finishing seventh in Corsica, and became European Ladies' champion, a run of events which earned her a semi-professional drive in the French championship the following year in an Elf-backed Group Four Alpine A310. Co-driven at this time by fellow-Frenchwoman Françoise Conconi, the performances of the all-girl crew not only caught the attention of Fiat France but also that of the Almeras Brothers, and in 1977 she took her first outright international win in Spain in a Porsche 911. A rare appearance in a Lancia Stratos on the 1978 Monte Carlo Rally gave her the *Coupe des Dames* and seventh overall on an event marked by heavy snow, but her three-year contract saw her mostly in the Abarth 131 with which

she won the 1978 Tour de France and the 1979 Lyon Charbonnières rallies. By the end of 1980 and the finish of her Fiat France contract, Mouton had held the European ladies' title a fairly routine five times, and the contract that was to make her name was just around the corner.

There was no reason to link the German manufacturer with Mouton's name before contracts were exchanged and for the driver herself the approach was a surprise, but she joined the Quattro team alongside Hannu Mikkola to give the four-wheel-drive phenomenon its world championship debut on the Monte Carlo Rally of 1981.

The event was a bad start to an association cynics were labelling as a publicity stunt. Mouton and Annie Arrii were forced to retire on the concentration run from Paris with a fuel blockage problem. With just Mikkola representing Audi in Sweden, Mouton had to wait for Portugal to get her car on the score-card, finishing fourth. More importantly, the event signalled the start of her relationship with Fabrizia Pons a young Italian co-driver with whom Mouton was to spend the rest of her career. Pons had been recommended by Mouton's boyfriend at the time, when Annie Arrii had been unable to make a commitment to full-time rallying around the world.

As well as the myth of her lack of skill, Mouton's detractors also labelled her as temperamental and difficult to work with, Walter Röhrl criticizing her for shouting at her mechanics. But the Mouton/Pons combination worked well and team spirit in the Audi camp was good between the driver and her team. A strong professional partnership developed between Mouton and Hannu Mikkola. During pre-Monte testing, the former learnt the left-foot braking technique they felt at the time essential for getting the best out of the big car from the vastly experienced Finn.

Just as 1981 seemed liable to fizzle out for Mouton, with mechanical failure in Corsica and the Audi débâcle in Greece and after a respectable debut in Finland where she finished 13th – and the best non-Finnish or Swedish driver – along came San Remo, an event she had last undertaken in 1976 in a Renault Alpine. The loose stages suited the Quattro, the speed and pace suited Mouton. Taking the lead halfway through the third leg, she opened out a three-minute advantage over Ari Vatanen, chasing the world title in an Escort. Just as it looked as if the Audi had an unassailable lead, first the brakes and then a driveshaft hit trouble, leaving her just 34 seconds in front of Vatanen, who scented another possible maximum score could be his. Despite the pressure the two frontrunners were under it was the Ford and not the Audi that left the road and Mouton had taken the historic first world championship rally win for a woman driver.

Michele Mouton gets to grips with the Fiat 131 Abarth on the Tour de Corse.

1982 was the year Mouton should have, indeed could have, become world champion, winning in Portugal, Greece and Brazil – more victories than any driver that year. And yet it was also a heartbreaking year, in more ways than one. It must have seemed that the year was to be ill-fated from the very first rally.

With its snow-covered mountainous stages, the Monte Carlo should have been tailor-made for Quattro traction, but this year the snow had been replaced by beautiful blue skies, and not a flake of snow fell anywhere. It was a combination of weather and the French tendency to do things their own way that ended her rally when up to fourth. Deciding to close the road making up the 11th special stage early, the police refused to allow Mouton's ice-note crew passage and so they tackled the stage almost blind, on ice-notes a day old. A patch of ice that had formed during the intervening hours rocketed the Quattro into a wall rendering Fabrizia Pons unconscious and giving Mouton an injured knee.

Sweden followed, and with it what Mouton was later to recall as being 'the most excruciating moment of my professional rally life.'

On a snow-covered Swedish Rally, team-mate Hannu Mikkola was firmly tipped to take his second victory on the event. Mikkola was leading by some six minutes, with Stig Blomqvist in the Quattro he rallied in the Swedish national series second, and Mouton third. On the longest stage of the rally, the 36th out of 40 stages that year, Mikkola stuck his car into a snowbank. Blomqvist managed to get past, and after a great deal of digging the Finn's Quattro was about to rejoin the competition when Mouton approached the corner a little too fast and shoved Mikkola back into the bank! It took Mouton minutes to get her Quattro out ... Mikkola almost half an hour. The Frenchwoman, however, managed to register her first world championship points of the season, finishing in fourth place.

Portugal was an altogether happier place and she took her second world championship victory by a staggering 13 minutes, setting fastest times on 18 out of 40 special stages. In fog, which only months earlier she had remarked on being her least favourite driving weather, she took the lead when team-mate Hannu Mikkola left the road. Pulling out a two-minute lead over Röhrl she didn't have to worry about the German threat for long when a terrifying accident as a result of steering failure put him out of the rally but remarkably left him and Christian Geistdorfer unhurt. With the charging Henri Toivonen unable to persuade his gallant Opel to carry on any more, Audi took the lead for the first time in the manufacturers'

Michele Mouton powers her way to mysterious retirement on the 1985 Ivory Coast Rally.

championship, but more importantly Mouton herself was just four points behind 1980 champion and arch-rival Walter Röhrl in the drivers' series.

With Audi missing the Safari Rally, Mouton's year continued in Corsica. Losing so comprehensively in Monte Carlo on dry tarmac, Audi had installed the new lightweight alloy block engine, saving precious kilograms. But for Mouton the rally was characterized by a frustrating series of problems that began with a leaking rear axle, continued with a broken shock absorber, worsened when she hit the side of a mountain, and ended when her seat broke loose from its mountings on the final stage. Fabrizia Pons provided as much stability as possible by hanging on to the back of her driver's seat. Mouton finished a discontented seventh, while Röhrl increased his lead by finishing fourth.

The Acropolis Rally, notorious for its huge demands on stamina and strength as drivers compete in searing heat over stages made up of boulders, gave Michele her third, and most glorious win. A victory in Greece was the final poke in the eye for her detractors, as she not only stood up physically to Greece's tough test but also mentally, as she led the rally with a trio of Opels on her tail, her Audi team-mates out of the event. Early trouble with the turbo was forgotten by the end of the rally which saw her return another 13-minute margin over her nearest challenger. Unfortunately for her world championship hopes, that challenger was Röhrl.

Politics and sport butting heads, Mouton's next world championship outing was in New Zealand – as opposed to the planned trip to Argentina, cancelled due to the Falklands War – but it was an awfully long way to travel for the Audi team to end in disappointment. For Mouton it was another frustrating rally, being forced to retire when leading after an oil line came adrift. There was nothing she could do but watch Röhrl pick up more points for a fourth place and extend his advantage.

The pressure was on both manufacturer and driver as they approached Brazil. A poor performance, indeed anything short of an outright win, and both makes and drivers' titles would have gone to Opel and Röhrl. It was hardly an appropriate arena for such an important test. Only eight days before the rally was due to start, the organizers had sacked their clerk of the course, Francisco Santos. For Santos the rally had been his mission, and when many officials walked off the course to protest against his removal, teams knew they were in for a rough ride.

Apart from Opel and Audi the entry was non-existent, with the exception of a Datsun from Shekhar Mehta and wife Yvonne. While local farm trucks wandered happily along competitive stages (Mouton was deliberately driven into by a VW Beetle on a road section), a classic battle developed between the French and German drivers. The rally would have merited mention only under 'chaos' if it hadn't been for the two front (and almost only) runners. Breaking a driveshaft on the first day gave the lead to Röhrl, who hung on grimly, driving as hard as he could. As the last day began, Mouton was still over half a minute behind Röhrl and to the team's exasperation, stages were being cancelled which of course reduced the opportunity she had to overhaul the German. On the 24th of 29 stages Mouton again hit the front with an eight second lead, a supreme effort over a 32 kilometre (20 mile) stage. Röhrl had no answer, and in fact drove into a deep hole breaking a track control arm and finishing the penultimate stage on three wheels. Mouton was behind him and saw it all. She had scored her fourth victory on an event where she set 18 fastest times compared to

Röhrl's five, and more importantly she had reeled Röhrl in on the drivers' front and Opel in the makes.

The 1000 Lakes Rally is so often rallying death or glory; for Mouton, up to fifth place on this fast and furious Finnish speciality, it wasn't the latter in 1982. A heavy landing on a previous yump had left her Quattro with only front-wheel drive. Blissfully ignorant of this she took the next corner only for the tail of the big car to shoot out, down a ditch with a resulting high-speed roll. Fortunately the two crew were shaken but otherwise okay but it was the end of their rally.

San Remo had only a year before been the backdrop to Mouton breaking her world championship duck. Twelve months on she was desperately trying to keep her world championship title bid alive. In order to keep the manufacturers' challenge on the boil, Audi had no fewer than six cars entered on the event, the idea being to block the Opels from scoring.

A first day puncture dropped her to 17th, a bad blow to suffer so early on in the event. Spins here and there dropped further time but, worse, team-mate Stig Blomqvist brought in to help bolster Mouton's position and secure manufacturers' points was proving the fastest of the Audi entries and, after 49 of the 56 stages, he led the event ahead of Mikkola, with Mouton in third place. The final night saw Audi's plan of dominating the top five places smashed to bits by the superiority of Michelin tyres on the Opels, the inability of the Quattros to perform well on tarmac, and the sheer determination of both Toivonen and Röhrl which saw the latter zoom into third place pushing Mouton – whose seat had broken – into fourth place by 44 seconds. The respective world championship scores in the drivers' table were now Röhrl 101 and Mouton 82 points.

The Ivory Coast was the most crucial rally of the year. If Mouton failed to win, Röhrl would take his second championship, if Mouton won, the advantage would be hers. The gods are not always kind. Just a few days before the Ivory Coast was due to begin, Michele's father, her mentor and source of encouragement from the earliest events, died. She had never competed in Africa, her team had never competed on the rally before and she knew Röhrl was waiting for her to fail. Despite the pressure, she took out an early lead, but turbo-boost problems meant the Quattro wasn't working on top form. However, with a lead of 59 minutes over Röhrl after team-mate Mikkola had retired, she faced the third leg of the rally second on the road, in the red dust behind Röhrl. The German lost a further 20 minutes when a rear shock absorber broke, and then he lost more time crossing a river.

For Mouton, first a front driveshaft had to be changed and then a problem getting the gearbox engaged lost her 58 minutes which meant, in African terms at 25 minutes behind, Röhrl was on her tail. And after a routine rear-strut change hit problems, the difference was down to 18 minutes going into the third and final leg.

As she took her position on the re-start ramp, disaster struck. The fuel injection system wasn't working, the car wouldn't start, had to be pushed over the ramp and the unit changed. Her lead had gone but she was not despairing; the last leg was the shortest, but there were still 645 kilometres (400 miles) in which she could catch her German adversary.

Fog rolled in and combined with the dust to make drivers totally reliant on their pace-notes. Ironically, Röhrl and Mouton went off the road at the same junction, but the difference was that the French driver had rolled her

Audi and Fabrizia Pons' pace-notes had disappeared out of the window. The conditions were simply atrocious and not the kind to be reading the route from a roadbook while travelling at competitive speed in a Quattro. She pressed on, but in the fog and dust they ended up in a ditch, breaking a front control arm. It was repaired but only just within maximum lateness; a sprained thumb was ignored but a subsequent front suspension breakage could not be. For Mouton 1982 was over, she had lost the world championship, albeit winning more rallies than any other driver, and she would never get close again

The following year she was eclipsed within Audi by team-mate Mikkola. While he had experienced a dreadful run of disappointments in 1982, everything came right for the Finn on his way to the world title. Michele meanwhile struggled to hit the top form she'd found the previous year. The year began with the third in a series of unlucky Monte Carlos for her with Audi, an accident again ending her rally. The year's best performance came in Portugal where she finished second to team-mate Mikkola, setting an equal number of fastest times as the winner. A third place on the Safari was followed by a string of non-finishes which ran from Corsica, where her new lightweight 360 bhp car caught fire when oil spilt onto the engine, through Greece where she crashed halfway through the opening stage and onto New Zealand where she was poised to take her fifth world championship win until the Audi's connecting rod broke to end her event after leading for 20 of the 33 stages. A third in Argentina was the best result for the remainder of the year, but worse than the run of bad luck was the news that she would have a new team-mate for 1984, the man who had declared that if the world championship was won by a woman, it would have no value: Walter Röhrl.

Her 1984 programme consisted of five events. Missing Monte Carlo to concentrate on preparation for the Swedish Rally, her second-place finish was the best result a non-Finnish or Swedish driver has returned on the specialist event, until the record was equalled in 1992 by Britain's Colin McRae. It was not however a result which gave her a great deal of pleasure.

Ill throughout the event, in common with the other Quattro drivers, she felt the gearing was too low and was not happy with the car at all.

Non-finishes on the Safari, Greece and 1000 Lakes left the RAC, on which she gave the Sport its debut, managing a gutsy and gritty fourth after problems throughout the event with the new car.

In 1985 Mouton was relegated to one world championship event, the Ivory Coast (to maintain her A-seeded status), and the British Open Championship. Neither projects were anything of a success. On the Ivory Coast a tale which instantly took its place in rallying folklore occurred. Mouton's Audi developed engine problems, all the indications being that a head gasket had gone and therefore the engine was finished as was Mouton's rally. Not so. Instead of having work carried out at the service point, the Audi spluttered through the control only to check in at the next control sounding as good as new, but with the chase car that had shadowed her nowhere to be seen. As she withdrew before the final control, no action was ever taken, or investigation undertaken but the transformation of a dead engine in a heavily strengthened car into a healthily engined Audi that was falling apart after the rough stages is the sort of miraculous transformation of which legends are made.

On the less glamorous stage of Britain's Open Championship, she had an unbelievably disastrous year,

finishing only one of the six rounds, coming second to British driver Malcolm Wilson on the Welsh Rally.

The following year, disassociated from Audi, she joined Peugeot and drove a T16 in the German Championship, winning the title. It wasn't for her however, and in only four years she had gone from one of rallying's brightest hopes to driving in a national series; it therefore came as no surprise when she announced her retirement from the sport in San Remo, after travelling to the event to have talks with Audi.

STIG BLOMQVIST

Even at 44, he had the instinct for pace of a hungry cat reluctant to leave its bed to eat. On the Mobil Super Challenge, a British made-for-TV event which took six drivers and put them over identical stages in identical cars, he was the last to go. Looking at the current leader's time he belted himself into his car, chugged down to the stage start and neatly sliced a second off the total, to win the event. There was no championship at stake, just competitive pride. Having done his job he returned to lie down on a bench where his back was being treated for an old injury.

Being Swedish, the start for Stig Blomqvist was naturally a front-wheel drive Saab 96, with which he used to compete with his father. To start with, Blomqvist senior was in the driver's seat until it became apparent that maybe Blomqvist junior had the greater driving talent of the two. He stayed with Saab right up until the Swedish Rally of 1981, giving a turbocharged car its first world championship victory when the Saab 99 Turbo won the 1979 Swedish. In fact, he was the only person ever able to coax any performance out of the 99T. In total he won the Swedish Rally a record seven times, taking his first victory in 1971 when he was 27.

1971 was a particularly good year for Stig, trying to break into full-time rallying, starting the year by winning the Swedish, ending it winning the RAC Rally beating fellow Swede Björn Waldegård in a Porsche 2.2 911 into second place.

A contemporary of Waldegård, the two Swedes not only carried on the tradition begun by Tom Trana, Erik Carlsson and Ove Andersson, but provided the role models for another generation of world-class Swedish drivers, including Ingvar Carlsson and Kenneth Eriksson.

It's a wholly wrong but fairly natural assumption to make that someone so quiet and unassuming outside a car couldn't possibly possess the raw aggression needed to become a world champion, but to see the Swede swinging first a succession of Saabs around stages, and then latterly Quattros and Fords, leaves no-one to question his speed or commitment.

While Waldegård has driven more different makes of cars in the world championship, Blomqvist, in common with probably Juha Kankkunen, has amazing versatility in driving different configurations to success. From the front-wheel drive Saab, through rear-wheel, mid-engined Stratos, then 4x4 with Audi and subsequently Peugeot and Ford, Blomqvist has managed to extract the maximum performance from them all..

A very snowy RAC Rally made an ideal event for Blomqvist and his Saab to win in 1971. He'd started the year winning the Swedish, pausing mid-season for the 1000 Lakes and the RAC was more of the same! Despite the fact that he had beaten the Finns on their home ground,

on one of the fastest and most specialized events of the championship, he still didn't enjoy the flurry of attention by other manufacturers that drivers both before and after have done. Not that Blomqvist was complaining, apart from anything it wasn't in his nature.

His style in the Saabs was breathtakingly sideways, the quiet man outside the car metamorphizing into a demon at the wheel of the 115 bhp front-wheel drive lightweight, which quite often ended on its roof *en route* to victory. He was invited to drive a Stratos on the 1978 Swedish, setting a string of 16 blistering fastest times, but finishing only fourth after several minor problems. Despite the good performance he was still regarded as too much of a specialist for a wider programme.

Talbot appeared in 1981, with the offer of a drive in Finland and on the RAC and despite adopting a role that would become familiar to him in future years, that of back-up driver, to in this case Henri Toivonen and Guy Frequelin, he brought valuable points to his team's quest for world championship glory, the only Sunbeam Lotus to finish either rally. Taking third place on the RAC attracted the attentions of Audi, looking for a third driver to strengthen its squad.

In 1982 he was an Audi driver, booked to join Mikkola and Mouton. Given a competitive car he immediately showed the talent that had been only glimpsed before. Winning in Sweden, slightly unexpectedly when his two Audi team-mates were shunted into a snowbank, he nonetheless took his sixth win on his home event.

At Audi, and subsequently Ford, Blomqvist was cast in a supporting role, a task he carried out diligently even when it evidently rankled as it surely must have on the 1000 Lakes that first year, when a charging Blomqvist was ordered by Roland Gumpert to keep behind team-mate Mikkola, despite the former setting 21 fastest stage times as opposed to Mikkola's 12. A Swede being forced to accede to a Finn when the smell of Finnish victory was in his nostrils – poor Stig was so fed-up he didn't bother fitting new rubber towards the end of the rally. If Audi had intended to issue the same instructions to their new recruit in San Remo, they were unable to due to the pace of the Opels. Sending five cars to Italy, Audi had intended to stack the odds against Opel in the manufacturers' championship, but the plan backfired when Michele Mouton lost a chunk of time with a puncture, and as Blomqvist set about the San Remo stages like a man possessed, all Audi's management could do was cheer his victory and reflect that the best laid plans ...

His team spirit paid off in 1984 when he was given a full crack at the drivers' title; ironically it was not a year when he was really at his peak, but Ingolstadt had decreed that it was to be Blomqvist's year, and after an initial stuttering start, it was indeed.

The Germans rewarded Blomqvist for his earlier patience with a programme of 11 events, and it took until the Ivory Coast before the world championship was safely up on the Blomqvist mantelpiece.

That he was a worthy champion was not in question. Wins in Sweden (again), Greece, New Zealand, Argentina and the Ivory Coast ensured that, despite the modesty of the man who didn't really consider events like Argentina, without a full works entry, 'proper rallies'. But even for a man with an appetite for testing and rallies such as Blomqvist, the year was a hard one, but accidents were still rare. 1985 still comprised eight tough events, but in the whole of the two seasons, a total of 19 events, he failed to finish through his own fault on only one occasion.

Blomqvist made his name initially with Saab, with whom he stayed beyond the competitive life of the car.

HANNU MIKKOLA

Everyone you speak to seems to have a good word to say about Hannu Mikkola. That's not to say he's a saint or sets out to give that impression, it's simply that through his team spirit and enduring skill he's a driver people are happy to have represent their sport. Managers sought his services because of his no-nonsense professionalism – and because he was quick. He was at the top of rallying for almost 20 years and was unlucky to win the drivers' title on just the one occasion in 1983. He was runner-up on three further occasions, once losing by a single point to Björn Waldegård in 1979.

By the time the official World Rally Championship was up and running, Mikkola was already the veteran of three 1000 Lakes wins – he remembers making his competition debut on the rally wearing a collar and tie! Indeed his first drive for Ford in 1968 saw victory. It was also the scene of some useful career advice by one of the Ford team. When Mikkola expressed surprise at the way the Escort's brake bias had been set up – towards the front, as opposed to the preferable rear-bias set-up for loose surfaces – he was told: 'Well, Roger Clark never complains; perhaps you'd be better off learning to drive like him!'

In total he spent 31 years rallying, starting his competitive career in a Volvo PV544 in 1963. He was third on the 1967 1000 Lakes and the hottest Finnish national champion foreign teams had seen for a long while. Ford, Lancia and Datsun all wanted him to drive for them, and after driving for Datsun in Monte Carlo he had a couple of outings in a Lancia Fulvia before plumping for Ford. More so than Audi, Ford is synonymous with the name of Mikkola, but out of a total of 123 world championship starts, only 21 were with the Boreham team, and of those only five were wins. In addition to world championship events with the Escort, he did of course win the World Cup Rally in 1970, the high profile London–Mexico marathon which grabbed attention worldwide.

Mikkola was certainly not the luckiest of drivers, his 1982 season with Audi when everything that could break, fall off or overheat did was proof in itself that you don't always make your own luck, sometimes you can be just plain, well, unlucky.

In 1973 and 1974 Ford's programme with the RS1600 was not a comprehensive one, the team throttling back to develop the RS1800, and so Mikkola, in addition to his Escort drives, expanded his programme with Volvo and then Peugeot on the following year's Safari Rally, hoping to repeat his success with Ford in 1972 when he and Gunnar Palm became the first non-African crew to win the rally. In 1975 Fiat pulled out of the 1000 Lakes, leaving Mikkola without a drive. Ove Andersson stepped in with a Toyota Corolla, and after covering almost 10,000 kilometres (6320 miles) in practice, Hannu won by 74 seconds from Simo Lampinen. For the team Mikkola had given a much-needed boost after a touch and go year in terms of funding for the rally programme. Of the car he said: 'You know this is the best injection I ever drive. It is very smooth power, not like when we try injection for Ford on Monte in 1973.' Unfortunately for Toyota, the car was only homologated with a 1600cc engine, which meant it was only competitive when there was no call for outright power from the bigger engines.

1976 and 1977 were not classic years for Mikkola. In fact there must have been times when he wondered if he was ever going to finish a rally. From the 1975 RAC Rally with Toyota when he retired with engine problems, to the 1976 1000 Lakes, when he was third in a Toyota, he failed to finish an event, and after the brief respite in Finland came another seven non-finishes with mechanical failure with Toyota, until the 1977 RAC Rally when he was second. It was a bad time for Mikkola. After having been hailed as a speed king, and sought after by every manufacturer, everything started to go wrong and he began

drinking heavily, letting it affect his professionalism and developing a reputation as a wild Finn.

By 1978 Mikkola had kicked his problems out of his life and Ford was back in full-time world championship rallying. In 1979 he enjoyed a tremendous season-long battle with Björn Waldegård for the first-ever drivers' title, losing by just one point to the Swede, but helping his team win its only world championship title to date.

1981 was the year he joined Audi with its revolutionary Quattro. He adapted quickly to four-wheel drive, and as the mainstay of the team was responsible for helping Michele Mouton get the best from the car.

Ironically it was Mouton who enjoyed the greater success with the car in 1981 and 1982, with Mikkola having an appalling run of mechanical failure throughout 1982. However, on the positive side he gave Audi its first world championship victory in Sweden, and took it to the RAC where British driver Tony Pond was prompted to comment: 'So long as Audi have no trouble, Hannu could easily win by 34 minutes.' The margin wasn't quite that great, a little over 11 minutes, but the combination of car and driver was just irresistible.

He spanned the ages in rallying, from a time when each round was almost a specialist event in itself and won

As he is best remembered: Hannu Mikkola at the wheel of a Ford Escort RS on the RAC Rally, usually winning.

73

by home-grown talent, into Group A and the rise of the southern European talent. Unlike some of his contemporaries, unable to contemplate life without rallying in some form or another – usually historic – Mikkola called final time on his career by winning the re-run of the World Cup Rally in 1995, retiring to the golf courses of Florida.

MARKKU ALÈN

'Such a raw – and frankly uncouth – talent.' Graham Robson (author and rally historian)

Tall, dark and brooding, if Markku Alèn had ever had to give up his day job he'd have earned a fantastic living as an alternative to Boris Karloff. Ninety per cent of this image was bluff and if the other 10% was genuine, well, his bark was always worse than his bite. If things were going badly on a rally you avoided Markku, and spoke to Kivimaki instead, but even then he was capable of springing a surprise. On the 1987 RAC Rally, his time through one of the early spectator stages was inexplicably slow to journalists waiting at the next service point. 'Markku, what was your problem?' someone asked. 'I have fuel problem,' came the reply. 'But Markku, your roof is dented, did you roll?' 'Sure,' came the laconic reply. 'Fuel not get through when car on roof!'

The son of a Finnish ice-racing champion, a young Markku decided to take to the ice and became champion in 1970, aged 19. His first 1000 Lakes Rally was in 1971 when he was third in a Volvo, in 1972 he was third again and then, with money from Marlboro, he travelled over to Britain for the RAC Rally. It wasn't a great success save to bring him to the attention of Ford and a certain persuasive Tony Mason, who was to enjoy success himself as Roger Clark's RAC winning co-driver in 1976. For now, however, Tony's job was as chief scout for Boreham; he remembers the young Finn vividly: 'Stuart [Turner] dispatched me to Finland to sign young Markku. He was not at all the self-assured star then that he is now, and didn't speak a word of English. He was living with his parents at the time, and we told him he had to learn English. After that, I kept getting postcards from Markku, wherever he was, with little messages telling me how much better his English was getting.' Even so, there was a communication problem and on the Welsh Rally, a round of the British championship, John Davenport could do little more than point his instructions. Far more suitable for Alèn was fellow Finn Ilkka Kivimaki, known as 'Kiki', with whom he has shared every world championship outing since Corsica 1974 creating an unusual all-Finnish crew.

His 1973 RAC drive is remembered as one of the great fightbacks and began his 14-year obsession with trying to win the British rally. Challenging Roger Clark over the first day's spectator stages, Alèn misjudged a corner in Sutton Park, sending his Escort off the stage into a triple roll and down into 177th place. The corner that year was a bit of an elephants' graveyard for Escorts, Hannu Mikkola and Russell Brookes both having an early roll out of the rally in the same place. Faced with a challenge Alèn began the task of scything through the field, catching cars on stages, and putting the car off again in Pickering Forest *en route* to the hardest won third place the rally is ever likely to see.

The RAC drive was a neon sign pointing to his talent,

Markku Alèn ploughs through a ford on his first visist to the RAC Rally in 1973.

and for 1974 Alèn was faced with a straight choice between Fiat and Ford. There were more rallies with the Italian manufacturer, a better car with Ford, but being number two at Lancia seemed preferable to being number three or four with Ford so Alèn and Kivimaki went to Abarth.

Despite their 15-year association with the Italian manufacturer, Alèn renewed his contract year by year, talking to other manufacturers but generally re-signing after San Remo each season.

He entered the team and drove the Abarth 124 Spyder, 'I loved the Fiat 124 Spyder,' he recalled in a *Rallysport* interview. 'To me, at that age, it was like driving a prototype round the streets.' The little car brought him his first world championship victory, in Portugal 1975. Morally, he should have broken his duck the year before in America's Press On Regardless Rally when Alèn led the rally from start to finish only to lose it when he received a time penalty for his service crew's alleged speeding.

He was then given the Abarth 131, with which he won the FIA Cup, the forerunner to the drivers' championship, in 1978. It was ironic that Alèn should win the drivers' title the year before it received its official world championship status, because he was doomed never to take the title once it had been made official.

It was a good time for Alèn to be at Fiat, the Abarth set-up simply dwarfing any other team's effort in terms of budget, manpower, expertise and resource. More than that, Alèn fitted into the lifestyle perfectly. While his command of English remained quixotic, 'Alèn go maximum attack' or 'Alèn not lucky' and then 'Povore Markku', his Italian ran the whole gamut of intonation, facial expression, shrugging and lots of hand waving. He became Finnish-Italian, dark shades, snappy and stylish casual clothes, good tan. Agreeing that the pace of life and philosophies suited him, 'I love everything Italian,' he said, '... I like the way you deal with them [Italians], for a few minutes you argue like hell, then you make decisions and immediately everything is back as it was.'

Of course Alèn is quick, you don't win world championship rallies if you're not, but the quality which really set him apart was his amazing ability to focus during an event. It was why he was so monosyllabic and unapproachable during a rally, the man was totally intent on the car and the stages.

Capable of furious outbursts on occasion, he was also quick to thank his team even when rallies didn't go according to plan, and could therefore get mechanics to do things for him which maybe they weren't so keen to do for his team-mates.

Labelled initially as a gravel specialist, he was the first Scandinavian to win Corsica when he took victory in 1983, a particularly satisfying time for the Finn as only months earlier his manager had written off his chances of even being in Corsica, let alone winning there.

It was the year when, against the odds, the Lancia two-wheel-drive 037 won the world championship, and to strengthen its hand Fiorio had brought in the reigning world champion Walter Röhrl. Alèn was not impressed at the attempt to shut him out and replied by winning in San Remo as well, which left him in third place in the drivers' championship, two points behind Röhrl and five behind Mikkola. Lancia's concern was for the makes title only and the hoped-for trip to the Ivory Coast for Alèn didn't materialize.

Alèn in the rear-wheel drive 037 struggled against Röhrl, in top form with the Quattro in 1984, only winning in Corsica when Vatanen crashed the debuting Peugeot

T16 in heavy rain; indeed visibility was so poor Alèn and Kivimaki didn't notice the Peugeot or its crew off the road. Despite its drive-handicap against Peugeot and Audi, the 037 handled well and throughout 1983 and 1984 was reliable too.

The handicap was too much for even Alèn to counterbalance, even on the 1000 Lakes Rally; but it wasn't for lack of trying. Raw aggression and skill gave the outdated Lancia a ten-second lead after the first Finnish leg, 'Here I am going flat out in a museum car,' commented Alèn as he was forced to take risk after risk on the fastest of events, only to be almost inevitably overhauled by Salonen's T16.

By the time the Delta S4 was ready to make its debut on the 1985 RAC Rally, Alèn and team-mate Toivonen had wrung every ounce from the 037. Both were simply fed-up with the delay in homologating the S4 and Alèn was talking to Jean Todt about a possible move to Peugeot, particularly when the S4 was refusing to shape up into anything like a world championship contender on its first three non-championship events. For Alèn, the watershed event was the Algarve Rally, the last test for the S4 before he had to choose whose contract to sign, the French or the Italian. The car's handling had made startling progress and it made a stunning debut, and yet Alèn seemed fated again not to win the RAC. When leading the rally as he had for most of the event, he went down a firebreak in Kielder and would have stayed there until Christmas if Toyota driver Juha Kankkunen had not decided to show Finnish solidarity in pushing him out. He was back in the RAC but team-mate Henri Toivonen had overtaken him, nonetheless giving the big Finn his best finish of the season.

Portugal 1986 was a difficult time for Alèn, shocked by the occurrence of what he had feared for so long in the death of four spectators, he was adamant that a withdrawal by the top drivers was essential to show the organizers the unacceptability of the situation. Boss Fiorio didn't agree and the Finn's name stayed absent from the drivers' declaration after an ultimatum was issued.

For 11 days at the end of that year, after winning in America on the Olympus Rally, Alèn was World Champion Driver. Keeping the title, however, hinged on the result of an appeal regarding the results from San Remo. The FIA decided that the points should be cancelled and Alèn, having won there, lost the points and the title.

Adapting quickly to the Group A Delta HF 4x4, he spent a further three years with Lancia before gradually being eclipsed by first Miki Biasion and subsequently Didier Auriol, at a time when Finns were waning in their fashionability to team managers and there were fewer seats available than top drivers. It was nonetheless difficult for the spectator to adjust to seeing Alèn in a Subaru, and his time there was not particularly happy. The Prodrive team were still perfecting ways in which to make the Legacy a winner and after two uncomfortable seasons which saw seven non-finishes from 12 rally starts he moved to Toyota for 1992. As the results started getting harder to come by, he started becoming ultra-fussy, worrying before stages about little things, changing his mind and not looking happy. His best result for Toyota was second on the 1993 Safari, his last drive for the team. He followed it the same year with an almighty accident in Finland, driving an Impreza, crashing on the first stage. 'It was the biggest accident of my career,' he said simply. It was the last time he was asked to drive for Subaru. He surprised everyone and turned to touring cars, where he drove an Alfa Romeo 155 on the German DTM circuit.

Opposite: He may have been Italian in looks, style and temperament, but Markku Alèn was always the archetypal Finn.

7
Supercars

'For me the original Group B cars were the maximum. Things started to get out of hand when the evolution versions came along.'

Björn Waldegård, 1979 World Champion

*Previous page:
The Lancia 037
Rally had just two-
wheel drive, but it
was clearly the
first of the Group
B supercars.
Below: the Audi
Quattro was the
first of the four-
wheel-drive
machines.
Bottom:
The 037 Rally was
so well-balanced
and driven so well
by the likes of
Henri Toivonen
that it held its own
against the four-
wheel-drive
Quattros for
several seasons.*

The supercars of Group B, those horribly short but wonderfully tumultuous years of motorsport hyperbole which embraced everything that was brave and new and audacious, began with the appearance of something of a carthorse.

The Audi Quattro's world championship debut in Monte Carlo in 1981 was the dawning of rallying's space age. Four-wheel drive had not been allowed by the FISA since 1971, but allied with a turbocharged engine, the Quattro was simply redefining the starting point for every designer for every future rally car. If it was heavy, had an uncomfortable 50:50 permanent drive split, and the engine was forward of its front wheels giving it a tendency to horrendous understeer, in those first three years of world championship rallying in the eighties it didn't matter, no other manufacturer had a serious competitor to the Quattro.

Lancia, for its part, sat in the opposite corner of the ring. Rejecting four-wheel drive as too heavy, and an advantage perceived as coming into play only in the very worst of loose stages, Sergio Limone, the 037's engineer, put his money on a racer, eschewing the possible technical complications of the Audi for a lightweight, powerful mid-engined thoroughbred, supercharged as opposed to turbo-charged and its inherent problems with turbo-lag. On paper it shouldn't have had a hope, but on the stages it

won, again and again. It was easy to drive and reliable. Mechanical failure caused works retirements only three times (two of those from the junior Jolly Club Totip team) from 27 starts and it enjoyed the biggest back-up operation outside Formula One. Limone had built a winner and the Fiat Group had demonstrated its superior team strengths in rallying over the *arriviste* Germans.

No victory was so illustrative of the Italian team's ingenuity and flair as the very first of that 1983 season, Monte Carlo. It was dry, which played into Lancia's hands. Under Cesare Fiorio's game plan, spectators watched amazed as mechanics gathered some 4 kilometres (2½ miles) in from the start of the second stage, Chamrousse, just where the icy section of the stage ended. All became clear when first Röhrl and subsequently Alèn and Andruet all had their soft studded Pirelli P7s – fitted to cope with the ice – changed to harder compound racing tyres for the remainder of the stage. It cost the cars about a minute apiece in standing time, and didn't really gain that much time as such, but illustrated the powers of lateral thinking of Fiorio, who had first introduced the blink-of-an-eye tyre swap in San Remo in 1969.

It was however an Indian summer for two-wheel-drive rallying: with power outputs topping 300 bhp, the traction of four-wheel drive was needed to direct the power. It was the last world championship title for two-wheel traction.

Audi's Teutonic nose had been given a severe Italian tweak by Fiat's world title win in 1983, and by 1984's Monte Carlo Rally the Ingolstadt team was determined to wrest back the world title which its technical advances deserved. It was all over by August. With Walter Röhrl in the team fresh from Lancia, the world championship ingénues were no more.

It was lucky for Audi that its early season dominance was so commanding because in Corsica Peugeot gave the world championship debut to its 205 T16. The king is dead, long live the king!

Audi and Lancia were powerless to stop Peugeot sashaying into the world championship arena with all eyes following. The T16 was beautiful, certainly elegant compared to the Audi. Surely it couldn't perform as well as it looked? But perform it did. It was a stunning debut by this French team headed by Jean Todt who only two years before (RAC 1981) had been co-driving for Guy Frequelin and who had built the PTS team up from scratch in the same period of time.

Ari Vatanen had been only one of a possible four drivers on Todt's shopping list and car and driver made a spectacular entrance together into world championship society in Corsica, leading until the last stage of the second day when Vatanen braked on water only to lose control and be thrown across the road and over the edge of a cliff, fortunately coming to rest on two huge rocks. Vatanen chipped his shoulder and the car caught fire, ending as a pile of distinctly inelegant charred metal. Of the incident Vatanen later said in his biography *Every Second Counts*: 'Professionally speaking I had committed some grave errors ... given the conditions I wasn't watching the road closely enough and I had braked when my tyres had nothing but water to grip on ...' But nothing could diminish the impact of the 205. Out of the hat, Peugeot had produced the rabbit of the future and over the tarmac surface on which Audi had always struggled to shine, Peugeot had succeeded.

Ironically enough, it was on the event that Audi recaptured the manufacturers' title, the 1000 Lakes, that Peugeot finally rendered the lumbering Quattro obsolete,

Dramatic looks and breathtaking performance: the Peugeot 205 T16 as driven by Timo Salonen in San Remo during the final days of Group B.

when Ari Vatanen – fully recovered from his Corsican injuries – gave the T16 its first of a total of 15 world championship victories. It was only the car's third world championship outing. After that event the Germans would take only two further world championship victories, beating the French team on only one of those occasions, San Remo in 1985 with the S1. The future was looking rather short and squat.

While even from the sides of stages the Quattro looked like a car that was hard work to drive, the T16 seemed to skip and skim over even the roughest of terrain, and when other drivers reached service points red-faced, sweaty and tired, Vatanen would climb from his Peugeot looking as if he'd covered half the distance.

The T16 was light, up to 240 kilograms (530 pounds) lighter in fact than the Audi, depending on the event. Its engine was fitted into the middle of the car, transversely sited to give a better placing for the dead weight in terms of both handling and weight than the Audi, but a configuration which caused problems of its own. Add to it an adjustable centre, rear and front diff., and the differences between adapted production car and made-to-win rally machine become the differences between winning and losing.

Of course it was by no means a perfect design. A tendency to peck on landing after jumps due in part to the transverse engine (with the engine rotating in the same direction as the wheels, the centrifugal force would throw the rear of the car up and the nose down if the driver lifted off the throttle), was just one handling idiosyncracy which was to have almost fatal consequences for Ari Vatanen in Argentina in 1985. It also had a certain left/right weight imbalance which could sometimes cause

unpredictable behaviour, but it had left the Audi offering looking like a relic from a past age.

Although Peugeot was the first manufacturer to actually deliver its new-born racer, first seen on a single stage French Rally in the October preceding Corsica, other manufacturers were keen that their babies were given an early chance to walk.

Lancia, having made a brave attempt at second-guessing the way FISA would dictate the sport by developing the two-wheel-drive 037, was not slow to recover ground. Having used every ounce of Italian wile and not a few million lire to bring the 1983 championship back to Abarth, Fiorio, Limone, Lombardi, Russo, Pianta et al. set about developing its four-wheel-drive challenger, the 038, later known as the Delta S4.

Across Europe and Japan, designers, engineers and team managers were designing, refining, testing, inventing, introducing. It was a heady time of mechanical and engineering decadence which would ultimately be allowed to develop unchecked and spiral into its own self-destruction. Four-wheel drive was a necessity, but of course the extra driving gear vastly increased the total weight of the car and so ludicrous amounts of money were spent on saving grams here and, exceptionally, kilograms there. Titanium was used where steel had been perfectly fine before, aluminium was thrown out to be replaced by magnesium. The accountants could do nothing as designers were allowed to indulge their ultimate engineering fantasies in pursuit of the world championship. Never before or after has rally car engineering been so absorbing to non-techno buffs, but the futuristic innovations were simply irresistible. And the guardians of dangerous excess did nothing.

Just like Audi, Peugeot did not have a permanant place in the sun. Winning seven world championship events equalled the achievements of Ingolstadt, but by the last event of 1985, Lancia and Austin Rover were ready to unveil their challengers. And although the T16 would win two world championships, the huge technical superiority that it first enjoyed was soon absorbed by the work of other engineers.

Before the S4, nothing in Lancia had used four-wheel drive so it was very much a blank sheet for the might of Abarth to start from. Deciding to use a supercharger in addition to a turbocharger was the Italian way of combating turbo-lag; the engine would be supercharged until the turbocharger could kick in, and each unit would have its own intercooler. It was an incredibly complex solution, but effective, producing a great deal of torque even at low revs. Sorting out the four-wheel drive's handling was not as easily overcome however, and coupled with arranging homologation, the much-awaited debut of the S4 was delayed from the San Remo Rally to the RAC, six weeks later.

It was a pretty spectacular first appearance, with S4s for Henri Toivonen and Markku Alèn. For British rally fans, the arrival of the 450+ bhp Lancias, coupled with the first appearance of the Austin Rover 6R4s which joined 460 bhp of Peugeot T16 E2 on the entry list, was almost too much to bear. Spectators everywhere, either watching on the stages or at frantic service areas, experienced sensory overkill. And as debuts go, they didn't really get any tougher than the 1985 RAC Rally.

Vociferously, foreign crews protested against the schedule of the event which not only remained secret, but demanded drivers undertook 32 of the total of 63 stages at night. Peugeot's Timo Salonen, reigning world champion and *agent provocateur* concerning the protests, actually announced he would withdraw from the rally, but in the

The MG Metro 6R4 could have been a winner, despite its lack of forced induction. Here Tony Pond makes a splash with the British public with his performance on the 1985 RAC Rally.

*Swede Kalle
Grundel makes the
most of the
RS200's handling
and traction on
the snowy 1986
Swedish Rally
(below and
opposite).*

best of traditions – call it poetic justice or sod's law – he was forced to retire by mechanical failure before he could make his dramatic flounce away from Britain. Toivonen's achievement in winning the event was a remarkable one on a rally that tested the stamina of drivers, mechanics and spectators alike. For a car's first event to take a one–two as the S4s did in conditions which often included treacherous patches of ice, indicated to everyone that the competition stakes had been raised.

It was difficult to know who the crowds were enthralled by most. The wayward young hero of the rally they loved from 1980 in the fire-spitting S4 or the home-grown stubby challenger from Cowley with Tony Pond.

Along the route Union Jacks were waved and spectators were out in their thousands to see an epic battle.

Austin Rover, reluctant at first to adopt a four-wheel-drive rally-car project, was persuaded by its competitions manager John Davenport that it could have a winner on its hands. While all around was turbo-whoosh, ARG decided to use a normally aspirated 3-litre V6 engine, reasoning that a) it would not be penalized by the FISA handicap on forced induction and b) response time would

be quicker than either turbo- or supercharging. While Lancia had decided the way to overcome turbo-lag was to fit both systems, ARG's fairly sanguine approach was to fit neither. Without turbocharging, how can you have turbo-lag? runs the logic. It was on the 6R4 that wings first sprouted, suggested from technology already used in Formula One, to provide the necessary downforce that would not only improve traction, but handling as well. The designers at ARG were canny. In order to obviate any problems with homologation of the rear wing, as for example were experienced by Peugeot, instead of building the necessary 200 road cars to satisfy Group B regulations and then turning a few into rally cars with all the inherent homologation problems, the British team simply built 220 rally cars, all with wings, all with front spoilers.

While the good response of the engine was to give that car some advantage, its power deficit was always going to be a handicap, but the 6R4's biggest problem was in perfecting its engine's performance. Engineers had been

given only 16 months to develop the unit and the speed with which it got from drawing board into rally car was evident in its lack of reliability. After its debut third place on the RAC with Tony Pond (team-mate Malcolm Wilson retiring with engine problems), there were non-finishes in Monte Carlo (Pond with a road accident, Wilson a broken transmission) Sweden (for Per Eklund's Schmidt Motorsports car) and Corsica where Didier Auriol, Pond and Wilson all retired with engine problems.

During the winter break between the 1985 and 1986 seasons, the next player to show its hand was Ford. After the success of the Escort, much was expected from the Boreham-based team, and the RS200 was duly delivered in Sweden in 1986. Its debut had been delayed several times, a sign that not all was well with the Essex supercar. The problem was the RS200 competed in basic as opposed to evolution form. Since other manufacturers were already using these latter type cars, it meant that the car had an initial disadvantage to overcome.

Style was its forte, its distinctive sleek shape owing more to Group C sports car design than anything previously on a rally, but for Ford it was too little too late. At 1140 kilograms (2510 pounds) powered by only a non-evolution 1800cc turbocharged unit, even on paper it looked underpowered and overweight. The Ford did have better weight distribution than other cars. Its gearbox was mounted towards the engine, and with twin shock absorbers at each corner, it had the potential of superb suspension. It was not a complete disaster, showing occasional glimpses of what it might be capable of, finishing third on its debut outing under Kalle Grundel and leading in Greece with both Blomqvist and Grundel before they retired, the former after an accident, the latter when Ford's back-up team, out of match practice, stripped a wheel nut at a service point. Time ran out before the hub could be replaced. It was a metaphor for the whole team.

There were planned weight reductions in evolution form, and an evolution engine which gave an additional 140 bhp would certainly have given the car a greater opportunity for world-beating performance but these never saw the light of day and the RS200's best performances were destined to be within a rallycross arena.

The biggest technical disaster of the era was the Group B Citroen BX 4TC, an ungainly creature from which Jean-Claude Andruet and Philippe Wambergue had to coax performance. Underpowered and lumbering, on paper it should have been a challenger, but the team made only three world championship appearances before headquarters decided enough was enough. Its only WCR top ten finish was in Sweden where it finished sixth – albeit behind two Group A Audis.

While Austin Rover, Ford and most notably Citroen struggled to come to terms with Group B, Lancia, Peugeot and Audi were still bounding ahead, but as technology began to outpace human reaction, muttered concerns could be heard ever more frequently. Like the chorus in a Greek tragedy, words like fire, accident and rocket began to form sinister undertones. And yet FISA did nothing to curb the excess of engineers and technicians. They did nothing to police the increasing use of special fuels, even to consider the potentially lethal consequence of sitting on 100 litres (22 gallons) of the Avgas hybrid which a turbocharger could use to produce over 550 bhp at full boost.

The kind of uncontrolled use of highly combustible lightweight alloy, huge fuel tanks with barely controlled fuel, combined with minimal fire extinguisher requirements would not have been allowed on racing circuits where marshals stood every few hundred yards. The concept of these Group B rally machines competing on unmanned stretches of stages was unbelievable to colleagues in the motor racing world.

The engineers' imagination in Group B was unfettered, but having built a car capable of awesome power and speed they then had to make the car drivable by human beings; and as more responsive engines were allied with greater traction, it seemed that there was little drivers could do to keep up with the advances of their cars. Steering and handling problems were common to all manufacturers, four wheels able to deliver more performance than even the most skilful driver would handle. This led to huge development in viscous couplings, essential in making the power usable; trying to stop more than 550 brake horsepower countless times through a stage was going to lead to huge heat production, potentially lethal when it came to brakes, and so both Lancia and Peugeot developed snap-on plates for their wheels designed to cool brake temperatures. The technical jiggery-pokery was phenomenal: Peugeot's rear wing was deemed illegal by FISA, Audi's passed without a second

glance. There were skirts, flaps, every kind of air re-directing device any factory member could think of, all designed to cool, direct and keep hold of the power produced. With four-wheel drive, Audi had produced the key to harnessing almost limitless power. What FISA did not produce were sufficient controls to curb developments in technology. By the end of 1986 development had reached such a point that turbo-driven Group B cars were so powerful they were capable of shredding any ill-judged choice of tarmac tyre in just 1.6 kilometres (1 mile).

In no time at all the snowball of Group B had created its own huge avalanche, and it was about to crash to the ground.

Even with the passage of time, the events that started in Portugal have a shocking inevitability about them. It wasn't so much that people were killed – in motorsport people have been killed throughout the years – it was that so many people had been predicting people would be killed, and the people that could have stopped 1986 ever being such a bleak, black year did nothing until it was too late.

First there was the body blow that left the sport reeling. Portugal, along with Monte Carlo and San Remo,

Following page: There was nothing more thrilling than a Lancia Delta S4 in full flight, especially with the likes of Markku Alèn at the wheel on the 1986 San Remo.

Below: The Lancia S4 produced over 550 bhp.

had always attracted fanatical crowds of supporters, but despite poster campaigns, and team threats to boycott events with poor crowd control, the 1986 Rally of Portugal had not even completed the first stage before four of those spectators were dead and many others injured. Triple Portuguese champion Joaquim Santos lost control of his RS200 when confronted by spectators on the stage and as a result had been unable to avoid a crowd who had been standing in a relatively sensible position. Although he was driving a Ford of Portugal RS200, both the official Ford entries were immediately withdrawn, and the remaining stages at Sintra cancelled. The works drivers called a meeting and decided they could not carry on, both as a mark of respect to the people killed and because there was no guarantee it would not happen again. The drivers were genuinely upset that they might turn a corner only to find spectators in front of them, and nowhere to go. They were also unsettled by a rally which had already provoked a meeting before the event started when crews learnt they were to drive past Attilo Bettega's memorial at full speed in Corsica. Walter Röhrl was blamed as being the main catalyst in the post-accident withdrawal but none of the drivers were in the mood to compete under such conditions.

The Safari followed and more tragedy, when Kenneth Eriksson's Group A Golf, without warning, dived off the track killing a spectator.

What happened in Corsica was not a competition accident, it was a horrible illustration of the crazy risks drivers were taking just by rallying their Group B fire-bombs. That it was Henri Toivonen, one of the most daredevil characters in the sport and Sergio Cresto his American co-driver, rocked everyone. His Lancia Delta S4 simply exploded after it left the road. What little remained of the car was unrecognizable. All of a sudden FISA sprang into action, but as Hannu Mikkola ruefully recalled later: 'There have been very few fires since they introduced safety tanks ... I remember a huge testing accident with Audi but not a drop of fuel was even spilled even after we rolled eight or ten times.'

Having sat back and watched from a distance as rallying bowled along its course of self-destruction, FISA announced the termination of Group B and the abortion of Group S, a more controlled formula of ten-off specially controlled rally cars which was scheduled to replace Group

B. Lancia, Ford, Peugeot and Austin Rover had poured millions of pounds into developing Group B contenders and in what many saw as a knee-jerk reaction to the Corsican tragedy, FISA threw the baby out with the bath water. Peugeot decided to take the ruling body to court to try and fight the ban, while Austin Rover, in conjunction with the discovery that its team manager had milked off thousands of pounds from the rally budget into his own pocket, has never returned to world championship rallying.

As Markku Alèn drove his Delta S4 onto the victory ramp after the Olympus Rally, his Lancia team had already been refining its new Group A contender: the Delta.

The king is dead, long live the king!

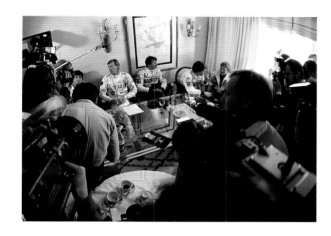

The events that would bring Group B to an end.
Clockwise from top opposite: Supercars drew huge crowds that often stood too close to the road, as witnessed here on the first stage of the 1985 Monte Carlo Rally. Walter Röhrl leads the famous press conference on the 1986 Portuguese Rally, when the drivers refused to continue. Alèn, Kankkunen and Toivonen, soon tragically to lose his own life, discuss withdrawal from Portugal on safety grounds.
The final straw – the loss of Henri Toivonen, rallying's fastest and youngest, remains the most bleak day in modern rallying. Cars with more raw power than a Formula One machine carved their way through a human armco in Portugal. It had to stop …

8

Dawning of Group A

'I tell you something quietly ... we have already been testing the new car and on gravel it is already faster than the 037. You know, that is fantastic.'

Cesare Fiorio, Lancia

It was a dank, cold morning. On the twisting road to the Italian side of the Matterhorn, a group of Italian, French and British journalists stood, huddled together, long faces frowning against the damp wind.

Lancia's chief engineer, Claudio Lombardi, stood apart. One British journalist noted: 'Look how white he is; how spotty his face is. Cesare [Fiorio] and the rest all look fit and suntanned, but you can tell when Claudio's been working hard on something – he's as pale as a ghost.'

We were awaiting Claudio's new baby. Normally, Lombardi would grin madly, eyes wide with enthusiasm when he brought out a new car like his last invention, the devastating Lancia Delta S4. But this time it was different. His eyes gave it away – while he talked of his 'great challenge to create a new car for the new rules' his eyes were dead and his mouth worked as if on automatic override, churning out a script carefully crafted by the Lancia spin doctors.

There was an air of gloom hanging over the occasion, and it wasn't just the weather. This was October 1986, and Group B – the supercar class – had recently been axed by the FIA. The fire-breathing monsters, now with a reputation for killing everything in their path, were to run for the last time the next month on the RAC Rally, and thereafter be banished for ever to the wilderness of hillclimbs, club rallies and rallycross. For many of the assembled journalists, this was the beginning of the end. Rallying had been neutered and the new Lancia, we expected, would be a tame gelding compared to the wayward, thoroughbred stallions that had made the sport great. Yes, the Group B cars had taken the lives of great drivers like Henri Toivonen, but they had made heroes of people like Vatanen, Salonen and Alèn. Who could be a hero in a shopping car?

Lancia team boss Cesare Fiorio was beaming as ever. His expensively tanned face gleamed with an aura of success. Only the likes of Enzo Ferrari commanded more respect in Italian motor sport (indeed, Fiorio was later to join the F1 Ferrari team for an unsuccessful few seasons).

As ever he was quiet and polite, nodding gently at familiar faces among the journalists. A junior reporter on *Motoring News* who had lucked into the trip to Italy by accident, hadn't yet learned that it wasn't the best practice to ask direct questions in a highly charged political atmosphere, especially when the target concerned possessed fiery Italian machismo, had lost a driver in a tragic Group B accident, and was politically bound to embrace Group A with conviction. He was asked: 'Will the new car be very slow? I mean, it won't be as exciting as the S4, will it?'

Fiorio smiled gently, put his arm around the brash youngster with more cheek than sense, and walked him gently away from the group of eager journalists. He knew how to deal with such situations. Motor sport is a dangerous sport for those with reputations to build and protect. Journalists can be young, opinionated and careless. Say the wrong thing to one, or have it misinterpreted; or worse still, upset the angry young person who may, with a touch of irresponsibility, carve you up in print, and you can find yourself in a very deep pool of hot water with sponsors, directors and bosses. He also understood the impassioned young journalist's emotions. As an Italian, he knew that all young men loved fast cars. He knew that in many eyes his team, his car, and indeed the whole sport of rallying had been emasculated. And he knew what to say, and how to say it, to put those fears to rest.

'I tell you something quietly,' drawled Fiorio. 'I would like this to be between you and me for the moment. But we have already been testing the new car and on gravel it is already faster than the 037. You know, that is fantastic. But please, do not write anything yet. If I were to tell everyone it is so fast, then perhaps they think that Group A is not the solution. Maybe after Monte Carlo you can say. It would not be good for me to say the car is so fast and then lose in Monte Carlo, you understand?'

I understood. I also understood that he would probably say the same thing, privately, to every journalist present. The whisper created excitement – the thought that Group A was not so bad after all.

But just as we were gradually becoming accustomed to the thought that, perhaps, there might be a future for rallying after all, the car arrived.

Gleaming, resplendent in its familiar Martini colours, the new Group A Lancia Delta HF4x4 arrived, with Massimo 'Miki' Biasion at the wheel. The Italian was the new favoured son of Fiorio. The driver, he believed, that would carry Lancia through the rest of the eighties and into the next, brave new decade of Group A rallying.

The sight of the car pricked the collective balloon of hope and excitement we had all begun to experience. It looked, well, it looked *ordinary*; like a road car, like something you could imagine parked in your driveway. In short, it was nothing special.

Certainly, those writers with an engineering background fell on it immediately. Lombardi became the centre of attention. 'What turbocharger have you used?' 'How have you tackled the turbo-lag problem?' 'Has the road car been built with the bigger intercooler?' 'What differentials have you used? Is the centre diff. viscous?'

Then came the killer question: 'What brake horse power are you getting?'

Lombardi almost mumbled the answer: 'We get over 200, maybe 250.'

'What?' Jaws fell to the floor with a clatter that echoed around the Matterhorn. This exciting new feat of motor sport engineering produced a pathetic third of the power

Ford's early efforts at Group A were less than spectacular, although Blomqvist tried hard in the underpowered Sierra XR4x4.

output of its predecessor. Only six months previously rumours of 700+ bhp were circulating for the top Group B cars. Fiorio, Jean Todt of Peugeot, and others had been seen deep in conversations with Formula One engine builders. More power, more power. Suddenly, the bubble had burst and we were left with a limp, whinging little machine that had about as much charisma as a wet fish.

Still, there was a job to be done. One by one, everyone was strapped in for a quick blast up through the hairpins to Cervinnia. The Lancia felt breathless. The familiar punch in the back of the Group B car became a gentle, polite shove in the Group A Delta. And while the Group B car tended to throw its passengers around like a rag doll with its fighter 'plane g-forces, you had the time to consider where the stereo system might be in the road version, and whether you would like a Delta as your next company car. As Miki threw the Delta into the hairpins, the little red hatchback didn't (couldn't) slide. There was no wheelspin, no sideways scrabble for grip, no life-threatening moments, and certainly nothing to make you hold your breath. Sure, the Delta was deceptively quick, but it brought the art of rally driving back down to something within the reach of mere mortals. The one thing that can kill interest in motor sport is the feeling generated in fans that 'I could do that'. Where once a passenger would sit helpless, unable to control his or her own body, while watching in awe as a blur of hands and feet controlled the rocketing rally car in death-defying slides, you were left to ponder whether it would be wise to strike up a conversation with the driver as you hurtled through the bends.

Biasion had time to talk. 'Watch my feet,' he said. 'The car is so balanced I can brake like normal, not with the left foot.' Interesting.

There was one breathtaking moment. Miki managed to pull a spectacular handbrake turn at the top of the hill. This was impressive, not because it was fun, rather that Lombardi had found a centre differential that would allow the driver to use the handbrake without locking up all four wheels on the all-wheel drive machine – something that earlier four-wheel-drive rally cars couldn't manage. But this was as impressive as it got.

In the meantime, we had the Lombard RAC Rally to look forward to in 1986. But that would be the last time we would see the fire-breathing, raucous Group B machines and all the raw excitement they generated. On that event, whole families lined the roads at motorway junctions and roundabouts in their thousands to watch. The cars, of course, were off-stage and doing about 48 kph (30 mph) but they provided a spectacle nonetheless. Would these people turn out to watch brightly painted hatchbacks? 1987 provided the answer when the RAC Rally could barely summon up a traffic jam on the Welsh lanes. The public, it seemed, had turned their backs on rallying.

While Lancia embraced the new Group-A-only regulations with enthusiasm (too much enthusiasm, the conspiracy theorists would later say), Peugeot simply walked off into the desert with the Peugeot 205 T16 to compete in events like the Paris–Dakar, where such cars were still allowed. The other manufacturers were left to struggle with whatever came to hand. Audi, the car manufacturer that started off the whole four-wheel drive turbo-engined spectacle, was left wallowing with its overweight and unwieldy Group A challenger, the 200 Quattro; it boasted 238 bhp from the engine, about the same

It took a while for some teams to get Group A right. Ford's first effort on the 1987 Monte Carlo ended in embarrassment when it was found that the paperwork was not in order and parts of the injection system were illegal.

as the Lancia. At just under 200 kilograms (440 pounds) lighter, the Quattro Coupé was a much more manageable machine, but without a homologated turbocharger, the nimbler Audi could manage less than 200 bhp.

Likewise, Ford had a Group A problem with two cars available, each with a weakness. The biggest weapon in the Ford armoury was its outrageously powerful and adaptable 2 litre turbocharged Cosworth engine. This beastie produced a quoted power output figure of 300 bhp. FISA, when banning Group B and clearing the way for Group A rallying, had declared that no car should produce more than 300 bhp – that was the upper limit – but never got round to announcing a method of policing this. The Cosworth engine, the rumour began to circulate, was capable of producing much more than 300 bhp. Indeed, figures of over 400 bhp were bandied around! But, Ford had a major problem: all that power had to be fed through two, rear wheels. The only place the Ford Sierra RS Cosworth, developed for Group A touring car racing, was going to win was on dry, fast tarmac.

But then there was the Ford Sierra XR4x4. It had four-wheel drive. But, like the Audi Coupé, it didn't have the engine to cope. The XR4x4 had a beautiful V6 fuel-injected unit, but without the blower, it simply wasn't going to be competitive.

Ford decided on a two-pronged attack. The XR4x4 would be used on rallies where traction was at a premium, such as Monte Carlo and Sweden, and roll out the powerful RS Cosworth on events such as the Tour de Corse. The plan was fatally flawed, of course, since the bulk of events demanded both power and traction.

Mazda, a new major player now that Group A represented the future of rallying, was faced with a similar problem to that of Ford with its XR4x4. It was a well-balanced car, had four-wheel drive, and even a turbocharged engine. But despite the fact that it quoted a higher power output figure than the Lancia Delta (by as early as January, these figures had become a standing joke amongst journalists and teams anyway as everyone claimed to be below the 300 bhp notional limit), it was clearly underpowered compared to its Italian rival. The Mazda, you see, featured a trifling little 1600cc engine, almost 400cc short of its rivals.

Others soon joined the fray, but it would be a long time before anyone caught up with Lancia. BMW made a half-hearted attempt with the M3 – great car, brilliant engine, but only rear-wheel drive; Toyota had the Supra –

again, powerful, but only rear-wheel drive; and of course there was a whole raft of front-wheel-drive Group A machines developed previously for the Group A championship won in 1986 by Volkswagen – these included the Opel Kadett, the VW Golf GTi, and the Renault 11 Turbo. Interestingly, there was one other manufacturer waiting in the wings with a car that seemed to be right for the job: Subaru. The Subaru Coupé 4WD Turbo with its flat-four turbocharged engine had the right configuration but when it first appeared on the 1987 Safari Rally with Ari Vatanen and Per Eklund in a two-car team, it proved to be terminally slow. We would hear more from this manufacturer later.

In the meantime, Lancia ran away with the show. In just six months the Delta HF4x4 had gone from a high performance road car to a fully fledged rally machine capable of winning world championship rallies – not just winning them, but dominating them to such an extent they were able to invent a new game: The Team Order Fiasco. Team orders were nothing new, especially at Lancia; the fiasco element was.

It was one of the most wintry Monte Carlos of recent years, and four-wheel drive was essential if you were going to figure in the results. Ford had opted for the Sierra

XR4x4 with Stig Blomqvist, and Walter Röhrl had an Audi 200 Quattro. Reigning world champion Timo Salonen presented himself in a Mazda 323 4WD, as did Ingvar Carlsson. Lancia fielded three of the new Deltas, one each for works drivers Miki Biasion and Juha Kankkunen and local hero Bruno Saby, drafted in as the tarmac specialist.

Lancia thrashed the opposition. The Italian team was better prepared, had a better car, and had better luck. Only Saby suffered from technical problems when his transmission (a potential weak point on all the new Group A four-wheel-drive cars) gave way on one of the few dry tarmac stages. The Ford and Audi Group A cars were too heavy and didn't have enough power to make a serious challenge as expected. However, the Mazda, which at the time was claiming more power than Lancia and boasted the light, nimble configuration needed in the new era, failed miserably in its challenge thanks to unreliability – a problem which was to plague Achim Warmbold's team for many years to come. Both Carlsson and Salonen were thwarted by loose turbo pipes, Salonen retiring after the fifth stage while Carlsson went on to finish fifth in the provisional results.

Lancia was therefore left to stage-manage the entire

The Ford Sierra Cosworth performed superbly on tarmac and Didier Auriol was able to win the Tour de Corse in the powerful two-wheel-drive machine in 1988.

Previous page: Ari Vatanen gets to grips with Group A in Africa on the Safari Rally.

event from the front, but the rally was made all the more interesting by the furore over team orders that resulted. Few people have any aversion to team orders; however unwelcome they may be, most understand that they are a necessary evil in all forms of motor sport. It's how they're handled that creates the friction and unpleasantness that can sometimes arise. Between them Cesare Fiorio, Miki Biasion and Juha Kankkunen managed to create a wave of controversy that kept journalists amused and scribbling for many months to come, although, as was clear from the sombre faces at Lancia's post-event press conference, no-one was laughing in Turin.

New boy at Lancia, Juha Kankkunen, and Miki Biasion had the rally to themselves. Naturally, a battle ensued between the two team-mates on the stages that could not be allowed to continue, and Fiorio stepped in with team orders. First he ordered 'we would freeze the positions', while Biasion was ahead, but Kankkunen failed to comply claiming that he had not understood the instruction. So, Fiorio tried again: 'I wanted a sporting method to choose who would win' and decreed that the fastest of the two Lancias over the classic Turini stage would be the one 'allowed' to win the event. It was a typically Latin thing to do, and to most rally fans, one that was easily understood and accepted; at least the result would be decided by a race of sorts. It didn't go to plan, however. As well as at least one British journalist describing the story of the Turini race as 'improbable', and a claim floating around that Biasion had been allowed to practise the stage more than Kankkunen during the recce, the Finn arrived at the finish of the Turini seething with rage; a temperature warning light had the temerity to illuminate itself during the stage and Kankkunen was forced to slow. Biasion had won Fiorio's blessing for a Monte victory.

Kankkunen, unused to Italian shenanigans, refused to accept the decision and ploughed ahead into the lead once more in a deliberate snub to his team boss. He was hardly proving a point since Biasion refused to pick up the gauntlet in the confident knowledge that Fiorio would look after him. Juha displayed his anger and frustration to

the world by slowing down dramatically on the final stage and stopping the Delta within sight of the finish so that Biasion could win. Later, he refused to confirm Fiorio's account of the story of the Turini race, adding further embarrassment to the team.

The Monte Carlo Rally had set the pattern which was followed for the rest of the first season of Group A rallying, with only a few notable exceptions. If you weren't in a Lancia, you weren't in the title race. Mazda should have come closer. Although its engine was smaller, it had the advantage of four valves per cylinder which gave it increased power and, indeed, should have led to greater reliability than the unit from Abarth. Petrol quality varied from rally to rally and was restricted to an octane rate of 99; having four valves allowed the Mazda to run poorer quality fuel if needed, while the Lancias were forced to run rich and reduce the boost of the turbocharger. The biggest advantage of all was that the Mazda's smaller engine put it in a lower capacity class, which meant that its weight limit was lower, allowing it to run 80 kilograms (176 pounds) lighter. Many of these advantages were lost on Mazda Rally Team Europe, however. The cars struggled with unreliability; they missed many of the important rounds of the series, and team boss Achim Warmbold's rage at anyone suggesting anything was wrong with the team suggested a touch of over-sensitivity. In fact, he accused the press of 'negative sensationalism' if it even came close to suggesting that MRTE had a problem.

There were more basic flaws, too. While the likes of Lancia began to investigate ways of controlling its three differentials (front, centre and rear), splitting the torque between front and rear and looking towards electronic controls, MRTE was faced with the prospect of extracting reliability and traction efficiency from a transmission system designed in the first instance without a centre differential.

Mazda did enjoy some success, however. A memorable victory on the Swedish Rally, a slippery, icy event that perhaps masked its traction deficiencies (it mattered less how the torque was split, so long as you had four wheels being turned by the engine) did much to lift morale and bring a smile to the face of the chain-smoking Timo Salonen. The win was more significant than merely confirming that Lancia had a serious challenger in Group A; this was also the first time a Japanese manufacturer had won a round of the world championship in Europe. It was all downhill from there, however. Until the team could find a solution to the transmission problem, there would be no more rallies for five months.

With Mazda out of the picture, Lancia was able to capitalize on the lack of opposition. The Italians did have weaknesses nevertheless, and the rules as they stood allowed other manufacturers into the frame, even if just briefly. In fact, after the doom and gloom of the closing months of 1986, it was encouraging to note that despite the predictions of the death of popular rallying, more manufacturers than for many years were encouraged to join in. In the late Group B days of supercar rallying, Lancia and Peugeot dominated, Audi struggled after an early head start, and Ford and Austin Rover had only just entered the fray. In 1987, we had Lancia, Mazda, Audi, Ford, Renault, Subaru, Toyota, Volkswagen, BMW, Opel, and Nissan all taking an interest.

Renault was, perhaps, the most astonishing of the 'new' performers. Although two-wheel-drive cars suffered a distinct handicap, the regulations handed them certain

advantages that, with an enthusiastic driver, could occasionally help them to challenge the four-wheel-drive cars. The main one was weight limits. The Renault 11 Turbo, a relatively unsophisticated machine with just two-wheel drive, was able to challenge for the lead of the 1987 Rally of Portugal in the hands of the mercurial and spectacular Jean Ragnotti. Granted, much of Ragnotti's charge had more to do with Lancia's Markku Alèn travelling backwards down the field thanks to damper problems on the Lancia; but on the Tour de Corse, the Renault's performance was purely and simply down to its superiority over the best four-wheel-drive machines. Equipped with new tyres from Michelin, developed specially for the 11 Turbo, Ragnotti led the event

which effectively moved the Renault 11 Turbo up a class, which meant a higher minimum weight limit. Added to this, changes in the engine regulations, such as the insistence that all cars use standard intercoolers, meant that the Renault suffered a loss of power, too. These changes barely affected the Mazdas and Lancias, but Renault was effectively out of the game, for the time being.

While Portugal and Corsica had revealed Renault's potential, both events had exposed Lancia's weaknesses. On tarmac, Lombardi needed to fit wide tyres to allow for softer compounds, especially at the front. However, with the bodywork in Group A restricted to standard dimensions, which were not that great on the Lancia,

This page and opposite: Markku Alèn uses the Lancia's superb traction and handling in icy conditions to take his first win on the 1988 RAC Rally.

initially before being caught out in a hail storm and picking up a puncture thanks to a brief excursion in the slippery conditions on the fifth stage. A further, similar incident on the 14th stage cost him more time, but he won the hearts of the French spectators with a spectacular drive in which the 'underdog' Renault 11 Turbo picked up 11 fastest stage times out of 24, two more than eventual winner Bernard Beguin. Despite his eight minutes lost through accidents, Ragnotti still managed a respectable fourth.

Renault's giant-killing feats were not to last for long, however. More rule changes followed for 1988, and the 11 Turbo's weight advantage disappeared. Previously, the equivalency rules meant that turbocharged cars had their cubic capacity multiplied by a factor of 1.4 to assess which class they entered. This was increased to 1.7:1 for 1988,

the team was forced to always run with a much harder compound 205mm (8 inch) wide tyre on the front; this led to a great deal of understeer. Furthermore, the smaller wheel arches restricted brake diameter and wheel travel, which contributed to Alèn's almost terminal damper problems in Portugal when a last-minute delivery of shock absorbers on the final leg prevented him from being overtaken for the lead by Ragnotti's Renault.

But Corsica was the scene of hope for other manufacturers. BMW, while not officially entering the World Rally Championship, had been backing a private team, Prodrive, in the development of the fabulous M3. In the hands of Bernard Beguin, the M3 won the Tour de Corse; but, while many pundits at the time felt that a powerful rear-wheel-drive car could easily match and even

surpass that of the new breed of four-wheel-drive machines, his was a far from easy victory. Jean Ragnotti's performance in the Renault had posed a major threat until 'Jeannot' started throwing it off the road. And, while Lancia had performed better than expected, BMW's victory owed more to the Delta's weaknesses on tarmac than a stunning dominance of the event. Had Lancia been able to widen their wheel arches to fit bigger tyres and brakes, then it might have been a different story.

Nevertheless, for a time it seemed that the M3 was a contender on tarmac. Like the Renault, without a turbocharger it could run lighter than the Lancia thanks to being in a lower class. It also had decent wheel arches on the standard body shell which allowed Prodrive to fit suitable brakes and tyres.

The BMW immediately had a great following. Those who remembered the Escort RS with affection switched their passions to the M3; it had all the right ingredients – rear-wheel drive, powerful, noisy, and it could be driven sideways, even on tarmac. Its beautifully tuned 2.3 litre, 4-cylinder 16-valve engine produced a claimed 275 bhp, and for those who loved and missed machines like the Opel Manta 400, the superficial similarity in specification was enough to evoke memories of a golden era. It was the first win for a normally aspirated car in four years, and one of the last for a two-wheel-drive machine.

However, like the Renault, the M3 had little future in the new order. The Sierra Cosworth won in Corsica the following year, but the four-wheel-drive brigade soon caught up with and passed those machines lacking such sophistication. Indeed, the speed at which the Delta improved was phenomenal, and any deficiencies in transmission or tarmac performance were quickly overcome. For example, at the beginning of 1987 Lancia could not possibly consider changing the gearbox on a rally; by the end of the season they could manage it in half an hour.

As might have been expected in such a climate of change and development, there were a few niggles over eligibility and more than the odd chant of 'cheat' directed at a number of teams. 'Interpretation' of the rules could be imaginative in many instances, but Ford was caught well and truly on the hop over homologation right at the very start of the Group A era; a false production declaration was uncovered relating to Stig Blomqvist's fuel injection system on the Monte Carlo Rally, and Ford had to cough up $250,000 in fines. Mazda also had problems when the Japanese manufacturer held up its hands in November 1987 and asked FISA to withdraw homologation of the evolution version of the 323 when it was unable to prove that 5000 identical models had been produced.

Fuel, too, became a major bone of contention. The only fuel permitted was that which could be obtained from 'roadside fuel pumps'. A number of petrol stations on certain rallies suddenly sprouted special pumps which were priced far out of the range of ordinary motorists where a variety of rally cars could be seen filling up!

Lancia, naturally, became the focus of much of the attention from those determined to identify who was overstepping the mark. The Italian cars had sprouted twin roof flaps at the rear, designed, they said, to draw air out of the cabin to help cool the crew. Other teams felt that they also had an aerodynamic effect which was illegal. Lancia shrugged and removed them, and said that they weren't that great an idea anyway.

Ford had problems again on the Safari Rally when the lightpods which appeared at scrutineering seemed to help with providing a cooling airflow for the intercooler.

Undeterred by the accusations, the Lancia steamroller pounded forward for the rest of the 1987 season, demolishing all before it. By the end of the summer, the Italians had already lifted the manufacturers' title, their fifth, and entered the record books by winning the series earlier in the season than ever before. Could anyone match them?

By September of 1987, hopes were growing in the Far East that the Italians wouldn't have it all their own way for much longer. Toyota had a car which fitted the Group A bill – the Celica GT4. This machine, they promised, would be available by mid-1988. It had four-wheel drive, a turbocharged engine, and the right balance to tackle the Lancias. Toyota needed a replacement for the Supra badly; it was a strong car, great for the African events, but it lacked power and it was simply outgunned on the Safari in 1987.

By the end of the first full season of Group A rallying, much of the talk centred on electronics; where the previous year everyone was aiming for raw power, now the engineers concentrated on using electronic wizardry and computer software to get what little power there was onto the road effectively and efficiently.

But the technological aspects of the birth of Group A did much to cloud some of the greatest performances by rally drivers in recent times. Swedish driver Kenneth Eriksson, the 1986 Group A world champion, pushed his Volkswagen Golf to the limits and earned the respect of his peers with some amazing performances. His win on the Ivory Coast Rally was clouded by the deaths of Toyota's Henry Liddon and Nigel Harris in an aircraft accident, leading to the team's withdrawal, but it was deserved nonetheless. Eriksson's skill behind the wheel never faltered throughout the season, although he wished the same could have been said about the Golf's transmission. He managed to set fastest times on the snow and ice of his home event in Sweden, despite the fact that he had just front-wheel drive. But he was noted not just for his brilliant driving, but his sheer commitment and dedication, even in the face of enormous problems; on the Safari, he changed a driveshaft shortly after the start and set off in hot pursuit of Mikkola and Waldegård only for his engine to blow up after making up 14 minutes on his rivals.

Ragnotti, mentioned in this chapter several times before, was the epitome of driver brilliance in the Renault as his second place in Portugal and fastest times in Corsica testify.

Franz Wittman became the first Austrian to win a world championship rally, in New Zealand, and the first since Walter Boyce in 1973 to win in his own car (a Lancia Delta).

And of course, there was the champion himself, Juha Kankkunen, who, after Cesare Fiorio announced his 'Equal Opportunity Scheme' halfway through the season (when the manufacturer's title was secure!) was able to fend off his Lancia team-mates Miki Biasion and Markku Alèn to take the world drivers' title by a mere six points from Biasion.

As Group A entered its second year as a fully fledged formula, much was to change although Lancia would remain at the top of the tree for some time to come. Audi, after deciding to return to world championship rallying after pressure from its marketing department in 1987, decided to withdraw properly this time, despite its 1–2 victory in the hands of Mikkola and Röhrl respectively in the Safari Rally. The 200 Quattro, even with its six-speed

Opposite: The last of the two-wheel-drive winners in Group A – Bernard Beguin took his BMW M3 to a solid victory on the 1987 Tour de Corse. However, there was no future for the charismatic M3 without four-wheel drive.

Victories on events such as the RAC Rally were commonplace for Lancia during the late eighties.

variable torque split transmission system, was too heavy and underpowered, and when the rules changed for 1988, forbidding the free intercoolers and restricting manufacturers to units that were standard on the road versions, all hope was lost.

Ford returned after its disastrous 1987 season with a lighter version of the Sierra Cosworth (by 60 kilograms/ 132 pounds), wider rear tyres (fitted thanks to suspension changes that allowed more space) and bigger brakes; but this machine didn't appear until the Tour de Corse which it promptly won. In the meantime, Ford drivers Stig Blomqvist and Carlos Sainz had to make do with the older version of the Sierra, while Stig managed second place in Sweden with the XR4x4, fitted with the right injection system this time!

It was the Corsican victory that gave rally fans the biggest cause for celebration: the Boreham boys had returned! BMW, after its victory in 1987, had no answer for the new, powerful Cossies and the three M3s, driven by Francois Chatriot, Marc Duez and Bernard Beguin failed to make an impression. Chatriot was fourth, Beguin a distant seventh and Duez retired after an accident. Much of the blame for the M3's failure lay with tyres – the new rules had effectively booted the Turbo machines up a class, while at the same time reducing tyre widths within the class structure; thanks to the equivalency rule 'bigger' machines such as the Cosworth retained the tyre widths they needed, while naturally aspirated machines like the BMW stayed in their class and had to make do with narrower rubber.

On gravel, this made little difference but the Sierra and BMW were not in that league anyway. Lancia was still having everything its own way, winning the Monte Carlo with tremendous ease against a distinct lack of opposition. Although it was one of the driest events for years (as opposed to the previous year's heavy snow) and qualified as an almost full, dry tarmac event, Ford and BMW, potential winners, stayed away for fear of slippery conditions. Local driver, Bruno Saby, took the honours for the Italians on this occasion.

Sweden fell to the Delta for the first time, while the previous year's winners, Mazda, began to suffer from those old reliability problems again.

Mazda was still there with the old 323, but after its homologation problem the previous year, it obtained special permission to run a new Xtrac six-speed transmission system which helped the team overcome the machine's weakness in this area. MRTE also had another new weapon in its armoury, Hannu Mikkola, lured to the team despite its problems after the legendary Finn lost his drive with Audi's withdrawal. Not that those changes seemed to make much difference to the team's fortunes; Salonen struggled home in fifth place after diesel inexplicably found its way into his fuel tank, Mikkola retired with engine failure after first suffering from suspension trouble and Ingvar Carlsson crashed on a road section. In Sweden, Salonen and Mikkola both retired with engine problems.

But it was in Portugal that Lancia dealt its demoralizing blow by updating the car which was already by far the best rally machine in the world: enter the Lancia Delta Integrale. This new version romped home to victory in the hands of Miki Biasion ahead of the older HF4x4 versions driven by Cesare Fiorio's son Alex in second place, and Frenchman Yves Loubet in third. The Integrale had a new 16-valve engine to replace the old 8-valve unit that Lombardi felt was such a disadvantage. And it had wide wheel arches as standard to give the

Abarth engineers more room to fit appropriately sized tyres and brakes, and give the suspension travel that they so badly needed.

Lancia's launch of the Integrale wasn't a total success, however. The five-speed gearbox was not strong enough to cope with the new-found power and torque and Mikael Ericsson retired his version with transmission failure. Alèn broke his transmission on the very first stage; luckily for him it was a superspecial (that day's only stage) and he was allowed to restart the next day! Abarth, normally well-prepared for any eventuality, was caught out slightly with the Integrale's transmission problems; the team was well aware that there might be a problem, but the switch from Pirelli to Michelin tyres at the start of the season meant a great deal of testing time was taken up with rubber assessment and not enough was left for trying out the new six-speed gearbox which was subsequently fitted in time for the Safari Rally. Indeed, armed with this unit, Lancia was able to take victory even in Kenya. It was a close run thing however. Erwin Weber managed to put his VW Golf in front for a time before his steering broke and then the big guns from Nissan and Toyota took over. Only a combination of accidents and mechanical failures stopped them in their tracks to allow Biasion through to win in the Integrale, and even then the new machine had transmission problems again, this time sticking in gear; Vic Preston Jnr retired his version with differential failure.

Ford's Corsican victory with rising new French star Didier Auriol at the wheel was the only fly in Lancia's ointment at the time. The Lancias finished second and third with Loubet and Saby respectively, but on the Acropolis Rally the *status quo* returned with Biasion heading home a magnificent 1–2–3–4.

Then came victory in America on the Olympus Rally, followed by Argentina with local man Jorge Recalde, then Finland with Markku Alèn taking the 1000 Lakes, and San Remo again fell to the Italians with Biasion back in front. Alèn's victory on the RAC Rally sealed it; Lancia was unbeatable. Biasion was world champion, and Lancia manufacturers' title-holder, again before the season's end.

But there were rumblings in the distance. While Josef Haider's victory in the two-wheel-drive Opel Kadett GSi in New Zealand, and Alain Ambrosino's win for Nissan in the Ivory Coast in the 200SX could be put down to the fact that Lancia didn't go to those events, there were two newcomers on the scene that posed a threat to Lancia. These were the cars that kept the Italians on their toes; that forced the birth of the Integrale: the Toyota Celica GT4 and the Mitsubishi Galant VR-4. One of these machines would eventually kill off the Integrale for good.

Fun to watch and to drive, but Didier Auriol had to leave Boreham for greater opportunities with Lancia's four-wheel-drive machine.

9

Japanese Invasion

*'The writing is on the wall –
in Japanese!'*

Mike Greasley, Motor Sports Journalist

Like many Japanese products, it took a long time for Europeans to accept them. At first, they were viewed as cheap imitations. Then, the Japanese added gadgets and gimmicks. Before long, they were turning out cars with which the European manufactuers could barely compete.

The process took a little longer in rallying; while Japanese cars were still perceived as characterless, by the late eighties few could deny that the quality of manufacturing and the high specification made them very good buys; but it wasn't until the nineties that Japanese cars began to dominate rallying.

Strangely, it was a Swede, working in Germany who acted as commander-in-chief for the invasion proper: Ove Andersson.

Andersson had been running Toyotas for many years, but with the arrival in 1988 of the Celica GT4, Toyota Team Europe (TTE) was ready to take on the world and meet Lancia head-on.

TTE had already been successful; indeed, the rear-wheel-drive Celica Turbo was one of the most successful rally cars to compete in Africa. But it never had a car which could win consistently in Europe. The Celica GT4 changed all that, but it took time.

The Celica GT4 couldn't come too soon. Even in Africa, TTE was losing its advantage; on the Safari Rally in 1988, Andersson was disappointed to see his Supra Turbos come home in fourth and fifth place in the hands of Kenneth Eriksson and Juha Kankkunen respectively, and the experienced Waldergård in seventh.

Andersson had specialized in Africa during the early eighties. In 1981, he went to Toyota in Japan with proposals to produce a specialized four-wheel-drive Group B machine that would become one of the supercars of the mid-eighties, but was rejected on the grounds that Toyota wanted to keep close links between its competition machines and the mass-produced vehicles it sold to the public. Ultimately, it was this philosophy which led to Toyota's support – and success – in Group A in the nineties. Andersson then developed the Group B Celica Twincam Turbo, which went from success to success in Africa, winning first the Ivory Coast Rally in 1983. Thanks to the machine's lack of four-wheel drive, it had little hope of competing against the top Group B cars in Europe. When Group A came along, Toyota's dominance of even the African backwaters was in jeopardy.

1987 was a year of great change and disruption for Andersson. TTE moved to shiny new premises in Cologne, and then tragedy struck on the Ivory Coast when his close friend and TTE co-ordinator Henry Liddon died in an air crash along with assistant Nigel Harris while overseeing the team's progress on the event.

But by 1988, the new Group A machine was helping the team pull together again after their loss, and the long hard struggle back to the top began in earnest. The GT4 was engineered by Karl-Heinz Goldstein and with its revolutionary hydraulic central diff., this was the machine on which Toyota's future would be based.

1988 was a difficult year. Throughout the turbulent development of TTE, Andersson had always stretched himself and his team to the limit and beyond; first he combined driving with running the team, moved from Sweden to Belgium to Germany and then new premises within Germany, and survived the horrible loss of Liddon. Then, in this transitional year, he developed and ran two completely different car models – the Celica GT4 on European events, and the Supra Turbo on the African rallies.

The GT4 first appeared in Corsica in 1988, and while it wasn't a resounding success, it was a solid start to a new era for Andersson and his team. Juha Kankkunen retired with a blown engine, but Kenneth Eriksson, hired after his exploits in the VW Golf in 1986 and 1987, survived to finish sixth after a succession of problems including punctures, thumping a bridge and a loose propshaft.

The Acropolis Rally shortly after gave the first indication that Lancia's dominance of Group A was

threatened by the newcomer when Kankkunen pushed his Toyota to score fastest time on the first proper stage of the event, and then engaged in a dogfight with the Lancias. His team-mate on this occasion, Björn Waldegård, had no such luck however, his GT4's transmission breaking unexpectedly almost as soon as the event got under way.

But Lancia drivers Mikael Ericsson and Miki Biasion soon began to feel the heat, not only from the Acropolis sun (which did much to exacerbate an overheating problem on the Lancias) but from the Finn in his German-run Japanese car. However, just as Kankkunen was about to strike, the Toyota's engine expired; back to the drawing board again, although with some enthusiasm. The car had proved itself competitive on gravel; all they had to do now was get the reliability.

Left: Toyota (this Celica driven by Juha Kankkunen on the Safari in 1988) were kings of Africa, but it took a few years and the development of the GT4 before the team could challenge Lancia in Europe.

The Olympus, New Zealand and Argentine Rallies were given a miss. TTE was sticking to less expensive rallies in Europe as this was 'a learning year' according to Andersson, so Kankkunen and Eriksson appeared with the GT4s again on the 1000 Lakes in Finland, and this time the story was even more encouraging. Kenneth retired with a broken gearbox on the second day after struggling with the Toyota's handling from the start – not that there was anything much wrong with the car; simply this was the first time the Swede had driven a car with four-wheel drive on gravel. However, Juha Kankkunen became embroiled in one of the hottest battles for the lead seen in many years when he pitted his Celica GT4 against Markku Alèn's Lancia Integrale.

Two Finns on home ground in cars which matched each other in terms of performance was a recipe for either a thrilling contest or disaster. They fought, second for second, and Lancia team boss Cesare Fiorio looked concerned for the first time in two years; he could only hope that the Celica's suspect reliability would hand him victory, because Alèn was beginning to reach the limits of his vast capabilities as the fight escalated. In the event, engine failure on the Toyota settled the issue, and Lancia was lucky to get away with its eighth victory in the world series that year. The Italians had dominated thus far, but it appeared they were no longer ahead of the game and the new boys were just as quick, if not quicker – all that remained was for TTE to work on the reliability of the Celica and a championship win could be on the cards.

TTE approached its next event with cautious optimism. The car was competitive, if unreliable, but the San Remo Rally was Lancia's home territory and the mix of gravel and tarmac stages was hardly ideal for the Celica GT4; it had proved itself on tarmac, but in Corsica earlier in the season it hadn't quite been on the pace of the Lancias. Nevertheless, Kankkunen provided a pleasant surprise.

It has to be said that the speed of the new Celica owed a good deal to the enthusiasm of its Finnish driver. Kankkunen, after an uneasy year in 1987 with Lancia, had signed for TTE, happy to get away from the politics and back-stabbing, as he saw it, at Lancia. He had been desperately unhappy with the team orders and manoeuvring by Fiorio, and had, at times, openly shown his disapproval of his team manager's tactics. Perhaps he had a point to prove or score to settle; certainly, his world championship crown in 1987 had been devalued by Lancia's policies because many saw it as a reward for obeying Fiorio, albeit grudgingly, and not the result of a straight fight with his rivals. He was unlikely to win the championship with Toyota in 1988, but he was keen to prove that he could beat the likes of Miki Biasion. Perhaps, too, he was enjoying the opportunity of taking Lancia on and giving the Italians a good thrashing. If that was the case, then his performance over the opening stages of San Remo must have been exceptionally satisfying. To arrive at the end of the first leg in Turin, home of Lancia, leading in a Toyota was quite a victory in itself.

While the Celica had merely been expected to hold its own and nothing more on tarmac, everyone, including TTE, was surprised to find Kankkunen leading (jointly with Dario Cerrato and Carlos Sainz) after the first seven stages on wet asphalt, although wider tyres led to improved suspension. With the rally

Juha Kankkunen slips through a watersplash in Australia with the sleek Toyota Celica that finally toppled Lancia.

moving onto gravel the following day, it looked increasingly likely that Juha could score TTE's first win for the Celica GT4. Carlos, the new face at Ford who was rapidly making an impression, couldn't possibly compete with the four-wheel-drive brigade on gravel in his Sierra Cosworth, and Cerrato, brilliant driver that he was, couldn't possibly hope to compete against the likes of Kankkunen, Lancia Delta Integrale or not.

Kankkunen was pushing hard, too hard. His moment of glory was over almost as soon as it began when he launched the Toyota into the trees close to the finish of the first stage the next day. The *status quo* returned, and Lancia romped home for a famous 1–2–3–4 victory on home ground. The Italians could breathe a sigh of relief, but it took some time to overcome the shock of being led by both Ford and Toyota on their own soil.

Again, Lancia took victory on the final round of the championship making it an astonishing record of 12 in 12 starts. But the results were hardly a true reflection of Lancia's standing as the Japanese closed in. Kankkunen led just before being caught out on the final leg by a patch of ice. Alèn had stretched out an almost unassailable lead in the Lancia when Kielder took its toll on the Finn once again, allowing Kankkunen to move in, only for the Toyota to strike trouble later.

That year's RAC was significant for a number of reasons. Not only had Lancia looked vulnerable once again, and Toyota looked strong only for bad luck and unreliability to hamper its progress, but Mazda had almost taken a memorable victory and Mitsubishi had burst onto the world scene with its Galant VR-4. It had been a trying RAC Rally to say the least. The night before the start of the event, all involved in the rally were surprised to see snow fall as they filed out of the restaurants and bars of Harrogate. The following morning, the whole of Yorkshire was covered in a blanket of white. The weather made the stages unpredictable; snow, slush, ice and relatively dry sections, combined to make tyre choice critical and caution essential. It also made it Mazda's kind of rally. Driving a nimble car with great handling and a basic transmission system that gave maximum grip, Hannu Mikkola and Timo Salonen revelled in the conditions. Mikkola was still able to lead the rally until he slid off the road when blinded by the low wintry sun. He might have recovered but for the gearbox exploding when he tried to reverse out of the ditch. Salonen, meanwhile, managed to cruise home in second place behind a fortunate Alèn. Björn Waldegård, meanwhile, gave TTE one of its best results so far by taking third place in the Celica GT4.

It was that great hero of modern rallying, Ari Vatanen, who raised most eyebrows, however, in the new Mitsubishi. The machine allowed Ari to set competitive times until its engine blew, but again, the omens were good for the future; the following season would pay dividends.

Ralliart Europe boss Andrew Cowan had trodden a similar path to Ove Andersson; he too had been a driver/manager, and he too used persuasion and persistence to talk a Japanese manufacturer into taking rallying seriously.

Initially, Mitsubishi had only been interested in Asia and the Pacific Rim (indeed, these remain a priority today). The company's first major foray into motor sport was the Macao Grand Prix with a class-winning 500cc racing car, and rallying started for Mitsubishi in 1967 in Australia, where the company had embarked on a major

export drive. The Southern Cross Rally, at the time Australia's biggest rally, was the main target and after five years Mitsubishi took its first international victory on the event in a 1600cc Galant in the capable hands of one Andrew Cowan. The same model won its class and finished seventh on the 1973 Safari Rally in Kenya with Satwant Singh, and then the Lancer 1600GSR, one of the great classic rally cars of the seventies, arrived and won the Safari Rally overall in 1974 with Joginder Singh.

For Mitsubishi, Andrew Cowan was the discovery of Ralliart Australia's manager, Doug Stewart, who brought the Scot in to drive on the Southern Cross. Ralliart is the competition arm of Mitsubishi, and certain regions have 'franchise' operations to run competition programmes in each country. Stewart had Australia, but Cowan went on to control Ralliart Europe, which, from its base in England, went on to handle the world championship programme, sometimes in conjunction with other Ralliart operations.

Cowan debuted the Lancer 2000 Turbo on the 1981 Acropolis Rally, but alternator failure stopped him on the dusty Greek tracks. This was the first venture for Mitsubishi into Europe, but the car was either ahead of its time or behind, depending on which way you looked at it; it was a Group 4 machine at a time when Group B was coming into its own, it was rear-wheel drive when four-wheel drive was clearly the way forward, yet the technology used and developed for the Lancer was later to spawn the prototype Starion four-wheel-drive car and eventually lead to the Galant VR-4. This was a trend for which Mitsubishi would become noted; by 1995, the Mitsubishi Lancer Evolution 3 was arguably the most technologically advanced rally car in the world.

During the mid-eighties, Mitsubishi Ralliart turned its attention to long-distance rally raids with the Pajero, or

Shogun as it is known in some countries. The powerful Starion Turbo, a rear-wheel-drive machine was used with limited success by national teams, regional Ralliart distributors and importers on national events. The Starion four-wheel-drive project enjoyed limited success in Asia but was never homologated, and Ralliart Europe turned its attention to the Galant VR4 in 1988. Potentially one step ahead of the competition, the new Group A machine from Mitsubishi had an 'advantage': four-wheel steering! This system was used on the road-going version for safety and stability, the rear wheels turning slightly in concert with the front to improve roadholding and handling. Needless to say like many other modern inventions for road cars, such as ABS braking, it quietly disappeared from the rally car.

Rumour at the time suggested that the Galant was immensely powerful, and Vatanen appeared to back it up: 'I tell you it's fantastic, the power is so much and it is there all the time. It's very fast,' he enthused after the RAC of 1988. With the notional and unpoliced 300 bhp limit still in place for Group A there were few boasts from any team that year regarding power outputs, and certainly the Sierra Cosworth had potentially enormous amounts of torque and bhp to propel it. Furthermore, while the Galants were built in Essex, the engines came from Japan,

so the team was unlikely to make any claims.

1989 was the golden year for the Galant as far as Mitsubishi was concerned, and while Lancia continued to enjoy the lion's share of success, the Italian team also had to face the prospect of stiff opposition from Toyota, Mitsubishi and yet another newcomer: Subaru.

To say that Subaru was totally new to rallying, or even Group A rallying for that matter, would not be totally correct. Like the other Japanese manufacturers, it had a history in the sport, notably with the RX Turbo which was driven in the main by New Zealander Possum Bourne, and entered frequently on the Safari Rally. But the new machine was announced in 1989 and due to make its debut in the world series in 1990. While Lancia didn't have to contend with the Subaru in the last months of the decade, it did at least have to keep an eye out for the machine which would be launched the following year.

Like Mitsubishi with Ralliart, Subaru has a separate competition department, known as Subaru Technica International, or STI. However, when the time came to launch and develop its first major attempt on the World Rally Championship, the engineering company and team which was to run the car kept its own identity; that team was Prodrive, managed by David Richards, world championship co-driver with Ari Vatanen in 1981.

Of the early attempts by the Japanese to secure a foothold in rallying, Mitsubishi made an impact from time to time, for example with Andrew Cowan on the 1977 Bandama. Interestingly, Cowan later became one of the vanguard of team managers bringing Japan to Europe with his creation of the Mitsubishi World Rally Championship programme run through Ralliart Europe.

Richards had built Prodrive from scratch. Along the lines of Formula One, he believed in creating a team which could run cars in its own right, but in rallying, hand-in-hand with the manufacturer. Richards' championship victory with Vatanen had laid the foundation for his new team. Their victory was the first for a private team; Vatanen's Escort was not a works machine, it was run by David Sutton and the finance, negotiated by Richards, came from Rothmans. David continued to sell sponsorship projects successfully and was able to build a centre of engineering excellence at his Banbury headquarters. He ran Porsches with Rothmans money, followed by Metro 6R4s; and then he struck the deal with BMW to develop the M3 Group A cars. His problem was that BMW was ambivalent towards rallying, and the two-wheel-drive M3 was inappropriate on loose surfaces, not that the Bavarian manufacturer wanted to see its cars muddied anyway. While Richards continued to run a Group A touring Car race programme for BMW, he needed a new project to revive his rallying ambitions – Subaru provided just that and the four-wheel-drive, turbocharged flat four-engined Legacy RS was born.

While Richards started his development programme, the world championship continued much as before in 1989. Lancia was still on top, but clinging by its fingernails. Toyota was fast coming up on the rails, and Mitsubishi was a thorn in the side. While this wasn't great news for Lancia, it was good for rallying. Mike Greasley, motor sport journalist, ex-team manager and motor sport entrepreneur (the man behind many of the commercial deals in rallying) was moved to write in his introduction to *Rallycourse* in 1989: 'Will the new decade bring an era of milk and honey? ... There is ... a note of optimism in the air.' Interestingly, he added: 'The writing is on the wall – in Japanese!'

Greasley had driven straight to the point: Group A rallying had a future – a big future, and it was largely due to Japanese investment. Nevertheless, the point is clearly made that it may be Japanese cars and money, but it was European expertise that made it work. Prodrive, Ralliart Europe, Toyota Team Europe, Mazda Rally Team Europe, and Nissan Motorsports Europe were all based in the EEC.

Lancia wasn't struggling just yet, while Mazda was fading quickly thanks to continuing problems at Mazda Rally Team Europe in Belgium throughout 1988. The team boss, Achim Warmbold, ruled MRTE with a rod of iron and fear; mechanics didn't like it and staff turnover was high; the specialist press didn't like it and ridiculed him; and Warmbold responded by becoming ever more aggressive and was beginning to be perceived as an eccentric. The team started to fall apart at the seams. In 1989, things changed for the better with Warmbold taking a step back and Andy Thorburn, the engineer, taking over direct control on events. Everyone relaxed a little, the programme was rationalized to concentrate on rallies on which the Mazda 323 was particularly competitive (slippery surfaces) and reliability improved. By the end of the year, a new 1800cc engine to replace the underpowered 1600cc unit was on the way and things looked much better.

While Mazda seemed to take strides forward, Toyota Team Europe continued to be thwarted ever more by reliability problems. The car was fast, the engineers and mechanics highly talented and the drivers skilful, but once again, Andersson appeared to be

Didier Auriol takes a step closer to becoming World Drivers' Champion with Toyota by winning the 1994 San Remo Rally.

stretched. Abarth, with its team of 284 people to run the Lancias, was cruising, while Ove had to make do with just 85. TTE had to struggle with inexperience, too. 1989 was the first year that the team had attempted a full world championship programme, and poor tyre choice, particularly on the Monte Carlo Rally revealed the team's inexperience.

There were high points, however. First and second place in Australia for Juha Kankkunen and Kenneth Eriksson respectively was a moment for rejoicing at TTE, although a loose wire, or, some said, a rag left in the air intake, caused Kenneth to suffer road penalties when his engine failed to fire in Parc Ferme and he had to push the machine. There was also a visible straining in his relationship with the team at this stage. The Australian victory did emphasize Toyota's superiority over Lancia when the cars were working, and even Markku Alèn had to concede that Lancia had had its day, although he was speaking too soon – Lancia had three more world titles ahead of it.

Alèn's suspicions were given further weight by Mitsubishi's victory, courtesy of Mikael Ericsson in Finland, Mazda's second place with Timo Salonen, and Toyota's third and fourth with Carlos Sainz and Kenneth Eriksson respectively. Mitsubishi made the point again on the RAC Rally with Pentti Airikkala's victory in the Galant. That result caused Toyota particular pain. Between them, Juha Kankkunen, Sainz and Kenneth Eriksson had led the event in their Toyotas. The Celicas were quickest by far, and certain victory had been lost through unreliability.

It was a particularly crushing blow for Sainz; the Spaniard, who was quickly making his mark as a future champion, had a particular love of the RAC Rally, one of the events that had brought him to the attention of the world only a couple of years previously in a Sierra. Carlos had been leading when, within sight of the finish, a driveshaft broke and Airikkala, who had been piling on the pressure anyway, slipped in front. Sainz entered the last stage in tears; Airikkala, at 44, had taken his first and last world championship victory and knew it.

Mazda did well through the year, too. Victory on the first round in Sweden with Ingvar Carlsson was followed by a 1–2 for Carlsson and local man Rod Millen in New Zealand.

Still, Lancia had its own way, thanks largely to the failures of others. Fiorio had moved on to pastures new at Ferrari, and Claudio Lombardi had taken the reins. Towards the end of 1988 he had admitted publicly that Lancia could wilt under pressure from the newcomers, but his prophecy came too soon and Miki Biasion was able to celebrate a second world championship victory after a string of wins in his Integrale.

Back in 1987, Lancia had produced a winner straight out of the box. Perhaps the Italians had been fortunate that there was little opposition at the time, no-one to expose the team's weaknesses, although there were undoubtedly few. It took Toyota three years, but the result was much the same: a car capable of winning rallies outright, consistently. By 1990, Group A had come of age. There was, at last, more than one make of car competing on relatively equal terms. 1990 was the year that Toyota came good and serious opposition to Lancia became more than a threat. Lombardi had to put away his little black book of team orders.

The cars were fast enough to entertain, too. Since Fiorio had whispered that his new Delta was already as

fast as an 037 on gravel, back in 1986, development had continued apace and the new 'slower', safer Group A machines were smashing stage records all over the world. By the mid-nineties, if you put a Group B supercar into a rally with the lastest Group A cars, the so-called supercar would be left for dead! It was in Portugal in 1988 that Stig Blomqvist studied the stage times and pointed out to David Williams of *Motoring News* that, 'He had noticed that the Lancias had broken some of his stage records at Fafe. These had been set three years previously in a Quattro, and no ordinary Quattro at that, but in a factory Quattro Sport, one of the late, lamented flame-spitting monsters,' recalled Williams in *Rallycourse*. While the Group B cars had raw energy and power, they perhaps had little balance and refinement; indeed, the drivers may not have been able to tame all that power. Group A cars had more sophisticated transmission systems, more efficient in

Carlos Sainz explains the intricacies of pushing the Toyota Celica to its limits to team-mate Mikael Ericsson on the 1990 Portuguese Rally.

putting whatever power was available on the road; tyre technology had helped, too, and the whole car was better tuned and finely balanced, making it much easier to drive and push to the limits. Group A has possibly become a case of less haste and more speed.

That same cliché could also be applied to Toyota. TTE had calmed down, taken a more methodical approach, built up its staff to more than 100, and put in place a specialized team that concentrated on testing only. Carlos Sainz became the number one driver and linchpin of the whole operation. His dedication and perfectionism made him the ideal choice to carry out much of the testing although at times he looked seriously overworked. His willingness to push himself to the limits and Ove Andersson's eagerness to capitalize on it would cost dearly later, but for the time being, they managed to keep some sort of balance in 1990.

TTE's approach paid rich rewards. The manufacturers' championship went down to the wire, with Lancia winning by a hair's breadth; but for once, it was not a Lancia driver on top of the podium at the end of the season, it was Toyota's Carlos Sainz .

There had been technical rule changes in 1990 which may have helped even the odds; a 40 millimetre (1½ inch) diameter air restrictor had been imposed on all turbocharged cars in an effort to cap power outputs. Restricting the amount of air entering the turbocharger was an effective method of keeping things under control. An engine will only produce the amount of power in proportion to the amount of air and fuel you can feed it.

The Toyota was still widely reckoned to be less powerful than Abarth's car, but its handling and traction were more than capable of pushing the red and white Japanese car to the front on many rallies. Add to that the considerable skill of Carlos Sainz, and Andersson had a recipe for success.

There were a number of surprising elements to Sainz's victorious season in the Celica. In the past, few could understand, let along match, Lancia's gamesmanship in rallying, but even on the Monte Carlo Rally TTE was able to pull an outflanking manoeuvre that left the Italians at a loss for an explanation. TTE's tyre man and later team manager, Maurice Guaslard, made judicious use of tyre warmers at the start of longer stages, allowing the Toyotas to run harder compounds without losing performance on the opening few miles. Lancia was left standing goggle-eyed for the first time in years! The second surprise was TTE's show of strength in resources, where Lancia had led in this respect since the dawn of rallying time. It seemed that Lancia's pockets knew no depth and it could summon up the cash, cars and personnel at a moment's notice when it was required to win. But once again Lancia opted out of the Rally of New Zealand – too far and too expensive – yet somehow the smaller TTE team managed to find the time to fly a car halfway around the world and hand Sainz an easy 20 points with an uncontested victory.

These were serious weaknesses in Lancia's approach, although Lombardi's boys would seldom make the same mistakes again. The Integrale was ageing, and they needed all the ingenuity they could muster to keep it out in front. The Lancia had always suffered from understeer and limited suspension travel which had to be overcome by driver skill and detailed fine tuning. Lancia's mountain of cash was shovelled into a hydraulic transmssion system, electronic clutch and telemetry systems, but not everything saw the light of day. But TTE, after suffering a couple of years of unreliability with the Celica started to produce a car that was more reliable than Lancia's. This could be partly explained by the fact that for the past four years, Abarth was able to run the Deltas and Integrales well within their tolerances, but when TTE emerged as a competitive force, Lancia was forced to run at maximum, 100% of the time, and the Integrale simply wasn't up to it on occasions.

Increasingly, Lancia was becoming swamped. Toyota was at full tilt, Mitsubishi, while it was only a minnow, still had a very competitive car on occasions, Subaru was joining the battle, Ford was combining the benefits of four-wheel drive with its superb Cosworth engine to produce the Sierra Sapphire Cosworth 4x4, and Nissan was working on the Pulsar GTi-R, a car that would replace the relatively unsuccessful March Turbo and the specialist African machine, the 200 SX.

While Lancia fielded Kankkunen (hungry for victory after frustration with Toyota, and welcomed back into the Lancia fold after Fiorio's departure), Biasion, and their new French star Didier Auriol, specialists such as Bruno Saby were once again brought in for events such as Monte Carlo. Toyota boasted Sainz, Mikael Ericsson, and German Armin Schwarz. For Mitsubishi, Vatanen was back, and Kenneth Eriksson left Toyota to join the Ralliart crew. Mazda retained Salonen and Mikkola once

more, and Ford reduced its programme for the two-wheel-drive Sierra while the new four-wheel-drive machine was developed for its launch later in the year, although Marc Duez made appearances in a Fina-supported car.

Subaru launched its Legacy RS on the Safari Rally in 1990, the scene of its previous successes in rallying. Markku Alèn had been poached from Abarth where he'd been for most of his career driving a variety of Lancias and Fiats, and on this occasion he was supported by Subaru

The Toyota Celica GT4, driven here by Sainz in 1990, thrived on rallies such as the Acropolis where Toyota's early work in Africa paid dividends in preparing cars for rough European events.

faithful Possum Bourne, and local experts Ian Duncan, Mike Kirkland, and Jim Heather-Hayes. All but Heather-Hayes' supported car failed to finish, although Alèn had given the fledgling new effort hope by leading on the early sections, retiring later with an overheating problem. Patrick Njiru won Group N in his private version of the Legacy. Alèn returned again on the Acropolis Rally and set two fastest stage times, but Ian Duncan upheld Subaru pride by winning Group N. Bourne took fifth on home

ground in New Zealand and then Alèn took a resounding fourth on the 1000 Lakes Rally, ahead of Kankkunen's Lancia and behind the two Mitsubishis of Vatanen and Eriksson in second and third respectively, and winner Carlos Sainz in the Toyota Celica GT4.

Sainz's victory in Finland was significant. It pointed to a great shift in tide in world championship rallying in that he was the first non-Scandinavian winner of the 1000 Lakes Rally. Like the crumbling European stronghold over car manufacturing, so, too, was the traditional dominance of Finns and Swedes over rally driving beginning to fade as the new breed of southern European driver epitomized by Biasion, Auriol and Sainz took over the mantle; beating the Finns on home ground made an emphatic point.

Sainz's performances in the Toyota were also strengthening hopes of a competitive sport in Group A; as the season wore on, he became locked in a head-to-head battle with Lancia's Juha Kankkunen, a fiercely fought drama which was to see an escalation of speeds, and accidents, as both pushed themselves and their cars to the limits and beyond. It was high drama that hadn't been seen in the world championship since the old Group B days. Sainz was virtually unassailable in the drivers' series, but each man brought out the other's competitiveness in the closing rallies of the season as they fought for event victories, keeping their own score-cards.

Sainz lost the battle in Australia when he clipped a rock while under pressure; in Italy he crashed again, but still recovered to finish third, behind Kankkunen, but it was enough to take the crown. Lancia, by this point, had picked up the manufacturers' title. That left the pair of rally gladiators to fight it out with one last fling on the Lombard RAC Rally. Neither had anything to lose; their responsibilities to championships and titles were settled and the scene was set for a dramatic battle in Britain.

It had been the first time that pace-notes had been allowed on the RAC Rally, a slow-speed recce giving drivers and co-drivers the opportunity to make detailed

Below: Driving a Japanese car brought Carlos Sainz his first taste of real success when he used the Toyota to win the 1990 World Drivers' Championship.

notes and mark important hazards. Sainz worked hard; he desperately wanted to win this event after victory had been snatched so cruelly from his grasp the year before. He had been given the rest of the season off by Andersson for winning the drivers' championship, but Sainz insisted he enter. Likewise Kankkunen wasn't going to ignore the gauntlet deftly cast in his direction.

The Lancia versus the Toyota; the Finn against the Spaniard. The pair set off from Harrogate at a tremendous pace, but they were not the only ones gunning for victory. Eleven different drivers set fastest stage times, five drivers in four different makes of car held the lead, and until the rally was settled on the 33rd of 42 stages, no driver managed to stretch out more than 22 seconds from the rest of the field. The RAC Rally of 1990 was a major indication of how competitive Group A rallying had become. It was at this point everyone was able to say with confidence that Group A had come of age; that it was a successful formula.

In the end, it was Sainz's victory, the first for a non-Scandinavian in Britain for 14 years. Both he and Kankkunen pulled away from the rest of the field on the third day, locked into a battle of epic proportions as they swapped seconds. Kankkunen's manager, Mike Greasley, predicted it would end in tears, and just a few moments later it did. Kankkunen flew off the road on stage 33 while flat in third in his Lancia and landed hard in a ditch. He and co-driver Juha Piironen were badly shaken, with cuts and bruises, but fortunately neither was seriously injured. Sainz was left to cruise through the rest of the final day, the battle won.

Subaru, in a major PR stunt, put Formula One driver Derek Warwick into one of its Legacy RSs, but that ended after a succession of off-road incidents. Markku Alèn had more success in his Legacy, leading from stages five to eight before retiring with engine failure after the 12th stage.

Union Jacks and St Andrew's crosses were waved high for a brave effort by a Scottish newcomer (relatively speaking), Colin McRae, as he bashed his way home to sixth place in what he coyly described as a 'Shed, well, it was by the time we got it home!' The analogy was appropriate, since after hitting a gate post and a variety of other objects down one side of the car, one of the doors was locked by mechanics with a shed-door bolt!

That car was the Ford Sierra Sapphire Cosworth 4x4, an interim machine while Ford got to work on what would be its first serious challenger in rallying since the RS200, or more accurately since that car barely saw the light of day before Group B was banned, the Mark 2 Escort RS.

The four-door Sapphire used a transmission system similar to that of the XR4x4, but with Cosworth power. It was homologated in August of 1990, and made its debut on the 1000 Lakes Rally in the hands of Pentti Airikkala, Malcolm Wilson and Franco Cunico. Backed by Q8 Oils, all three machines retired, Airikkala's with gearbox failure and Cunico's with accident damage. Wilson withdrew his after a gearbox failure forced the team to replace it in the middle of the stage so that they could continue for more experience. Wilson was pulled for 'safety reasons' according to Ford, although the team was probably mindful that by attempting to finish the event they would achieve nothing other than attracting unwanted attention from the organizers for the gearbox swap.

Colin McRae first made his name in world championship terms by finishing sixth on the RAC Rally in 1990, despite tangles with the scenery!

The gearbox itself represented an interesting departure; to get the maximum use from the engine, Ford developed a seven-speed gearbox. Whether this achieved anything or not was uncertain, but it certainly kept the drivers busy!

Mazda looked for improvements on the 1000 Lakes. The new 323 GTX with its bigger (1800cc) engine had arrived at last and was homologated that August, but at first it was a disappointment, producing much less power than expected.

VW had made an attempt at four-wheel drive, too, with the Rallye G60, but its supercharged 8-valve engine boasted less power than the 16-valve machines at the top. Erwin Weber scored a distant third behind Sainz's Toyota and Ingvar Carlsson's Mazda in New Zealand, but the machine was excluded on its next outing in Australia when an electrical failure shut the engine down in a 'control zone' where no assistance was allowed, and he had to be pushed.

One of the few teams still pursuing the front-wheel-drive route during this time was GM with its Astra. Malcolm Wilson campaigned it (before moving back to Ford) with great success considering its lack of power from the normally aspirated engine and the lack of drive to the rear wheels. But 1990 was its final official year in the world championship and the car was supplied to Louise Aitken-Walker, the objective to win the ladies'

world championship. She faced opposition from Paola de Martini's Audi 90 Quattro, and then in March 1990 Louise and co-driver Tina Thorner's car dived over a massive drop in Portugal and plunged into a lake. Both were lucky to survive, but it deeply affected Louise for some time after and she refused to talk about it; she merely said that coming so close to death was a deeply personal thing and she just wanted to forget about it. It did little to affect her driving, however, and GM's swansong season was rewarded with a world title for Louise and eventually the Scottish driver picked up an OBE in recognition of her bravery and achievement.

1991 brought a tingle back to those whose fervent hope was the continuing success of Group A rallying. Ford's exciting new Escort RS Cosworth was due to make its appearance in testing, and Nissan was making a serious attempt with its new Pulsar GTI-R.

Like most Japanese car manufacturers, Nissan's motor sport history can be traced back to the sixties and even the fifties, but as always, their first forays were in Australia and Africa. Nissan was the first Japanese manufacturer to finish the Safari Rally with its Cedric model. Datsun became its more familiar name and it was the 240Z sports car in the hands of Rauno Aaltonen on the 1971 Monte Carlo that first brought this Japanese manufacturer to prominence in Europe when he finished fifth.

The Violet followed in the seventies and the immensely strong, reliable and inexpensive 240RS rally car of the early Group B days enjoyed an enormous popularity with privateers, even if it was a little unwieldy and underpowered. The works team enjoyed success in Africa and the Nissan 200SX continued that tradition. However, the Pulsar was to be Nissan's first attempt at grappling with the Group A rules and tackling European rounds of the world championship with the possibility of success. Naturally for a Japanese company, its debut was pegged

for the Safari Rally, but a full programme was planned in 1992.

As with other Japanese car makers, Nissan put the programme with a European team, using Nissan Motorsports Europe in Milton Keynes, the home of its successful Group C sports car racing operation.

On paper the Sunny looked as competitive as anything in rallying; it was high-tech, complex, and boasted full telemetry for testing. Nissan, it seemed, had thought of everything. In reality, the story was very different, quite the opposite, in fact. The Nissan was an unmitigated disaster when measured by the team's own expectations. One would have thought that with a new car Nissan might have expected a learning year or two before getting it right, but the team expected it to win rallies. This it did not.

Basic engineering flaws emerged almost immediately. The complex transmission system could have been good, but needed development, but it was the intercooler that created the biggest embarrassment. This device was used to keeping the intake charge temperatures down – the cooler the intake, the more power you could expect. Naturally, the answer was to fit as big a unit as possible; the bigger the intercooler, the more power you could extract. Nissan got that bit right, but where do you put it? Right on top of the hottest part of the engine, they thought ...

The result was that on the Acropolis Rally, the Nissans were a full three seconds a mile slower than the best Group A cars as the engines wilted in the heat. Britain's David Llewellin described the performance thus: 'At the start of the stage, it was great; bags of torque. Then halfway through the thing just died and it felt slower than a Group N car. At times I thought it simply wasn't going to pull through to the end of the stage. Then it would cool down, and we'd be off on the next stage, only for it all to happen again.'

More telling was a reported story from the press office on the Acropolis, when an angry Nissan executive managed to get through on the team's high-tech satellite 'phone to speak to the team in the field: 'How come my rally winning car is not winning the rally?' he is said to have screamed over the ether. The reply is not recorded, but the expectations were clear; and his anger had been fired by the fact that at the time Greek driver 'Stratissino' was quicker in his standard Group N version. Both Nissans dropped valves, Blomqvist retiring while Llewellin struggled through for ninth place. The Greek driver won Group N for Nissan, but there was little cheering.

The Safari Rally was perhaps responsible for the misplaced optimism in Greece. On the car's launch Blomqvist finished fifth overall which was more than creditable given that it was a new car. The Japanese were nonetheless slightly disappointed.

Perhaps one could understand Nissan's impatience, when it seemed that Lancia and Toyota were progressing at such a phenomenal rate. During the previous two years, Lancia had seemed vulnerable, but now that Toyota's attack was being felt with full force, somehow the Italians managed to find that extra 10% to keep on top of the situation. The ageing Integrale seemed to be reborn in 1991, and it often led to allegations of creative interpretation of the rules. Sainz often wondered aloud how Lancia could find the extra performance on many occasions, and there were counter-allegations. Soon, rumours of special fuel additives circulated, and everyone began to speculate just where the top teams hid their alleged caches of nitrous oxide – in the fire extinguishers? In the lamp pods? Just what was in the washer bottles? Could they even run nitrous through the hollows of the roll cage? The championship had become so aggressive and so hotly contested that it seemed everyone was capable of going to whatever lengths it took to win.

While allegations of cheating were never proved, spiralling costs were very evident. Toyota and Lancia, it was said, were working with blank cheques and win-at-all-costs budgets. Certainly, Andersson admitted that his budgets were reviewed with increasing frequency by Toyota

Motor Company and increased when necessary, and Abarth had always appeared to have total financial commitment from Fiat Group.

The Big Two were beginning to leave everyone else behind. Mazda was on the way out, Ford was taking its time in producing the new Escort and its servicing arrangements were becoming a standing joke, Nissan was too naïve, Subaru would need another year or two, and Mitsubishi was contesting only five or six rallies a year and couldn't keep up with the pace of development.

Ralliart's launch of the Galant Evolution model on the Acropolis Rally set the rally world alight. Kenneth Eriksson blew his chances when a road accident, caused by an organizer's gaffe that sent rally cars hurtling through an Athens Monday morning rush hour at high speed while attempting to reach the first stage of the day on time, made him late for the next time control. He nevertheless proceeded to blast his way back through the field, setting a record number of fastest stage times, and, despite losing a wheel on the final day, he would have won by a comfortable margin had it not been for the subsequent road penalties. However, by the 1000 Lakes, a lack of match practice for the drivers, exacerbated by Ralliart being out of the game too long and not keeping up with the pace of development, left Mitsubishi struggling to put its cars in the top five, never mind win. After so much promise, Andrew Cowan's team was despairing; it was all a far cry from the celebrations that had ensued when Kenneth Eriksson won the Swedish Rally earlier that year.

Subaru made steady if unspectacular progress, and while the Legacy never looked as competitive as the Galant, there was a sense of direction at Prodrive that was missing at Ralliart. The Subaru crew were aiming for the future, a full programme that they hoped would bring them titles within a few years. Mitsubishi was simply picking the odd rally to win and capitalize on for the marketing people at MMC in Japan. Furthermore, Prodrive suffered that old Japanese handicap of having its engines produced in the East, and, as Toyota had found out in the past and corrected, this never works. Reliability of the engine seemed to be of more importance than winning, and at the slightest hint of heat in the engine the electronics would kick in engine-life prolonging tuning which retarded the ignition and almost halved power output. Alèn summed up the situation in Australia when he jumped from the car and shouted: 'It's no good. It's coming like in Group N car!'

Ford's problems were of an entirely different nature. For the British-based team, the season couldn't have started with more drama. Peter Ashcroft had signed a brash young Frenchman to drive a Q8 Sierra 4x4, François Delecour. He had been the doyen of the French championship with his giant-killing performances in a Peugeot 309, and while he could claim to know every inch of the Alps, no-one at Ford expected him to put the Sierra into the same league as Sainz's or Auriol's Toyota and Lancia. But that's exactly what the fiery blue-eyed driver did; and on the last night he was beating them. Delecour had forged his way past Sainz with four stages to go. However, after the final pass over the infamous Turini, within sight of the finish at Monaco, Delecour arrived at the stage finish in floods of tears. Television spotlights glared as the previously icy-cool Frenchman broke down and poured his anguish out for all to see; his moment of glory had disappeared with his rear suspension into the night and he dropped back to third. Ford couldn't produce that form again during the season. Alex Fiorio, Delecour and Malcolm Wilson were the drivers, and good ones at

*The fiery German
Armin Schwarz
takes victory for
Toyota on the
1991 Rally of
Catalonia – a rare
moment of success
in an otherwise
miserable season
that promised
much, but
delivered only
accidents.*

that, but the management left a good deal to be desired, as did the cars' reliability. All three cars retired in Portugal, Fiorio with oil-cooler failure and the other two with accidents. On the Acropolis, the team was devastated by persistent front driveshaft failures and all eventually retired again. The San Remo Rally contrived to make fools of the entire team with badly placed servicing, inadequate numbers of mechanics in some places and a surfeit in others – it was a complete nightmare.

Catalonia was better, with Delecour taking third and Mia Bardolet fourth, despite suffering a blown turbo and yet more transmission breakages.

Delecour took sixth on the RAC Rally in the sole surviving works Sierra to complete a miserable season for the Boreham team.

While Ford ended the year on a low note, Subaru enjoyed quite a different RAC Rally – no result, but an astonishing performance from Colin McRae and new Prodrive-built engines that made the Legacy look better than ever before. McRae pulled the nation onto its feet to watch a Brit lead a world championship rally on home soil, and although his two rolls, the second of which put him out of the event, gave Roger Clark the opportunity to breathe a sigh of relief that he remained the only British driver to have won the modern RAC, the performance pointed to a great future for Subaru and especially for McRae.

While the others had, on balance, made some progress, Toyota and Lancia were left to themselves to fight it out once more; but again, Lancia mastered the championship and went one better than the previous season by taking the manufacturers' crown and the drivers' title for Juha Kankkunen (his third). Sainz and Kankkunen were fairly evenly matched in their respective cars, but Sainz was more a victim of the relentless pace of the season. Exhausted, both drivers slumped into their hotels in Harrogate at the finish glad it was all over, but Sainz had suffered the most and it had cost him the title. TTE had made a mistake by relying too heavily on Sainz in its attempt to win the manufacturers' series. When he wasn't competing he was testing, when he wasn't testing he was travelling; the Spaniard was on a relentless treadmill and by the end of the season he was making mistakes, big ones, at high speed – a prime example was his massive roll in Australia which was simply caused by driver error. Lancia had three good points-scoring drivers in Kankkunen, Biasion and Auriol. Toyota had Armin Schwarz, who admittedly won in Catalonia, but he wasn't a back-up man, rather he was a fiery youngster out to prove himself, a charger like Sainz, but one who hadn't yet learned to temper his enthusiasm. The resultant accidents, such as that when leading in Corsica, indicated that he could not be relied upon just yet and Carlos was left to shoulder the entire responsibility for the team's success while the younger talent was fostered. Additionally, FISA, while promising only a year before that the number of rallies counting towards the championship would be reduced, had actually increased the spread of the series to include no less than 14 events! Things would have to change.

Tough cars these new Japanese Group A things. Despite this roll by Carlos Sainz in San Remo, he managed to continue and finish high enough in the results to secure the World Drivers' Championship.

10

The Nineties

Manufacturers had by now developed their Group A cars to be faster than the old Group B supercar formula. Despite worldwide recession the sport suddenly had the strongest entry at world championship level for years.

Previous page:
Back to the good
old days? The
modern Group A
cars are often
faster than the old
Group B
machines.
They spit fire, and
still attract big
crowds. But
somehow, it's all
more controlled.

After contesting 20 years of world championship rallies, Lancia's last year of official representation at rallying's highest level was 1991. At first, it was impossible to imagine the sport without the Abarth force, until it became evident that the 'junior-team' Jolly Club was to take over running the team and maintain financial backing from Martini. Furthermore, a high percentage of personnel shifted over from Lancia to Jolly Club, and so, initially anyway, it was *plus ça change.*

The latest model Integrale, the 16-valve HF Turbo, was given its debut as planned in Monte Carlo in 1992 and with Didier Auriol won the first of ten rounds that would give the manufacturer its last world championship title to date. It was not the most exciting year's motor sport. You saw the podium celebrations, and it was difficult to determine which event you were looking at; it was too much a case of same winners, different rally. It was a contrast to 1991 when rallies had been won by seconds and Toyota had come so close to taking the manufacturers' title to Japan.

On the same rally that the HF Integrale was given its debut, Toyota unveiled its futuristic new round shape Celica Turbo, but in its initial appearances it was overweight and wouldn't handle properly. The rampant success of the Integrale only highlighted the failure of TTE to make its new racer work. Morale in the camp was low, chief engineer Karl-Heinz Goldstein had left the company, and the German-based team, normally so ebullient, was floundering.

Winning the manufacturers' title on the 1000 Lakes Rally by August the Jolly Club Lancia team found it had time on its hands, and so, just to see how the Integrale would handle, it went to Australia 100 kilograms (220 pounds) heavier in preparation for the new, higher weight restrictions for 1993.

Toyota meanwhile had turned the corner, winning at Easter with Sainz on the Safari. The team moved forward, losing 40 kilograms (88 pounds) from the car by fitting a new tubular sub-frame and also taking victory in New Zealand. By shaving off kilos here and there it actually ended the year 20 kilograms (44 pounds) lighter than the Integrale. Although the handling on the new Celica was not totally free of problems it was working sufficiently well for Sainz to take the drivers' championship lead after New Zealand. It was a most extraordinary situation, the Lancia sweeping all before it, while Sainz had something of the tortoise's year, picking up momentum towards the tail-end of the season with wins in Spain and Great Britain.

No other manufacturer had even a peep at victory that year, although Nissan had a ray of hope – which they later decided was of the false variety – when Stig Blomqvist set five fastest times on the Swedish Rally, finishing third, the best world championship result for the Pulsar GTI-R. The result was achieved when the car was on Pirelli, as opposed to its usual Dunlop, tyres. The combination of a new car under public development and a tyre manufacturer that had been out of rallying for many years was never going to be ideal, and the Japanese simply lost patience with waiting for their little car to come right. Mid-season they announced they would be pulling out of rallying and the 1992 RAC Rally was the last event they undertook in an official capacity.

Of the other Japanese manufacturers, Subaru still seemed some way off becoming a serious challenger to Toyota. In the hands of Colin McRae, the Legacy had taken second place in Sweden, but neither of the Big Two had been present. Far more significant was McRae's

Left: Lancia in its death throes. Carlos Sainz's efforts in the Lancia in 1993 brought appalling results. The Lancia had finally been outgunned by the new Japanese machines.

Following page: Mitsubishi continued to concentrate on classic events and took as much pleasure in seeing Kenjiro Shinozuka bringing home a decent result on the Safari as watching Eriksson set fastest time on a European event.

performance in Greece, not so much for the end result of fourth, but for the 11 scratch times he had set *en route*. While neither car nor driver were world beaters yet, the signs were promising.

Mitsubishi's sole consolation was a win on the Ivory Coast with Kenjiro Shinozuka in Galant VR-4. It was a frustrating time for the Ralliart team. After Eriksson's explosive speed the previous year in Greece, the team was sure it had a winner with its Evolution Galant, but it never fulfilled its potential, and work was already well underway on the Lancer which would debut in 1993.

And what of Ford? Having abandoned the XR4x4 and Sierra projects in favour of the Sapphire Cosworth 4x4, a star driver was brought in to drive it. Indeed, Ford seemed to have woken up to modern rallying as it signed Miki Biasion to join Delecour in its world championship assault. Boreham had been given a facelift, there was much talk about a whole new attitude within the team, but it was rudely awoken to the facts of world championship life when its star driver and former champion pronounced the Sapphire Cosworth 'a pile of shit' on his opening event. Nonetheless, it managed two runner-up spots, and two third places. While no-one was really thinking the Sapphire could be a winner on anything more than a one-off basis, the hands-on world championship experience was invaluable for a team so short of match practice and it was indicative of a new realization of the demands of world championship rallying in the 1990s that Ford actually acknowledged it had much to learn from Toyota and Lancia. Meanwhile the excited whispers about the new Escort Cosworth were getting louder, and by January 1 1993 it was at last homologated.

Monte Carlo is always a rally full of anticipation. After the winter break even the biggest cynics look forward to seeing how new cars will fare on the Championship opener, and 1993 presented two new debutantes: Ford's Escort Cosworth, and Mitsubishi's Lancer Evolution. Of the two it was the former that presented the biggest challenge to the continuing efforts of Italy (albeit with development in limbo) and Cologne. It was a spectacular world championship debut for the Escort, with Delecour leading the rally by over a minute with four stages remaining in the first car Ford had produced since the seventies that looked capable of winning. Didier Auriol thought otherwise and he produced another miraculous Monte win, this time in the Toyota.

The car's performance came as something of a relief to the team, none more so than John Wheeler, the car's designer, but the congratulations had to wait until the next outing in Portugal when Ford led the event from start to finish, Delecour winning by 55 seconds from his team-mate.

It was the first world championship win for Ford since 1988, and the lengthy testing and development programme in which the company had invested to produce a winner from the outset, seemed to be paying off. The thousands of miles that test drivers like the experienced British driver Malcolm Wilson and former world champion Stig Blomqvist had put into the car, often taking it over the same roads as rally stages in order to compare times, seemed to be money well spent.

Before his retirement Peter Ashcroft had predicted the car would be a world champion on its second full season, but as 1993 progressed it looked as if it might fulfil its potential a year earlier, lying equal with Toyota on points as teams started the 1000 Lakes Rally.

The mid-nineties belonged to Juha Kankkunen and Toyota.

This page: Ford finally began to find success with the Escort RS, which at last looked like a rally-winning machine. Here, Cunico takes victory in San Remo.

For 1993, the TTE welcomed back its favourite son, Juha Kankkunen, as Carlos Sainz left for Jolly Club. The latter's decision to move in order to retain his sponsor Repsol was to cost him dear. With development of the HF Integrale at a standstill, it could not progress and with Ford, Subaru and Mitsubishi all having competitive cars, Sainz didn't manage a single rally win throughout the year.

No-one, not even Ford, whose hopes of marking the inaugural season of the Escort Cosworth with a championship title had been raised by rally victories, could begrudge Ove Andersson's crowning moment as he

directed Toyota to its first world championship, the first ever for a Japanese manufacturer. Whatever his official title at Toyota, president of TTE, he is simply the heart of the team. Having overseen operations since its first world championship rally in 1972, he has driven, prepared, ordered parts, made tea and orchestrated tactics for the team ever since, at times almost single-handedly fulfilling all roles at one time. Having seen so many bad times, here was the best time of all. The fact that the team had the biggest operation in the world championship was a testimony to Andersson's recognition of the tools necessary to do a job correctly.

Even while Toyota was clearing a space for the new trophy, events in New Zealand were to present it with a new threat. While the Integrale ended a whole era of Lancia involvement in the world championship, Colin McRae began a new chapter for Subaru, winning its first ever world rally in a Legacy, a feat that marked the young Scot's maiden victory at world level as well. It placed the foundations for a Japan versus Japan showdown for the following year.

Ford grabbed the 1994 rally headlines for all the wrong reasons. When its incorrigible star Delecour won in Monte Carlo, the first time for Ford in 41 years, it seemed the sky was the limit for this odd couple of civil service team and recalcitrant driver. But only a few weeks later the Frenchman's foot was almost severed in a road accident and he was out of competition until San Remo. It made the announcement that came in June all the more depressing. Ford was pulling out of rallying. All the months spent developing and refining the Escort to make it into a world champion were to be forfeited it seemed so that the team could go chasing touring car success. There was a furore at the staff meeting to announce the decision to Boreham: mechanics were furious at being left high and dry in the middle of a programme. As it transpired, it was not even a clean break. The rallying operation would be farmed out to Belgian satellite operation RAS in a move that would shave hundreds of thousands of pounds from the bottom-line cost of the rally programme. Chapters were closing thick and fast. This latest was the end of the last factory team's involvement with the sport that had made the Escort name synonymous with sporting performance.

It wasn't all doom and gloom on the rally front, for while the old firm had decided to shut up shop, the newcomer Subaru was gradually challenging Toyota's supremacy. The vast experience and knowledge of Ove Andersson was set against the slick business acumen and sharp ambition of David Richards. The potentially lethal combination of Sainz and McRae jousted with Juha Kankkunen and Didier Auriol, vastly experienced, but known quantities. And while Mitsubishi continued to show flashes of brilliance, the title fight was between the blue and yellow Subarus and the white, red and green of Toyota.

Subaru finally broke through with the high-tech Impreza 555. Not only did it bring Group A rallying to life, it also fired the imagination of the British public when Colin McRae won the New Zealand Rally three times in the row for Subaru, and the 1994 RAC Rally.

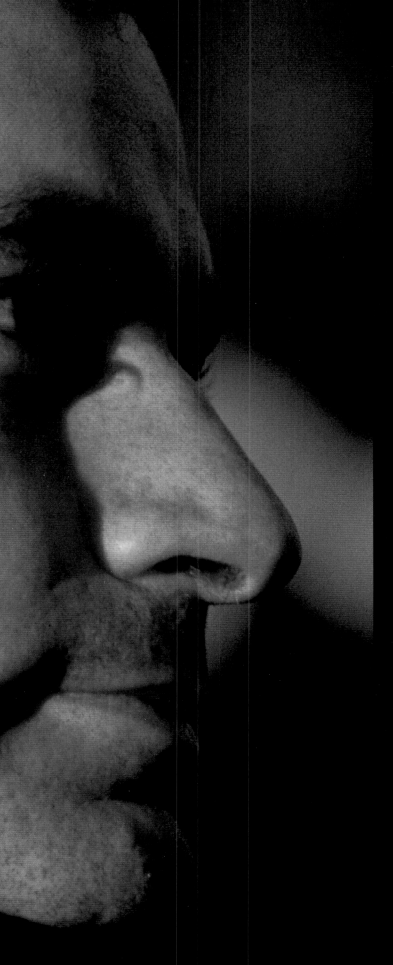

11

Modern Gladiators

In the 1970s and 1980s the Scandinavians dominated rallying, then a new front from southern Europe led by Miki Biasion, Carlos Sainz, Didier Auriol and François Delecour took the sport by storm.

143

JUHA KANKKUNEN

One minute it seemed Björn Waldegård was the Toyota expert on Africa, the next newspaper copytakers worldwide were being told 'Yes, that's K-a-n-k for Kenneth – K for Kenneth ...' Always looking older than his actual years (possibly the moustache), Juha Kankkunen seemed to accept his sudden leap into rallying's premier league in his stride to the extent that he'd only been around a season or two and it seemed like he'd been there for ever.

1985 was the year that he zoomed into everyone's consciousness, winning the Safari Rally on his first visit to Kenya, an achievement that a decade later still seems remarkable, but Kankkunen is simply a modern rallying phenomenon. Four times world champion with Peugeot, Lancia (twice) and Toyota he is a driver without equal in the way he has transferred his skill from team to team. In his early years he was compared to Walter Röhrl, and in his cool approach to driving there is a similarity, but Kankkunen has none of his German forerunner's hang-ups. He is usually polite and easygoing, happy to carry out sponsorship and public relations duties and a good team player. He's no saint, of course, the equal of any of his countrymen when it comes to celebrating, but it has never been more than high jinks and even his public disagreement with his new team Lancia in 1987 was

patched up to the extent that he returned to the Italian team four years later.

He was the first of a new generation of Finnish drivers – natural flair tempered with a judgement for pace – and enjoyed the patronage of Björn Waldegård in his first years with Toyota. The influence of the Swede paid off handsomely in that first Safari victory, the youngster acknowledging the help and advice he'd received.

The tall Finn could have been made to order, growing up on his family's farm only a ten-minute drive from Jyvaskyla, centre of the 1000 Lakes Rally under the watchful eye of Timo Mäkinen, a friend of Kankkunen senior. Even when he failed to finish in early rallies he was often streets ahead of the opposition and was soon offered a drive with Toyota Finland.

Very much under the wing of Ove Andersson, Kankkunen grew with every rally he undertook for the Cologne-based team. Andersson for his part had been shrewd enough to snap up the young Finn before Italy beat him to it. A fifth spot on the 1000 Lakes was the highlight of 1984, and then came the Safari win the following year. That Toyota should win for the second year in succession despite its lack of previous experience should have surprised no-one: Ove Andersson had accumulated some of the oldest African hands in rallying in his team. The fact that Kankkunen's team-mate Björn Waldegård's car hit trouble, and successive rally leaders fell

Previous page: Carlos Sainz: highly paid and highly motivated.

Below: Juha Kankkunen celebrates victory on the 1985 Safari.

by the wayside does not greatly diminish his achievement. After a run of bad luck it was certainly Kankkunen's turn for a place in the sun.

Taking an African double after victory on the Ivory Coast, Kankkunen was a target for Jean Todt and so the Finn joined Peugeot for 1986 alongside Timo Salonen.

In no time at all he had eclipsed his team-mate, in the same way that only a year before Salonen had won the title over the favoured Ari Vatanen. But his road to that first drivers' title was tortuously long-winded, up against not only his fellow-Finn Markku Alèn, but the ditherings of FISA to boot. Both had their chances to wrap the title up earlier in the season, but both squandered them for different reasons. In Kankkunen's case, after wins in Sweden, Greece and New Zealand he was second in Argentina and then rolled on the RAC and had to be given an ordered third place. Nonetheless, while people were itching to see Alèn take the drivers' crown after so many years of trying, most observers decided that, sentiment apart, Kankkunen was a deserving title-holder.

With the foreshortening of Group B, Lancia was Kankkunen's next stop for 1987, but his career with the Turin team got off to a wobbly start in Monte Carlo when he became embroiled in a public squabble with Cesare Fiorio after Biasion had taken an orchestrated win. Those in the Kankkunen camp slapped their foreheads in horror: it was a daft thing to do, so early in the season, so soon

after joining. Team orders were a part of Lancia and Fiorio folklore, a fact that Kankkunen must have been well aware of before he joined. Nonetheless, ever the politician, Fiorio gave his latest Finnish signing the nod on the Olympus Rally to win from Alèn and Biasion. The idiosyncratic Italian further surprised when he announced his plan to give each of his drivers an equal crack at the drivers' championship, which left Kankkunen on the RAC Rally – already signed for Toyota in 1988 – heading for his double of titles. While many cynics thought his Delta HF 4x4's engine might develop an inexplicable fault on the last leg and give Alèn the championship, it was not to be and there was much gracious congratulating of the double-champion in the Lake District service area after the final stage.

His return to his Toyota family in 1988 and 1989 was neither happy nor successful as TTE struggled to make its Group A challenger, the Celica 2000 GT4, a winner. It failed to finish any of its rallies with Kankkunen and he was so disillusioned that even when it began to show distinct promise, winning the Rally of Australia, he had already made plans to return to Lancia.

It wasn't until returning to Australia, that Kankkunen hit winning form again, the 12-month gap between wins an uncomfortable length of time for Lancia and the former multiple champion. It was something of an ironic win – victory on the rally where he had gained valuable

Kankkunen gets to grips with the powerful Peugeot 205 T16 in the USA in 1986.

experience with TTE the year before – pushing Lancia further ahead in the makes championship, the goal Ove Andersson had set his heart on scoring for Toyota.

A second victory on the Safari in 1991 made the contrast with a lacklustre fifth on Monte Carlo more noticeable. Never a fan of tarmac, his lack of ability to win as well on rallies such as Monte Carlo or Corsica was his Achilles' heel. His programme was such however that wins in Greece, Finland, Australia and Great Britain made sure he lifted the drivers' title yet again. It was becoming something of a habit. By this time Kankkunen was the highest paid of all the rally drivers, breaking the £1 million barrier, previously only the preserve of Formula One drivers; but Kankkunen, despite his rural background, knew how to make the most of an opportunity, even if it was by employing the best manager around to negotiate for him!

He said later that none of his world championship wins gave him as much satisfaction as that in 1993 when, as well as becoming individual champion, he helped Andersson achieve his managerial ambition by giving

Toyota the manufacturers' title. It was a touching moment, no matter how many times you saw Kankkunen in the Martini overalls of Lancia, he still looked more at home in the white of Toyota with Andersson behind him like a benevolent father.

His partnership with Juha Piironen was a straight man-funny man combination, with Piironen's wicked humour turning them into a rallying Reeves and Mortimer. He had first met the older Finn when he was studying English in Helsinki and teamed up with him in 1986 after Fred Gallagher decided he was more suited to Björn Waldegård's programme of events. Personally, Kankkunen was devastated when his friend collapsed with a brain haemorrhage mid-way through 1993 but professionally he didn't falter, dedicating his fourth world championship title to the still recuperating Piironen while striking up an altogether different partnership with the less experienced, but more openly ambitious, Nicky Grist. More surprisingly, he found new impetus with his new partner, even to the extent of improving his tarmac performances to finish second in Monte Carlo (his highest finish).

Miki Biasion takes the Lancia to victory in Argentina.

MIKI BIASION

The expected career path for the first Italian World Rally Champion would be via the popular Fiat one-make series chased by hundreds of hopeful young Italian drivers each year. Not for young Massimo Biasion. Writing off his mother's Renault 5, he then tried a Group 1 Opel Kadett, winning his local series with it, and moving up to an Ascona for 1980, with which he won the Italian Group 2 Championship. Opel Italy was now involved for whom he drove an Ascona 400 on, most notably, the San Remo, finishing sixth. The following year he returned to San Remo and again clinched a top ten finish, this time eighth. The drive was enough to pave the way to Lancia, via the Jolly Club team who gave him the opportunity for a full tilt at the European championship, which he won in 1983, one of the few holders of the title to go on to better things.

His rise through the ranks at Jolly Club to take his place in the Lancia team was as inevitable as it was unhurried, so that by 1985 his foreign experience was already extensive, courtesy of the 037. The junior member of the squad, which included Henri Toivonen and Markku Alèn, drove a Delta S4 in 1985 and 1986, taking his first world championship victory in Argentina, much to the annoyance of Markku Alèn, who was ordered by Fiorio to stay in second place. Biasion saw team orders in a different light in San Remo when, poised to take victory, Fiorio dictated otherwise and he had to be content with second.

Nonetheless, the most successful Italian drivers since Sandro Munari had driven the Stratos, Biasion and long-time co-driver Tiziano Siviero were soon lionized by the *tifosi*, and given a full programme in the newborn Group A Delta. They soon had the sports pages of *Corriere della Serra* following their every move.

Lancia took the manufacturers' title as a matter of course in 1987, but team-mate Kankkunen beat Biasion to the drivers' championship. There was little love lost between the two men from the start, Biasion irritated at Kankkunen's refusal to abide by Fiorio's 'race of Turini' diktat, dismissing the Finn's claim to have misunderstood. He could be satisfied by the end of 1988, however, when the world title was his. An Italian world champion in an Italian car and securing the championship in Italy! He had won in style, flattening any opposition, winning five times from seven starts with a second in Argentina. It made for fairly predictable but compulsive rallying, as the Biasion Integrale forged through 1988 and into 1989, hardly pausing for breath and collecting a total of ten rally wins from 13 starts.

There was no doubt that Biasion was in the right place at the right time. At no other time in the championship's history has one manufacturer been so dominant, and Biasion was the man behind the wheel, but to his credit, he had Alèn and latterly Auriol in the same team, and despite Fiorio's orders, their pace had to be beaten too.

By the end of 1991, Biasion could no longer enjoy his unchallenged domination as Auriol came to terms with the Integrale. The announcement, however, of a big money transfer to the Ford team for 1992 still came as something of a surprise. Had the Italian dream turned sour?

Ford had not had a highly paid number one driver before and was looking to Biasion to make the Sierra a winner. Monte Carlo was to be the start of three frustrating years at Ford for Biasion. A difficult eighth had Biasion talking about the Sierra as a 'Third World car', an inauspicious start for driver-management relations. Worse still was Ford's supposed number two driver François Delecour, who finished four places in front of Biasion.

The two drivers never really did get along: Delecour resented the amount of money Biasion was able to command for a three-year contract, while later at Ford Biasion began to feel he was getting the poorer treatment from the engineers. Biasion did his best in the Sierra, stringing together seven top-ten finishes to claim fourth place in the championship, but Delecour was consistently quicker.

With the arrival of the Escort Cosworth, Biasion was much happier now that Ford had a car 'more like the Lancia'. He was to become competitive again, but still regularly behind his Ford team-mate Delecour.

If Biasion was becoming disenchanted with Ford, Ford also found it difficult to work with Miki. In testing, Ford's engineer Philip Dunabin preferred to sit with the driver and experience for himself what was happening, but Biasion insisted on having Siviero. Indeed, the feelings in the Ford camp were that the more volatile Siviero was at the bottom of any ill-feeling between team and driver.

It was Siviero who seemingly chose the suspension settings for each event after a day's testing, but once the event started it wouldn't be long before Miki was looking to try different settings in an effort to make up lost time on the leaders. There was a definite tension between Biasion and some members of the Ford team: the mechanics often thought he wasn't trying, while Miki was at a loss to explain why he should suffer four engine failures in his last five rallies. However, the quiet Italian was trying hard to become a team player in a side that has been notoriously partisan of its drivers over the years – indeed he wrote to Malcolm Wilson to personally thank him for all the work he'd put into setting up the Escort so well.

He suffered badly in direct comparison to Delecour, both on stage times and at service areas. Delecour would arrive at a service point, jumping out of his Cosworth, ranting and raving at the mechanics after a bad time. He looked to the technicians as if he was really trying, as if he really cared. Miki on the other hand would quietly get out of the car, shrug his shoulders and disappear into the motorhome with a cluster of Italian journalists. Ranting and raving were simply not his style.

In his time at Ford, he was a notoriously slow starter, but often finished faster than any of the other drivers. His drive in Portugal in 1994 proved he could still hold his own against the best, when he finished second; but it was unfortunately one of the few times he really seemed committed during a difficult time at Ford. It is apparent now that his continued beatings at the hands of Delecour were simply due to the exceptional speed of the Frenchman.

CARLOS SAINZ

Arguably rallying's biggest star, and earning over £2 million a year certainly the highest paid, Carlos Sainz is Spain's leading sporting hero. He commands the front page of his national newspapers for his every victory since becoming the first Spaniard to win the World Rally Championship for Drivers in 1990. He had come a long

way since Peter Ashcroft signed him for Ford amid much criticism in 1988.

Unfortunately for Ashcroft, the Ford Sierra Cosworth Sainz used in 1989 was never going to be a serious world championship contender, despite Didier Auriol's Corsica victory in 1988, and despite Sainz leading the 1987 Rally of Portugal (for one stage) in his Marlboro-Spain backed entry. Nonetheless, even if he had to wait to see his decision vindicated, it was a satisfying moment.

As the trend for talent-spotting away from Scandinavia hit its height, the interest Sainz had created after three world championship outings backed by Marlboro Spain was immense. His results had not been drop-dead spectacular – a win on the Corte Ingles in a Renault 5 Turbo and a couple of runner-up spots behind Fabrizio Tabaton in the European championship – but his speed in the little Renault had marked him out as a definite catch to be landed, and there was always the cynical view that Ford might have wanted to establish a better presence in an under-serviced car market ...

Baby Carlos was a happy child, from a wealthy Spanish family who numbered King Juan Carlos amongst its contacts. Despite being sent to law school, the writing was on the wall that young Carlos would more than likely make his mark as a sportsman. But at which sport? A junior and senior Spanish squash champion, Sainz could have made a comfortable living as a footballer, or developed his fencing or skiing talents. Instead, motor sport captured his imagination even during his schooldays.

He started rallying in a Fiat (or Seat as it was Spain) Panda in 1980 but it was in the two-wheel-drive Renault 5 Turbo that he began to really attract attention.

His time at Boreham was cut short when an offer from Ove Andersson came along to drive the Celica GT4 in its last year of development just as it became a winner. Sainz was the junior support to Juha Kankkunen but when the former champion's patience with the car snapped and he left for Lancia in 1990, Sainz was once more thrust into the spotlight. The error of judgement on Kankkunen's part – to leave a team just when the car was about to realize its potential – was a stroke of good fortune for the Spaniard. Sharing billing with Armin Schwarz and Mikael Ericsson, Sainz undertook a massive programme of eleven events – an unbelievable schedule of constant recce, testing and competition.

The year started with a psychological blow on the Monte Carlo Rally. Sainz was engaged in a second-for-second duel with Didier Auriol from the very first stage. It was a famous battle, the first time the GT4 had been able to launch a serious attack on Lancia's domination. Andersson had scored a significant early goal, producing tyre warmers for the GT4. Michelin specialist Maurice Guaslard had joined TTE and borrowed the idea from F1. Seeing the rows and rows of red-wrapped tyres waiting in the service area, was a moment of quiet triumph over Lancia. For once, Lancia had been out-trumped, and its team, used to having the best and the first of everything were distinctly wrong-footed ... it wasn't long before news of the tactic filtered back through the service area, and a private crew decided their driver wasn't to be outshone by the might of the works Toyota's. Okay, so TTE had the full electronic warmers, but wrapping their tyres in blankets, even if it didn't help their driver, certainly gave everyone something to smile about!

Meanwhile, the battle with Auriol was hotting up, and as the final night began Sainz led after the first run over the Col de Turini. Throughout the rally there had been only seconds separating the two drivers. Halfway through the final night's stages, Lancia changed Auriol's turbo, and suddenly the Frenchman was able to beat Sainz by a second a kilometre, cutting the time from his first run over the Turini by an astonishing 27 seconds, smashing records for the stage made by Group B cars.

Poor Sainz could do nothing. He had given his all, snatched a second here and a second there by driving to the edge of his capabilities, only to see his lead literally blown away. Ove Andersson was in turn furious and disgusted, Toyota launched a protest but the result stood, albeit still not to everyone's satisfaction. Even years after, Sainz admits to wanting to know the real truth of what happened that night.

It was an inauspicious start to what was to become a momentous year. Sainz's first world championship was taken in the same year he took the world driver's title, and for a labelled tarmac specialist it was, most satisfactorily, taken on the roughest gravel of all, Greece. The occasion was a dream for statisticians and champagne houses alike, the first world championship win for a Spaniard, first major rally win for Sainz, first European win for Toyota for 15 years. Ove Andersson's quiet delight was understandable. After initial hiccups in settling into the team, Sainz was now an integral part of the Cologne factory and after two years of searching for speed and reliability and 1001 other changes the Celica too launched its serious attack on the Integrale. Lancia began to look vulnerable.

Straight from Greece, TTE went to New Zealand, despite the rally being only a counter towards the drivers' championship. Without Kankkunen, Auriol or Biasion, Sainz's opposition was thin on the ground, the greatest challenge coming from Ingvar Carlsson's Mazda which he got the measure of by the mid-point. The Antipodean victory gave him an advantage of 25 points over Didier Auriol in the drivers' table. Argentina was another extra trip, and although Sainz increased his advantage over the Frenchman by a further three points, two accidents in practice and a hefty roll on the rally suggested that the heavy demands on the driver were beginning to tell.

Getting into his Celica in Finland, Sainz looked ready for a holiday and a bit of repair work himself. Nursing bruised tendons after an accident in practice, he wore a trainer on his injured foot, a racing boot on the other. Ready to contest the fastest rally in the world? You wouldn't really have wanted to be Luis Moya sitting next to a peg-legged Sainz, on a rally which has caused countless problems for fully fit drivers. The problems made the Spaniard's victory on a rally which for 40 years had been the legendary preserve of Scandinavian drivers all the more remarkable, especially in the face of a strong challenge from Ari Vatanen. Each time Sainz started a rally it seemed he was creating new precedents; by the end of the year what would there be left to exclaim about?

Plenty as it transpired; third place in San Remo – despite an accident – was sufficient to make Sainz champion, and the Spanish sports pages made the most of the occasion. Single-handedly Sainz had sparked off thousands of Spanish youngsters' daydreams.

Rounding off his year by winning the RAC Rally, an event which the year before had left him in tears as propshaft failure lost him the lead with only three stages remaining, it seemed as if a long stretch of rest and recuperation was in order, but Spain's first rally champion was in far too much demand on the media front to even think about rest. As a champion, and an ambassador for Spain, Sainz is ideal. Goodlooking, articulate and confident his popularity and success took a country and

Opposite: Extreme talent required! Carlos Sainz on the edge in New Zealand.

gave it a full world championship qualifier for the first time in 1991. After his mercurial elevation to champion in 1990 so much was expected of him that it was no surprise when he began to get a little more elusive to the press. His close-knit entourage closed around him like a protective outer shell.

It seemed incredible but Sainz's 1991 programme included a further rally, Catalonia. It pushed the Spaniard too far. Despite victories in Monte Carlo, Portugal, Corsica, New Zealand and Argentina, he had a high-speed barrel roll of an accident in Australia, a result of trying to win the manufacturers' title single-handedly for Toyota as well as successfully defend his drivers' crown. The team was relying far too much on the huge strengths of one driver. Going next to Spain, hoping to win the title on home ground, he instead handed the advantage to Juha Kankkunen when the Toyota refused to start on the rally's second day. Toyota and Sainz were doomed to end the year with precious little to show for their huge efforts.

The new, rounded Celica Turbo made its debut in Monte Carlo in 1992; initially overweight, its handling problems were unresolved before its full competition year began. The team had lost a key member of its set-up when Karl-Heinz Goldstein had left for Volkswagen and his loss grew. Unusually in the Toyota camp, tensions grew and the atmosphere was not its usual one of unity. All this changed on the Safari, when Sainz took his first victory in Africa, and gave the new-shaped car its inaugural win. His hat-trick win in New Zealand gave him valuable points but even on the San Remo Rally, both Auriol and Kankkunen had the advantage over him. Winning in Spain meant everything hinged on the RAC Rally, and when he heard of the abandoned Auriol Integrale, Sainz knew that barring a catastrophe a second drivers' title would be his.

He made a surprise transfer to Jolly Club/Lancia for 1993, as Toyota was adopted by Castrol, a conflict with Sainz's long-standing personal sponsor, Repsol. He had a barren year however, and as Lancia in whatever guise withdrew from the world championship, Sainz opted to join Subaru for the 1994 season, where a good win in Greece eased his 12 rally drought. In San Remo came a bizarre occurrence, when he lost his lead to a flu-stricken Auriol: driving superbly in a car that was showing no sign of problems, he had realized Auriol was on his tail and could do nothing about it. He insisted there was something wrong with the car, while the engineers found it was working perfectly. The machine was human after all. It had been a closely fought season in 1994, and Sainz came within a hair's breadth of winning the drivers' championship again. But just when it seemed that he might get a little help from his team-mate, Colin McRae, who was leading the final round RAC Rally, a few wayward members of the British public, looking for their first RAC victory for a Brit since Clark, intervened and put logs on the stage. Sainz managed to avoid them, but slid off, concentration disturbed, shortly after.

FRANÇOIS DELECOUR

A vivid scar weaves its way insidiously around François Delecour's left ankle. The fact that it stops short by some 2 centimetres (³/₄ inch) of completing its circumference is the reason why the Frenchman still has a left foot.

In terms of highs and lows if this man's 1994 was

made into a theme park ride people would be queuing until Christmas. In January he delivered to the Essex-based Ford team one of the most prized titles of all, the Monte Carlo Rally, the first time that the team had taken victory on that most evocative of events since 1953. He was going to become world champion driver, he declared, and ensure that his team took the manufacturers' prize. With his searing speed, few were taking bets against him achieving at least the former.

Ten weeks after that champagne-soaked Monte Carlo visit, a short trip to buy some bread near his home, then in the north of France, ended with the 31-year-old's feet wrapped around the front of what minutes earlier had been a Ferrari F40. A clubman, practising for a local rally in a Citroen, had chosen the same stretch of road to race along, stopped only by Delecour's car. The other driver was not seriously hurt but the impact almost severed the sportsman's left foot and wrapped its partner around the accelerator. 'I saw my foot, and saw the bone sticking out, and I thought maybe they must cut it off, I knew it was bad,' he remembers.

The foot was saved and ten weeks later Delecour was doing speed trials in a standard car on a closed road behind his new home in the south of France.

The accident came at a crucial time in his career. In the midst of Delecour's fightback to fitness, came Ford's announcement that it was to quit rallying again. Now Bernie Ecclestone might not be the most popular man in rallying, but he simply wouldn't stand for that kind of behaviour in Grand Prix racing. When Alain Prost made the first of several 'retirements', the dealmaker was disgusted. 'Who does he think he is?' he stormed. 'The way he's popping in and out of Formula One, he's treating it like a public convenience.'

Signed by Peter Ashcroft after a blinding run on the 1990 Monte Carlo Rally in a two-wheel-drive Peugeot 309 gave him a top ten finish, Delecour was under close scrutiny as the world waited to see just why Ashcroft had signed this Frenchman who hadn't even won a rally. Despite some good drives in 1991 and 1992, notably in Monte Carlo where he very nearly pulled off a dream start to his partnership with Ford, he had led Carlos Sainz going into the final stage, only for the Sierra Cosworth's rear suspension to break under stress on the Col de Turini. He finished totally distraught and in third place.

After the initial plaudits from Monte Carlo, too many rallies passed without victory. Delecour recalls the period well: 'It was terrible,' he remembers. 'Everybody needed to win. The pressure was very, very great. I needed to win, Ford needed to win and I know that people were beginning to say: 'Maybe François, he cannot do it after all'.' The most crushing moment came on the 1993 Monte Carlo Rally when Delecour and Ford had led from the second stage right through to the 20th of the total 22 stages entering the last night-time leg with a two-minute advantage, only to see certain victory snatched from him when Auriol produced an explosive turn of speed in his Toyota to win the rally by 15 seconds. It was the second time he had placed one hand on the magnificent Monte Carlo trophy only to have it pulled off.

He broke his duck at last in Portugal the same year, giving the Escort Cosworth its first world championship win, breaking a five-year drought. The win did wonders for the confidence not just of Delecour, but the Ford team as well, and he proceeded to further victories that year in Corsica and Spain. It was all looking so good for 1994, a million pound-plus contract in his pocket and then the accident spelt disaster.

Didier Auriol (right) and Carlos Sainz exchange pleasantries in Monte Carlo.

His single-minded recovery came as no great surprise to Ford's chief engineer and Delecour-mentor, Philip Dunabin. 'He's the type of person that has to win a walk across a room,' he observes wryly. The two enjoy a close relationship. It helps that Dunabin is something of a Francophile and Delecour's co-driver is now Dunabin's girlfriend, but their mutual respect is apparent in their dealings together, Delecour trusting no-one in the team above Dunabin.

Despite trying his utmost to persuade Colin Dobinson that he was fit for New Zealand and almost collapsing from the effort, Delecour's comeback was in Finland – the fastest rally of the year. Few doubted that Delecour would come out of his corner fighting but his gritty drive into fourth place was breathtaking for the raw courage it exposed.

Unfortunately in San Remo, his mutterings about Miki Biasion's co-driver Tiziano Siviero didn't endear him to many: he accused the Italian of using his influence with the organizers to ensure their car would run down the order, on stages cleared of slippery surface gravel.

It is this juxtaposition of Delecour's talent with his ill-judged outbursts that leads those in his camp into occasional despair. Indeed, the British journalist David Williams observed in *Rallycourse* that Delecour's problems began when he got out of the car, and to a large extent

that is so – at least one big sponsor refusing to have anything to do with a driver who seems to have a knack for sticking his Sparco-shod foot well into his mouth. He tried to open negotiations for a new contract by drawing a parallel with Manchester United's multi-million pound Frenchman Eric Cantona, he has called drivers who beat him cheats, and in Portugal after a fuel check by FISA had left him with no fuel, he blocked the stage with his Cosworth until chief scrutineer Gabriele Cadringher was summoned. On the same rally, with a clear lead over team-mate Biasion, Colin Dobinson told his two drivers to hold station, and not to risk a rare one-two for Ford. Delecour was having none of this, and with a clear lead, proceeded to risk it all by setting fastest times on the first four stages of the final day. Biasion meanwhile backed off to preserve the car. When Biasion finally cracked on the fifth stage of the day, beating Delecour by one second, the Frenchman – whose lead was well over a minute – felt justified in his disregard for team orders. 'You see,' he retorted, 'I told you he would try to win still.'

More seriously when Carlos Sainz, duelling with Didier Auriol (who would have been the first French world champion) broke down on the early stages of the 1994 RAC Rally in a no-service zone, Delecour happily broadcast on French television that it was his Ford that had pushed the Spaniard into service, only to deny it just as hotly hours later when quizzed about the matter by his team.

While it all makes for good copy some managers might feel that sometimes the liability might outweigh the advantage.

DIDIER AURIOL

It had been a hard season and one for which Auriol had waited for more years than he would probably care to count, but here in Chester he was at last being crowned world champion. But where was the elation, the jigging, the exuberance that had marked his celebrations in the past? 'Winning a title is a different feeling ... it's not the sort you can live at the moment. You have to live it afterwards, quietly, with people you like,' he said, standing on the platform in the RAC's press centre immediately after the rally. But perhaps his overriding feeling was one of relief, thankful that he would not end up as the Markku Alèn of his generation, immensely talented and successful, but just unable to make it the final few yards to the championship title. Thankfully for Auriol, Alèn's destiny was not to be his.

He first became the focus of interest in the 33 Export Metro 6R4 in 1986 when he won the French championship from François Chatriot in a full works Renault. Prepared by British specialists Rally Engineering Developments (R-E-D), the three-cornered partnership of driver, sponsor and team continued when the 6R4 was swapped for a Sierra Cosworth, and he ventured to San Remo for his first foreign world championship event, finishing fourth.

Venturing even further afield in 1988, after winning in Corsica, giving the RS Cosworth its sole world championship victory – he grabbed all the pressroom babble in Finland with an extraordinary drive, finishing third on his first ever visit to the famous jumps and in a two-wheel-drive car to boot! That he was too good for Ford to hold onto was inevitable, that Lancia would grab hold of this sensation even more of a foregone conclusion.

A driver from the south of France, with a pedigree from the French championship would have had to have boasted a Scandinavian mother in order not to be labelled a tarmac specialist. It was the standard rally rejoinder; northern Europeans good on gravel, southern Europeans good on tarmac, and never the twain should meet. It was particularly frustrating for Auriol but a second place in Greece in his first year with Lancia went part way to ensuring his programme included some off-road rubber.

He was a late starter in terms of full world championship baptism. Miki Biasion, his Lancia team-mate, is only seven months older than him and yet while he (Auriol) was taking his first world championship win with the Cosworth in Corsica in 1988, Biasion was winning his first of two consecutive drivers' titles. Another contemporary of his, Carlos Sainz, was his team-mate while at Ford. In fact Auriol had seemed the better prospect of the two, actually persuading the Cosworth to be a winner, a feat Sainz could never manage, but while Sainz was collecting his first world title in 1990 Auriol was still writing large his reputation as an all-or-nothing merchant.

It all so nearly changed in 1992. Auriol and Bernard Occelli – his partner from the very earliest Renault days – collected a staggering six wins that year, but somehow contrived not to become champions, by virtue of the fact that if they didn't win, they didn't finish. Unbelievably the pair only finished third in the league that year, behind both Sainz, who won four rallies, and Kankkunen, who won one.

Auriol's turn of speed in the final throes of events means he can never be discounted if in contention, but even his phenomenal speed has been called into question at times, notably in Monte Carlo in 1990 when a timely turbo-boost change prior to the final stages resulted in his gaining a second a kilometre over a helpless Carlos Sainz.

Two years later he was to grab another victory from under the nose of the Spaniard, zooming through uphill sections of stages faster than the downhill sections. Sainz has had cause to rue the day Auriol gets within scent of him at the end of a rally. The 1994 San Remo Rally, which Sainz had almost sewn up, was a case in point: Auriol won despite a severe bout of flu, after grinding the Subaru driver's lead down to nothing.

The final clincher for the drivers' title came on the RAC. It was between Sainz and Auriol, and the latter had to finish at least fourth to ensure his name would be 1994 world champion. But the man from Millau looked as if he'd blown it again when on only the third stage he hit a rock and lost four minutes. Bottles of champagne must have been placed in the Sainz family freezer when news came through that the Frenchman had rolled, losing a further ten minutes and dropping through the ranks into three figures. Few people would have bet against a third title for Sainz. Then on the final morning came news that Sainz had encountered logs on a stage, he had continued but been so shaken by the discovery his Impreza had left the road on the following stage. It was all over, Auriol in his battered Toyota had taken the championship. He was happy but not deliriously so: 'Now I'm equal ...' He wasn't to be the second member of Markku Alèn's unfortunate club.

Auriol's major breakthrough came with victory for Ford on the 1988 Tour de Corse.

12

Looking to the Future

The new waiting to replace the old.

*Previous page:
Colin McRae
carries the hopes
of the British
nation in rallying.*

*Below: It hasn't
been a smooth
ride for McRae, as
this heartbreaking
moment on the
1991 RAC Rally
demonstrates.*

*Opposite:
Evidence that
McRae is a future
world champion,
as he calmly eases
his Subaru
Impreza home to
his third New
Zealand Rally
victory in a row in
1995.*

Reaching mid-point in the nineties, the sparkling new order of talent that swept up from the Mediterranean is now the Establishment, challenged by an ever-younger band of drivers.

It used to be that rallying was a sport dominated by men in their late thirties and forties, but as the nature of the events has moved the emphasis away from the ability to drive without sleep for day upon day to speed and sprinting, laser-like reflexes are needed and rally drivers, like policemen, are getting younger every day.

At the age of 27, Colin McRae had already won five world championship qualifiers – three in New Zealand, a Formula Two event in Australia, and on the RAC of 1994. The latter was a tremendous triumph, the first victory on the rally for a British driver since Roger Clark in 1976, and while he wasn't quite invited to parade his Subaru at the London Palladium, it certainly brought his name into pub-talk across the country.

In his home country, McRae was already a familiar and successful motor sporting name; father Jim won the British Rally Championship a record five times and Colin became something of a rally legend in Scotland for his speed – and crashes – in a Vauxhall Nova. A sixth place on the 1990 RAC – totally against the odds in a Sierra held together by a gate bolt and masking tape by the end of the rally – prompted Prodrive's David Richards to sign him for Subaru. Joining Richards' organization was the best move the driver could have made. His first years with the Banbury team were spent winning the British championship in the new Legacy, while the rest of the time was spent as part of the service crew on world championship events for Carlos Sainz. It was astute planning on the part of Richards, who recognized the quantum leap from British to world events and wanted to give the youngster an idea of the scale and pace of the premier league. Winning the British championship in 1991 and 1992, he was given a limited programme of five world championship events for 1992, and on his first outing returned second on the Swedish Rally, joining Michele Mouton in the Audi Quattro as the best ever performance by a non-Scandinavian on the event. A good fourth on his first Acropolis drive was followed by a further two respectable top ten finishes. The following year, Asian–Pacific championship duties were added to a total programme of eight world championship rallies, and McRae won his first world qualifier, in New Zealand in the face of a full entry from all five works teams. It was a fantastic result for the Scot, not only his first win, but the first success at world championship level for Subaru.

The New Zealand win was the last bright spot for many months for Colin. The honeymoon period with Prodrive was coming to a close. The prankish Luis Moya, Sainz's co-driver, was seen by insiders to be a mischievous influence in many of Colin's high-spirited exploits out of the rally car but even allowing for the natural exuberance of a twenty-something let loose on a world of money, travel and hero-worship, David Richards was beginning to come down hard on his protégé. Having given McRae 'growing room', a gentle introduction to the rigours of top-flight rallying, he now expected a decent return on his investment, starting in 1994.

The year began badly for McRae and Derek Ringer in Monte Carlo when French spectators threw snow onto a corner, putting both McRae and early leader Armin Schwarz into a snowbank. It wasn't McRae's fault, but it went down as the first off-road manoeuvre of the year. Portugal was next, and an engine fire ended McRae's rally. In Corsica he crashed, and then in Greece he was excluded

after a messy incident, while leading. Scrutineers didn't replace the bonnet pins on his Impreza after a routine spot check and predictably the bonnet flew up cracking the windscreen. Blocking the stage with his car, McRae insisted that a Subaru service crew be allowed in a 'no-service' area to replace his now dangerously damaged windscreen. The marshals agreed, the windscreen was replaced, and McRae carried on. It was only later that night while McRae was asleep that the stewards decided to exclude him for 'unsporting behaviour'.

Misery in Argentina followed, crashing out again after setting some spectacular times, and starting speculation that Richards was losing patience with his shooting star's inability to keep on the road.

While rumours of his departure from Subaru were greatly exaggerated, the shrewd team boss knew that keeping McRae's wilder driving in check could be no bad thing; he was pulled from the 1000 Lakes Rally and promptly took his second consecutive win in New Zealand in distinctly un-McRae fashion. Under strict orders to simply finish the rally, he won it by two and a half minutes from Juha Kankkunen. From the fifth stage he found himself in the uncomfortable position of leading the rally and after the 15th being the sole Subaru survivor. His controlled and paced drive was the best retort for those who were beginning to think his upkeep in bodywork made him too expensive.

Victory in Australia after a hard-fought tussle with four-times rally winner Juha Kankkunen paved the way for the historic RAC victory, and a swift move to Monaco, via Switzerland.

It's easy to try to label McRae as 'early Vatanen' but after a short time these tags peel off. Yes, he's had more accidents than his mother would like, yes he's lost the chance of victory when maybe caution could have bagged it; but he outgrew the experience his father could pass onto him years ago and, much like the later years of Group B technology, the question seems to be not just how much speed he possesses, but how long will it take him to cope with its limits?

His lifestyle couldn't contrast more with that of his co-driver of the last eight years. While McRae revels in his bachelordom – despite the best efforts of his mother – Derek Ringer, 12 years his senior, is the happily married father of three, nowhere to be seen in wee hours in the nightclubs and hotspots where many of the other team members do their relaxing. He is as articulate and forthcoming as McRae is reserved, but the two enjoy a knockabout humour of a very Scottish kind.

Despite no longer living in Lanark, the family connection is still a close one. Jim and Margaret are often present on rallies and were naturally the first to congratulate their son at the finish of the 1994 RAC in Chester on achieving what his father would so dearly have loved to do. The parents must experience split loyalties since younger brother Alister started appearing on world championship rallies, in a F2 Nissan Sunny GTi, winning the category in San Remo while still cutting his teeth on the British championship series.

To loosely borrow a Wildean sentiment, 'To have one son in rallying is unfortunate, to have two is sheer madness.'

The gauntlet for the future from the UK has been thrown down, but drivers from Finland's Tommi Mäkinen, the winner of the 1994 1000 Lakes Rally, to Germany's Armin Schwarz who first won a top-class rally in Spain in 1992, are already vying for world-championship honours.

It is as things have always been, the new waiting to replace the old, in sport as in life. Whether the future of world championship rallying consists of kit-cars, rules advocating four-wheel drive or those pressing for two-wheel drive, it now has 21 years to draw on and spit out any attempts to neuter it for good. Drivers, teams and cars have bustled into the sport to be captured by its spotlight only to vanish just as quickly into the darkness once again. BMC, Rootes, Ford, Peugeot, Lancia, have all come, left their mark and then gone again, but rallying continues. And if one day, the manufacturers did all decide to pack up and devote their millions elsewhere, it wouldn't be long before someone jumped into a car and decided to drive across country, as fast as they could, just for the sheer hell of it. Isn't that where we came in?

APPENDICES

1973 World Rally Championship Results

Monte Carlo Rally 19-26 January

1. Jean-Claude Andruet/'Biche'	F	Renault Alpine A110
2. Ove Andersson/Jean Todt	S/F	Renault Alpine A110
3. Jean-Pierre Nicolas/Michel Vial	F	Renault Alpine A110
4. Hannu Mikkola/Jim Porter	SF/GB	Ford Escort RS1600
5. Jean-Luc Therier/Marcel Callewaert	F	Renault Alpine A110

Swedish Rally 15-17 February

1. Stig Blomqvist/Arne Hertz	S	Saab 96 V4
2. Per Eklund/Rolf Carlsson	S	Saab 96 V4
3. Jean-Luc Therier/Marcel Callewaert	F	Renault Alpine A110
4. Harry Kallstrom/Claes Billstam	S	Lancia Fulvia
5. Hakan Lindberg/Solve Andreasson	S	Fiat Abarth 124

Rally of Portugal (TAP Rally) 13-18 March

1. Jean-Luc Therier/Jacques Jaubert	F	Renault Alpine A110
2. Jean-Pierre Nicolas/Michel Vial	F	Renault Alpine A110
3. Franscisco Romaozinho/Jose Bernardo	P	Citroen DS21
4. Luis Netto/Manuel Coentro	P	Fiat Abarth 124
5. Americo Nunes/Antonio Morais	P	Porsche 911

Safari Rally 19-23 April

1. Shekhar Mehta/Lofty Drews	EAK	Datsun 240Z
2. Harry Kallstrom/Claes Billstam	S	Datsun 1800SSS
3. Ove Andersson/Jean Todt	S/F	Peugeot 504
4. Tony Fall/Mike Wood	GB	Datsun 1800 SSS
5. Peter Huth/John McConnell	EAK	Peugeot 504

Moroccan Rally 8-13 May

1. Bernard Darniche/Alain Mahe	F	Renault Alpine A110
2. Robert Neyret/Jacques Terramorsi	F	Citroen DS23
3. Richard Bochnicek/Sepp-Dieter Kernmayer	A	Citroen DS23
4. Raymond Ponnelle/Pierre de Serpos	MA	Citroen DS23
5. Jean-Pierre Nicolas/Michel Vial	F	Renault Alpine A110

Acropolis Rally 23-27 May

1. Jean-Luc Therier/Christian Delferrier	F/B	Renault Alpine A110
2. Rauno Aaltonen/Robin Turvey	SF/GB	Fiat Abarth 124
3. Jean-Pierre Nicolas/Michel Vial	F	Renault Alpine A110
4. Hakan Lindberg/Arne Hertz	S	Fiat Abarth 124
5. Georg Fischer/Hans Siebert	A	VW1303S

Polish Rally 12-15 July

1. Achim Warmbold/Jean Todt	D/F	Fiat Abarth 124
2. Egon Culmbacher/Werner Ernst	DDR	Wartburg 353
3. Maciej Stawowiak/Jan Czyzyk	PL	Polski-Fiat 125p

Only 3 finishers.

Rally of 1000 Lakes 3-5 August

1. Timo Makinen/Henry Liddon	SF/GB	Ford Escort RS1600
2. Markku Alèn/Juhani Toivonen	SF	Volvo 142
3. Leo Kinnunen/Atso Aho	SF	Porsche 911
4. Simo Lampinen/John Davenport	SF/GB	Saab 96 V4
5. Antti Ojanen/Heikki Miikki	SF	Opel Ascona

Austrian Alpine Rally 12-15 September

1. Achim Warmbold/Jean Todt	D/F	BMW 2002 tii
2. Bernard Darniche/Alain Mahe	F	Renault Alpine A110
3. Per Eklund/Bo Reinicke	S	Saab 96 V4
4. Björn Waldegård/Hans Thorszelius	S	BMW 2002 tii
5. Jean-Pierre Nicolas/Michel Vial	F	Renault Alpine A110

Rallye San Remo 10-13 October

1. Jean-Luc Therier/Jacques Jaubert	F	Renault Alpine A110
2. Maurizio Verini/Angelo Torriani	I	Fiat Abarth 124
3. Jean-Pierre Nicolas/Michel Vial	F	Renault Alpine A110
4. Giulio Bisulli/Arturo Zanuccoli	I	Fiat abarth 124
5. Sergio Barbasio/Bruno Scabini	I	Fiat Abarth 124

Press-On Regardless 1-4 November

1. Walter Boyce/Doug Woods	CDN	Toyota Corolla
2. Jim Walker/Terry Palmer	USA	Volvo 142S
3. Jim Smiskol/Carol Smiskol	USA	Datsun 240z
4. John Buffum/Wayne Zitkus	USA	Ford Escort RS1600
5. John Rodgers/Erik Brooks	USA	Datsun 1600 SSS

RAC Rally 17-21 November

1. Timo Makinen/Henry Liddon	SF/GB	Ford Escort RS1600
2. Roger Clark/Tony Mason	GB	Ford Escort RS1600
3. Markku Alèn/IlkkaKivimaki	SF	Ford Escort 1600
4. Per-Inge Walfridsson/John Jensen	S/GB	Volvo 142
5. Jean-Pierre Nicolas/Claude Roure	F	Renault Alpine A110

Tour de Corse 1-2 December

1. Jean-Pierre Nicolas/Michel Vial	F	Renault Alpine A110
2. Jean-François Piot/Jean de Alexandris	F	Renault Alpine A110
3. Jean-Luc Therier/Marcel Callewaert	F	Renault Alpine A110
4. Guy Chausseuil/Christian Baron	F	Ford Escort RS1600
5. Francis Serpaggi/Felix Mariani	F	Renault Alpine

1974 World Rally Championship Results

Rally of Portugal (TAP) 20-23 March

1. Rafaelle Pinto/Arnaldo Bernacchini	I	Fiat Abarth 124
2. Acide Paganelli/Ninni Russo	I	Fiat Abarth 124
3. Markku Alèn/IlkkaKivimaki	SF	Fiat Abarth 124
4. Ove Andersson/Arne Hertz	S	Toyota Corolla
5. Harry Kallstrom/Claes Billstam	S	Datsun 260Z

Safari Rally 11-15 April

1. Joginder Singh/David Doig	EAK	Mitsubishi Colt Lancer
2. Björn Waldegard/Hans Thorszelius	S	Porsche 911
3. Sandro Munari/Lofty Drews	I/EAK	Lancia Fulvia
4. Harry Kallstrom/Claes Billstam	S	Datsun 260Z
5. Zully Remtulla/Nizar Jivani	EAT	Datsun 260Z

Rally of 1000 Lakes 2-4 August

1. Hannu Mikkola/John Davenport	SF/GB	Ford Escort RS1600
2. Timo Makinen/Henry Liddon	SF/GB	Ford Escort RS1600
3. Marku Alèn/IlkkaKivimaki	SF	Fiat Abarth 124
4. Stig Blomqvist/Hans Sylvan	S	Saab 96 V4
5. Simo Lampinen/Juhani Markkanen	SF	Saab 96 V4

Rallye San Remo 2-5 October

1. Sandro Munari/Mario Mannucci	I	Lancia Stratos
2. Giulio Bisulli/Francesco Rossetti	I	Fiat abarth 124
3. Alfredo Fagnola/Elvio Novarese	I	Opel Ascona
4. Shekhar Mehta/Martin Holmes	EAK/GB	Lancia Beta Coupé
5. 'Iccudrac'/Dino Defendenti	I	Porsche 911

Rideau Lakes Rally 16-20 October

1. Sandro Munari/Mario Mannucci	I	Lancia Stratos
2. Simo Lampinen/John Davenport	SF/GB	Lancia Beta Coupé
3. Walter Boyce/Stuart Gray	CDN/GB	Toyota Celica
4. Keith Billows/John Campbell	GB/USA	Ford Escort RS1600
5. Eric Jones/Mark Hathaway	USA	Datsun 510 SSS

Press-On Regardless 30 October-3 November

1. Jean-Luc Therier/Christian Delferrier	F	Renault 17 Gordini
2. Markku Alèn/Atso Aho	SF	Fiat Abarth 124
3. Jean-Pierre Nicolas/Geraint Philips	F/GB	Renault 17 Gordini
4. Simo Lampinen/John Davenport	SF/GB	Lancia Beta Coupé
5. Guy Chasseuil/Jean-Pierre Rouget	F	Renault Alpine A110

Lombard RAC Rally 16-20 November

1. Timo Makinen/Henry Liddon	SF/GB	Ford Escort RS1600
2. Stig Blomqvist/Hans Sylvan	S	Saab 96 V4
3. Sandro Munari/Piero Sodano	I	Lancia Stratos
4. Björn Waldegård/Hans Thorszelius	S	Toyota Corolla
5. Walter Röhrl/Jochen Berger	D	Opel Ascona

Tour de Corse 30 November-1 December

1. Jean-Claude Andruet/'Biche'	F	Lancia Stratos
2. Jean-Pierre Nicolas/Vincent Laverne	F	Renault Alpine A110
3. Jean-Luc Therier/Michel Vial	F	Renault Alpine A310
4. Jean-Pierre Manzagol/Jean-François Fillippi	F	Renault Alpine A110
5. Gerard Larousse/Christian Delferrier	F	Renault Alpine A110

1975 World Rally Championship Results

Monte Carlo Rally 15-24 January

1. Sandro Munari/Mario Mannucci	I	Lancia Stratos
2. Hannu Mikkola/Jean Todt	SF/F	Fiat Abarth 124
3. Markku Alèn/IlkkaKivimaki	F	Fiat Abarth 124
4. Fulvio Bacchelli/Bruno Scabini	I	Fiat Abarth 124
5. Jean-François Piot/Jean de Alexandris	F	Renault 17 Gordini

Swedish Rally 13-15 February

1. Björn Walegard/Hans Thorszelius	S	Lancia Stratos
2. Stig Blomqvist/Hans Sylvan	S	Saab 96 V4
3. Simo Lampinen/Solve Andersson	SF/S	Lancia Beta Coupé
4. Per Eklund/Björn Cederberg	S	Saab 96 V4
5. Ingvar Carlsson/Claes Billstam	S	Fiat Abarth 124

Safari Rally 27-31 March

1. Ove Andersson/Arne Hertz	S	Peugeot 504
2. Sandro Munari/Lofty Drews	I/EAK	Lancia Stratos
3. Björn Waldegård/Hans Thorszelius	S	Lancia Stratos
4. Andrew Cowan/ John Mitchell	GB	Mitsubishi Colt Lancer
5. Bert Shankland/Chris Bates	EAT/K	Peugeot 504

Acropolis Rally 24-31 May

1. Walter Röhrl/Jochen Berger	D	Opel Ascona
2. 'Siroco'/Miltos Andriopoulos	GR	Renault Alpine A110
3. Michael Koumas/Peter Dimitriadis	CY	Mitsubishi Galant
4. J. Pesmazoglou/Dimitris Georgitsis	GR	Opel Ascona
5. 'Leonidas'/John Lekkas	GR	Audi 80GT

Moroccan Rally 24-28 June

1. Hannu Mikkola/Jean Todt	SF/F	Peugeot 504
2. Bernard Consten/Gerard Flocon	F	Peugeot 504
3. Robert Neyret/Jacques Terramorsi	F	Renault Alpine A110
4. Jean Deschaseaux/Jean Plassard	MA	Citroen DS23
5. Timo Makinen/Henry Liddon	SF/GB	Peugeot 504

Vinho do Porto Rallye de Portugal 18-21 July

1. Markku Alèn/IlkkaKivimaki	SF	Fiat Abarth 124
2. Hannu Mikkola/Jean Todt	SF/F	Fiat Abarth 124
3. Ove Andersson/Arne Hertz	S	Toyota Corolla
4. Rauno Aaltonen/Claes Billstam	SF/S	Opel Ascona
5. Pedro Cortes/Teixeira Gomes	P	Datsun 260Z

Rally of 1000 Lakes 29-31 August

1. Hannu Mikkola/Atso Aho	SF	Toyota Corolla
2. Simo Lampinen/Juhani Markkanen	SF	Saab 96 V4
3. Timo Makinen/Henry Liddon	SF/GB	Ford Escort RS 1.8
4. Per Eklund/Björn Cederberg	S	Saab 96 V4
5. Anders Kullang/Claes-Goran Andersson	S	Opel Ascona

Rallye San Remo 1-4 October

1. Björn Waldegård/ Hans Thorszelius	S	Lancia Stratos
2. Maurizio Verini/Francesco Rossetti	I	Fiat Abarth 124
3. Jean-Luc Therier/Michel Vial	F	Renault Alpine A110
4. Mauro Pregliasco/Piero Sodano	I	Lancia Beta Coupé
5. Carlo Bianchi/Maro Mannini	I	Porsche 911

Tour de Corse 8-9 November

1. Bernard Darniche/Alain Mahe	F	Lancia Startos
2. Jean-Pierre Nicolas/Vincent Laverne	F	Renault Alpine A110
3. Jean-Claude Andruet/Yves Jouanny	F	Alfa Romeo Alfetta GT
4. Jean-Pierre Manzagol/Jean François Filippi	F	Renault Alpine A110
5. Jacques Henry/Maurice Gelin	F	Renault Alpine A110

Lombard RAC Rally 22-26 November

1. Timo Makinen/Henry Liddon	SF/GB	Ford Escort RS 1.8
2. Roger Clark/Tony Mason	GB	Ford Escort RS 1.8
3. Tony Fowkes/Bryan Harris	GB	Ford Escort RS 1.6
4. Tony Pond/David Richards	GB	Opel Kadett GTE
5. Erik Aaby/Per-Odvar Nyborg	N	Ford Escort RS 1.6

1976 World Rally Championship Results

Monte Carlo Rally 17-24 January

1. Sandro Munari/Silvio Maiga	I	Lancia Startos
2. Björn Waldegård/Hans Thorszelius	S	Lancia Stratos
3. Bernard Darniche/Alain Mahe	F	Lancia Stratos
4. Walter rohrl/Jochen Berger	D	Opel Kadett GTE
5. Roger Clark/Jim Porter	GB	Ford Escort RS 1.8

Swedish Rally 20-22 February

1. Per Eklund/Björn Cederberg	S	Saab 96 V4
2. Stig Blomqvist/Hans Sylvan	S	Saab 96V4
3. Anders Kullang/Claes-Goran Andersson	S	Opel Ascona
4. Simo Lampinen/Arne Hertz	SF/S	Lancia Stratos
5. Ulf Sundberg/Mats Nordstrom	S	Saab 99 EMS

Vinho do Porto Rallye de Portugal 10-14 March

1. Sandro Munari/Silvio Maiga	I	Lancia Stratos
2. Ove Andersson/Arne Hertz	S	Toyota Celica
3. 'Meqepe'/Joao Baptista	P	Opel Kadett GTE
4. Rafaelle Pinto/Arnaldo Bernacchini	I	Lancia Stratos
5. Santinho Mendes/Lemos Nobre	P	Opel Kadett GTE

Safari Rally 15-19 April

1. Joginder Singh/David Doig	EAK	Mitsubishi Lancer
2. Robin Ulyate/Chris Bates	EAK	Mitsubishi Lancer
3. Andrew Cowan/Johnstone Syer	GB	Mitsubishi Lancer
4. Bert Shankland/Brian Barton	EAT	Peugeot 504
5. Simo Lampinen/Arne Hertz	SF/S	Peugeot 504

Acropolis Rally 22-28 May

1. Harry Kallstrom/Claes-Goran Andersson	S	Datsun Violet
2. 'Siroco'/Miltos Andriopoulos	GR	Renault Alpine A110
3. Shekhar Mehta/Henry Liddon	EAK/GB	Datsun Violet
4. George Moschous/Dimitri Arvanitakis	GR	Alfa Romeo Alfetta GT
5. Klaus Russling/Manfred Essig	A	Opel Ascona

Moroccan Rally 22-27 June

1. Jean-Pierre Nicolas/Michel Gamet	F	Peugeot 504
2. Simo Lampinen/Atso Aho	SF	Peugeot 504
3. Sandro Munari/Silvio Maiga	I	Lancia Stratos
4. Jean Deschaseaux/Jean Plassard	F	Citroen CX2200
5. Jean-Claude Lefebvre/Gerard Flocon	F	Peugeot 504

1977 World Rally Championship Results

Monte Carlo Rally 22-28 January

1. Sandro Munari/Silvio Maiga	I	Lancia Stratos
2. Jean-Claude Andruet/'Biche'	F	Fiat Abarth 131
3. Antonio Zanini/Juan Petisco	E	SEAT 124 Especial
4. Salvador Canellas/Daniel Ferrater	E	SEAT 124 Especial
5. Gerard Swaton/Bernard Cordesse	F	Porsche 911

Swedish Rally 11-13 February

1. Stig Blomqvist/Hans Sylvan	S	Saab 99EMS
2. Bror Danielsson/Ulf Sundberg	S	Opel Kadett GTE
3. Anders Kullang/Bruno Berglumd	S	Opel Kadett GTE
4. Simo Lampinen/Solve Andreasson	SF/S	Fiat Abarth 131
5. Kyosti Hamalainen/Juhani Korhonen	SF	Ford Escort RS 2000

Vinho do Porto Rallye de Portugal 1-6 March

1. Markku Alèn/IlkkaKivimaki	SF	Fiat Abarth 131
2. Björn Waldegård/Hans Thorszelius	S	Ford Escort RS
3. Ove Andersson/Henry Liddon	S/GB	Toyota Celica
4. Jean-Claude Andruet/Christian Delferrier	F/B	Fiat Abarth 131
5. Maurizio Verini/Ninni Russo	I	Fiat Abarth 131

Safari Rally 7-11 April

1. Björn Waldergard/Hans Thorszelius	S	Ford Escort RS1800
2. Rauno Aaltonen/Lofty Drews	SF/EAK	Datsun Violet
3. Sandro Munari/Piero Sodano	I	Lancia Stratos
4. Andrew Cowan/Paul White	GB	Mitsubishi Colt Lancer
5. Joginder Singh/David Doig	EAK	Mitsubishi Colt Lancer

South Pacific Rally 1-7 May

1. Fulvio Bacchelli/Fransesco Rossetti	I	Fiat Abarth 131
2. Ari Vatanen/Jim Scott	SF/NZ	Ford Escort RS1800
3. Markku Alèn/IlkkaKivimaki	SF	Fiat Abarth 131
4. Simo Lampinen/Solve Andreasson	SF/S	Fiat Abarth 131
5. Rod Millen/Mike Franchi	NZ	Mazda RX3

Acropolis Rally 28 May-3 June

1. Björn Waldegård/Hans Thorszelius	S	Ford Escort RS1800
2. Roger Clark/Jim Porter	GB	Ford Escort 1800
3. Harry Kallstrom/Claes Billstam	S	Datsun Violet
4. Simo Lampinen/Solve Andreasson	SF/S	Fiat Abarth 131
5. 'Siroco'/Manolis Makrinos	GR	Datsun Violet

Rally of 1000 Lakes 26-28 August

1. Kyosti Hamalainen/Martti Tiukkanen	SF	Ford Escort RS1800
2. Timo Salonen/Jaakko Markkula	SF	Fiat Abarth 131
3. Björn Waldegård/Claes Billstam	S	Ford Escort RS1800
4. Markku Saaristo/Timo Alanen	SF	Toyota Corolla
5. Henri Toivonen/Antero Lindqvist	SF	Chrysler Avenger

Criterium Molson de Quebec Rally 14-18 September

1. Timo Salonen/Jaakko Markkula	SF	Fiat Abarth 131
2. Simo Lampinen/Solve Andreasson	SF/S	Fiat Abarth 131
3. Roger Clark/Jim Porter	GB	Ford Escort RS
4. John Buffum/'Vicki'	USA	Triumph TR7
5. Jean-Paul Perusse/John Bellefleur	CDN	Saab 99 EMS

Rallye San Remo 4-8 October

1. Jean-Claude Andruet/Christian Delferrier	F/B	Fiat Abarth 131
2. Maurizio Verini/Bruno Scabini	I	Fiat Abarth 131
3. 'Tony'/Mauro Mannini	I	Fiat Abarth 131
4. Mauro Pregliasco/Vittorio Reisoli	I	Lancia Stratos
5. Björn Waldegård/Hans Thorszelius	S	Ford Escort RS1800

Tour de Corse 5-6 November

1. Bernard Darniche/Alain Mahe	F	Fiat Abarth 131
2. Rafaelle Pinto/Arnaldo Bernacchini	I	Lancia Stratos
3. Fulvio Bacchelli/Bruno Scabini	I	Fiat Abarth 131
4. Tony Carello/Maurizio Perissinot	I	Lancia Stratos
5. Francis Vincent/Francis Calvier	F	Fiat Abarth 131

Lombard RAC Rally 20-24 November

1. Björn Waldegård/Hans Thorszelius	S	Ford Escort RS1800
2. Hannu Mikkola/Arne Hertz	SF/S	Toyota Celica
3. Russell Brookes/John Brown	GB	Ford Escort RS1800
4. Roger Clark/Stuart Pegg	GB	Ford Escort RS1800
5. Andy Dawson/Andrew Marriott	GB	Ford Escort RS1800

1978 World Rally Championship Results

Monte Carlo Rally 21-28 January

1. Jean-Pierre Nicolas/Vincent Laverne	F	Porsche 911
2. Jean Ragnotti/Jean-Marc Andrie	F	Renault 5 Alpine
3. Guy Frequelin/Jacques Delaval	F	Renault 5 Alpine
4. Walter Röhrl/Christian Geistdorfer	D	Fiat Abarth 131
5. Bernard darniche/Alain Mahe	F	Fiat Abarth 131

Swedish Rally 10-12 February

1. Björn Waldegård/Hans Thorszelius	S	Ford Escort RS
2. Hannu Mikkola/Arne Hertz	SF/S	Ford Escort RS
3. Markku Alèn/IlkkaKivimaki	SF	Fiat Abarth 131
4. Stig Blomqvist/Hans Sylvan	S	Lancia Stratos
5. Ari Vatanen/Atso Aho	SF	Ford Escort RS

Safari Rally 23-27 March

1. Jean-Pierre Nicolas/Jean-Claude Lefebvre	F	Peugeot 504 V6 Coupé
2. Vic Preston/John Lyall	EAK	Porsche 911
3. Rauno Aaltonen/Lofty Drews	SF/EAK	Datsun 160 J
4. Björn Waldegård/Hans Thorszelius	S	Porsche 911
5. Simo Lampinen/Henry Liddon	SF/GB	Peugeot 504 V6 Coupé

Vinho do Porto Rallye de Portugal 19-23 April

1. Markku Alèn/IlkkaKivimaki	SF	Fiat Abarth 131
2. Hannu Mikkola/Arne Hertz	SF/S	Ford Escort RS
3. Jean-Pierre Nicolas/Vincent laverne	F	Ford Escort RS
4. Ove Andersson/Henry Liddon	S/GB	Toyota Celica
5. Achim Warmbold/Claes Billstam	D/S	Opel Kadett GTE

Acropolis Rally29 May-2 June

1. Walter Röhrl/Christian Geistdorfer	D	Fiat Abarth 131
2. Markku Alèn/IlkkaKivimaki	SF	Fiat Abarth 131
3. Shekhar Mehta/Yvonne Mehta	EAK	Datsun 160J
4. Harry Kallstrom/Claes Billstam	S	Datsun 160J
5. Achim Warmbold/Hans Sylvan	D/S	Opel Kadett GTE

Rally of 1000 Lakes 25-27 August

1. Markku Alèn/IlkkaKivimaki	SF	Fiat Abarth 131
2. Timo Salonen/Erkki Nyman	SF	Fiat Abarth 131
3. Pentti Airikkala/Risto Vitanen	SF	Vauxhall Chevette 2300HS
4. Per Eklund/Björn cederberg	S	Porsche 911
5. Simo Lampinen/Juhani markkanen	SF	Fiat Abarth 131

Criterium Molson du Quebec Rally 13-17 September

1 Walter Röhrl/Christian Geistdorfer	D	Fiat abarth 131
2. Markku Alèn/IlkkaKivimaki	SF	Fiat Abarth
3. Anders Kullang/Bruno Berglund	S	Opel Kadett GTE
4. Taisto Heinonen/John Bellefleur	CDN	Toyota Celica
5. Jean-Paul Perusse/Louis Belanger	CDN	Triumph TR7

Rallye San Remo 3-7 October

1. Markku Alèn/IlkkaKivimaki	SF	Lancia Startos
2. Maurizio Verini/Arnaldo Bernacchini	I	Fiat Abarth
3. Francis Vincent/Willy Lux	F/B	Porsche 911
4. 'Bip-Bip'/Mirko Perissutti	I	Porsche 911
5. Mauro Pregliasco/Vittorio Reisoli	I	Alfa Romeo Alfetta GT

Rally Bandama Cote d'Ivoire 21-24 October

1. Jean-Pierre Nicolas/Michel Gamet	F	Peugeot 504 V6
2. Timo Makinen/Jean Todt	SF/F	Peugeot 504 V6 Coupé
3. Jean Ragnotti/Jean-Marc Andrie	F	Renault 5 Alpine
4. Simo Lampinen/Atso Aho	SF	Peugeot 504 V6 Coupé
5. Guy Frequelin/Jacques Delaval	F	Renault 5 Alpine

Tour de Corse 4-5 November

1. Bernard Darniche/Alain Mahe	F	Fiat Abarth 131
2. Jean-Claude Andruet/'Biche'	F	Fiat Abarth 131
3. Sandro Munari/Mario Mannucci	I	Fiat Abarth 131
4. Jacques Almeras/Jean-Claude Perramond	F	Porsche 911
5. Michele Mouton/François Conconi	F	Fiat Abarth 131

Lombard RAC Rally 19-23 November

1. Hannu Mikkola/Arne Hertz	SF/S	Ford Escort RS
2. Björn Waldegård/Hans Thorszelius	S	Ford Escort RS
3. Russell Brookes/Derek Tucker	GB	Ford Escort Rs
4. Tony Pond/Fred Gallagher	GB	Triumph TR7 V8
5. Anders Kullang/Bruno Berglund	S	Opel Kadett GTE

1979 World Rally Championship Results

Rallye Monte Carlo 20-26 January

1. Bernard Darniche/Alain Mahe	F	Lancia Stratos
2. Björn Waldegård/Hans Thorszelius	S	Ford Escort RS
3. Markku Alèn/IlkkaKivimaki	SF	Fiat Abarth 131
4. Jean-Claude Andruet/Chantal Lienard	F	Fiat Abarth 131
5. Hannu Mikkola/Arne Hertz	SF/S	Ford Escort RS

Swedish Rally 16-18 February

1. Stig Blomqvist/Björn Cederberg	S	Saab 99 Turbo
2. Björn Waldegård/Hans Thorszelius	S	Ford Escort RS
3. Pentti Airikkala/Risto Virtanen	SF	Vauxhall Chevette 2300HS
4. Markku Alèn/IlkkaKivimaki	SF	Fiat Abarth 131
5. Hannu Mikkola/Arne Hertz	SF/S	Ford Escort RS

Vinho do Porto Rallye de Portugal 6-11 March

1. Hannu Mikkola/Arne Hertz	SF/S	Ford Escort RS
2. Björn Waldegård/Hans Thorszelius	S	Ford Escort RS
3. Ove Andersson/Henry Liddon	S/GB	Toyota Celica
4. Andy Dawson/Martin Holmes	GB	Datsun 160j
5. Carlos Torres/Pedro de Almeida	P	Ford Escort RS

Safari Rally 12-16 April

1. Shekhar Mehta/Mike Doughty	EAK	Datsun 160J
2. Hannu Mikkola/Arne Hertz	SF/S	Mercedes-Benz 450SL
3. Markku Alèn/IlkkaKivimaki	SF	Fiat Abarth 131
4. Andrew Cowan/Johnstone Syer	GB	Mercedes-Benz 280E
5. Rauno Aaltonen/Lofty Drews	SF/EAK	Datsun 160J

Acropolis Rally 28-31 May

1. Björn Waldegård/Hans Thorszelius	S	Ford Escort RS
2. Timo Salonen/Sepo Harjanne	SF	Datsun 160J
3. Harry Kallstrom/Claes Billstam	S	Datsun 160J
4. Jean Ragnotti/Jean-Marc Andrie	F	Renault 5 Alpine
5. 'Iaveris'/Costas Stefanis	GR	Ford Escort Rs

Motogard Rally Of New Zealand 14-18 July

1=. HAnnu Mikkola/Arne Hertz	SF/S	Ford Escort RS
1=. Timo Salonen/Seppo Harjanne	SF	Datsun 160J
3. Blair Robson/Chris Porter	NZ	Ford Escort RS
4. Ari Vatanen/David Richards	SF/GB	Ford Escort RS
5. Paul Adams/Mike Franchi	NZ	Ford Escort Rs
5= Andy Dawson/Kevin Gormley	GB	Datsun 160J

Jyvaskylan Suurajot Rally of 1000 Lakes 24-28 August

1. Markku Alèn/IlkkaKivimaki	SF	Fiat Abarth 131
2. Ari Vatanen/David Richards	SF/GB	Ford Escort RS
3. Björn Waldegård/Claes Billstam	S	Ford Escort RS
4. Ulf Gronholm/Bob Rehnstrom	SF	Fiat Abarth 131
5. Timo Salonen/Seppo Harjanne	SF	Datsun 160J

Criterium Molson Du Quebec 13-16 September

1. Björn Waldegård/Hans Thorszelius	S	Ford Escort RS
2. Timo Salonen/Seppo Harjanne	SF	Datsun 160J
3. Ari Vatanen/David Richards	SF./GB	Ford Escort RS
4. Andy Dawson/Kevin Gormley	GB	Datsun 160J
5. Taisto Heinonen/Erkki Nyman	SF	Toyota Celica

Rallye San Remo 1-7 October

1. 'Tony'/Mauro Mannini	I	Lancia Startos
2. Walter Röhrl/Christian Geistdorfer	D	Fiat Abarth 131
3. Attilio Bettega/Maurizio Perissinot	I	Fiat Abarth 131
4. Tony Pond/Ian Grindrod	GB	Talbot Sunbeam

Tour de Corse 2-4 November

1. Bernard Darniche/Alain Mahe	F	Lancia Stratos
2. Jean Ragnotti/Jean-Marc Andrie	F	Renault 5 Alpine
3. Pierre-Louis Moreau/Patrice Baron	F	Porsche 911
4. Alain Coppier/Josepha laloz	F	Porsche 911
5. Michele Mouton/Françoise Conconi	F	Fiat Abarth 131

Lombard RAC Rally 18-21 November

1. Hannu Mikkola/Arne Hertz	SF	Ford Escort RS
2. Russell Brookes/Paul White	GB	Ford Escort RS
3. Timo Salonen/Stuart Pegg	SF/GB	Datsun 160J
4. Ari Vatanen/David Richards	SF/GB	Ford Escort RS
5. Markku Alèn/IlkkaKivimaki	SF	Lancia Stratos

Bandama Rally 9-14 December

1. Hannu Mikkola/Arne Hertz	SF/S	Mercedes-Benz 450 SLC
2. Björn Waldegård/Hans Thorszelius	S	Mercedes-Benz 450 SLC
3. Andrew Cowan/Klaus Kaiser	GB/D	Mercedes-Benz 450 SLC
4. Vic Preston Jnr/Mike Doughty	EAK	Mercedes-Benz 450 SLC
5. Ove Andersson/Henry Liddon	S/GB	Toyota Celica (Liftback)

1980 World Rally Championship Results

Rallye Monte Carlo 19-25 January

1. Walter Röhrl/Christian Geistdorfer	D	Fiat Abarth 131
2. Bernard Darniche/Alain Mahe	F	Lancia Stratos
3. Björn Waldegård/Hans Thorszelius	S	Fiat Abarth 131
4. Anders Kullang/Bruno Berglund	S	Opel Ascona
5. Per Eklund/Hans Sylvan	S	VW Golf Gti

International Swedish Rally 15-17 February

1. Anders Kullang/Bruno Berglund	S	Opel Ascona
2. Stig Blomqvist/Björn Cederberg	S	Saab 99 Turbo
3. Björn Waldegård/Hans Thorszelius	S	Fiat Abarth 131
4. Hannu Mikkola/Arne Hertz	SF/S	Ford Escort RS
5. Björn Johansson/Ragnar Spjuth	S	Opel Kadett G/E

Vinho do Porto Rallye de Portugal 4-9 March

1. Walter Röhrl/Cristian Geistdorfer	D	Fiat Abarth 131
2. Markku Alèn/IlkkaKivimaki	SF	Fiat Abarth 131
3. Guy Frequelin/Jean Todt	F	Talbot Sunbeam Lotus
4. Björn Waldegård/Hans Thorszelius	S	Mercedes-Benz 450 SLC 5.0
5. Ingvar Carlsson/Claes Billstam	S	Mercedes-Benz 450 SLC 5.0

Marlboro Safari Rally 3-7 April

1. Shekhar Mehta/Mike Doughty	EAK	Datsun 160J
2. Rauno Aaltonen/Lofty Drews	SF/EAK	Datsun 160J
3. Vic Preston Jnr/John Lyall	EAK	Mercedes-Benz 450 SLC
4. Mike Kirkland/David Haworth	EAK	Datsun 160J
5. Jean-Pierre Nicolas/Henry Liddon	EAK	Datsun 160J

Acropolis Rally 26-29 May

1. Ari Vatanen/David Richards	SF/GB	Ford Escort RS
2. Timo Salonen/Seppo Harjanne	SF	Datsun 160J
3. Markku Alèn/IlkkaKivimaki	SF	Fiat Abarth 131
4. Anders Kullang/Bruno Berglund	S	Opel Ascona 400
5. Walter Röhrl/Christian Geistdorfer	D	Fiat Abarth 131

Rally of Argentina 19-24 July

1. Walter Röhrl/Christian Geistdorfer	D	Fiat Abarth 131
2. Hannu Mikkola/Arne Hertz	SF/S	Mercedes-Benz 500
3. Carlos Reutemann/Mirko Perissutti	RA/I	Fiat Abarth 131
4. Shekhar Mehta/Yvone Mehta	EAK	Datsun 160J
5. Jean-Claude Lefebvre/Christian Delferrier	F/B	Peugeot 504 V6 Coupé

Rally of 1000 Lakes 29-31 August

1. Markku Alèn/IlkkaKivimaki	SF	Fiat Abarth 131
2. Ari Vatanen/David Richards	SF/GB	Ford Escort RS
3. Per Eklund/Hans Sylvan	S	Triumph TR7V8
4. Björn Johansson/Ragnar Spjuth	S	Opel Ascona 400
5. Lasse Lampi/Pentti Kuukkala	SF	Ford Escort RS

Motorgard Rally of New Zealand 13-17 September

1. Timo Salonen/Seppo Harjanne	SF	Datsun 160J
2. Walter Röhrl/Christian Geistdorfer	D	Fiat Abarth 131
3. Hannu Mikkola/Arne Hertz	SF/S	Mercedes Benz 500 SLC
4. George Fury/Monty Suffern	AUS	Datsun 160J
5. Björn Waldegård/Hans Thorszelius	S	Mercedes-Benz 500SLC

Rallye San Remo 6-11 October

1. Walter Röhrl/Christian Geistdorfer	D	Fiat Abarth 131
2. Ari Vatanen/David Richards	SF/GB	Ford Escort RS
3. Hannu Mikkola/Arne Hertz	SF/S	Ford Escort RS
4. Guy Frequelin/Jean Todt	F	Talbot Sunbeam Lotus
5. Henri Toivonen/Antero Lindqvist	SF	Talbot Sunbeam Lotus

Tour de Corse 24-25 October

1. Jean-Luc Therier/Michel Vial	F	Porsche 911
2. Walter Röhrl/Christian Geistdorfer	D	Fiat Abarth 911
3. Alain Coppier/Josepha Laloz	F	Porsche 911
4. Bruno Saby/'Tilber'	F	Renault 5 Turbo
5. Michele Mouton/Annie Arrii	F	Fiat Abarth 131

Lombard RAC Rally 16-19 November

1. Henri Toivonen/Paul White	SF/GB	Talbot Sunbeam Lotus
2. Hannu Mikkola/Arne Hertz	S/SF	Ford Escort RS
3. Guy Frequelin/Jean Todt	F	Talbot Sunbeam Lotus
4. Russell Brookes/Peter Bryant	GB	Talbot Sunbeam Lotus
5. Anders Kullang Bruno Berglund	S	Opel Ascona 400

Rallye Cote d'Ivoire (Bandama) 9-14 December

1. Björn Waldegård/Hans Thorszelius	S	Mercedes-Benz 500 SLC
2. Jorge Recalde/Nestor Straimel	RA	Mercedes-Benz 500 SLC
3. Alain Ambrosino/Jean-Robert Bureau	F	Peugeot 504 Coupé V6
4. Samir Assef/Gilbert Fourcade	RL/F	Toyota Celica
5. Vic Preston Jnr/Claes Billstam	EAK/S	Mercedes-Benz 500

1981 World Rally Championship Results

Monte Carlo Rally 24-30 January

1. Jean Ragnotti/Jean-Marc Andrie	F	Renault 5 Turbo
2. Guy Frequelin/Jean Todt	F	Talbot Sunbeam Lotus
3. Jochi Kleint/Gunter Wanger	D	Opel Ascona 400
4. Anders Kullang/Bruno Berglund	S	Opel Ascona 400
5. Henri Toivonen/Fred Gallagher	SF/GB	Talbot Sunbeam Lotus

Swedish Rally 13-15 February

1. Hannu Mikkola/Arne Hertz	SF/S	Audi Quattro
2. Ari Vatanen/David Richards	SF/GB	Ford Escort Rs
3. Pentti Airikala/Risto Virtanen	SF	Ford Escort RS
4. Anders Kullang/Bruno Berglund	S	Opel Ascona 400
5. Stig Blomqvist/Björn Cederberg	S	Saab 99 Turbo

Vinho do Porto Rallye de Portugal 4-7 March

1. Markku Alèn/IlkkaKivimaki	SF	FiatAbarth 131
2. Henri Toivonen/Fred Gallagher	SF/GB	Talbot Sunbeam Lotus
3. Björn Waldegård/Hans Thorszelis	S	Toyota Celica
4. Michele Mouton/Fabrizia Pons	F/I	Audi Quattro
5. Tony Pond/Ian Grindrod	GB	Datsun 160J

Marlboro Safari Rally 16-20 April

1. Shekhar Mehta/Mike Doughty	EAK	Datsun Violet GT
2. Rauno Aaltonen/Lofty Drews	SF/EAK	Datsun Violet Gt
3. Mike Kirkland/Dave Haworth	EAK	Datsun 160J
4. Timo Salonen/Seppo Harjanne	SF	Datsun Silvia
5. Jochi Kleint/Gunter Wanger	D	Opel Ascona 400

Tour de Corse 30 April-2 May

1. Bernard Darniche/Alain Mahe	F	Lancia Stratos
2. Guy Frequelin/Jean Todt	F	Talbot Sunbeam Lotus
3. Tony Pond/Ian Grindrod	GB	Datsun Sunbeam 80
4. Jean-Pierre Ballet/Jacky Guinchard	F	Porsche 911SC
5. Terry Kaby/Rob Arthur	GB	Datsun 160J

Acropolis Rally 1-4 June

1. Ari Vatanen/David Richards	SF/GB	Ford Escort RS
2. Markku Alèn/IlkkaKivimaki	SF	Fiat Abarth 131
3. Attilio Bettega/Maurizio Perissinot	I	Fiat Abarth 131
4. Guy Frequelin/Jean Todt	F	Talbot Sunbeam lotus
5. Shekhar Mehta/Yvonne Mehta	EAK	Datsun 160J

Rally Codasur (Argentina) 18-23 July

1. Guy Frequelin/Jean Todt	F	Talbot Sunbeam Lotus
2. Shekhar Mehta/Yvonne Mehta	EAK	Datsun Violet GT
3. Jorge Recalde/Jorge del Buono	RA	Datsun 160J
4. Ernesto Soto/Carlos Silva	RA	Renault 12 TS
5. Ricardo Albertengo/Ricardo Alberto	RA	Peugeot 504

Marlboro Rallye do Brazil 6-8 August

1. Ari Vatanen/David Richards	SF/GB	Ford Escort Rs
2. Guy Frequelin/Jean Todt	F	Talbot Sunbeam Lotus
3. Domingo de Vitta/Danial Muzio	U	Ford Escort RS
4. Jorge Recalde/Jorge del Buono	RA	Datsun 160J
5. Carlos Torres/Antonio Morais	P	Ford Escort RS

Rally of 1000 Lakes 28-30 August

1. Ari vatanen/David Richards	SF/GB	Ford Escort Rs
2. Markku Alèn/IlkkaKivimaki	SF	Fiat Abarth 131
3. Hannu Mikkola/Arne Hertz	Sf/S	Audi Quattro
4. Timo Salonen/Seppo Harjanne	SF	Datsun Violet Gt
5. Pentti Airikkala/Risto Virtanen	SF	Ford Escort RS

Rallye San Remo 5-10 October

1. Michele Mouton./Fabrizio Pons	F/I	Audi Quattro
2. Henri Toivonen/Fred Gallagher	SF/GB	Talbot Sunbeam Lotus
3. 'Tony' Fassina/'Rudy'	I	Opel Ascona 400
4. Hannu Mikkola/Arne Hertz	SF/S	Audi Quattro
5. 'Lucky'/Fabio Penariol	I	Opel Ascona 400

Rallye Cote d'Ivoire 26-31 October

1. Timo Salonen/Seppo Harjanne	SF	Datsun Violet GT
2. Per Eklund/Ragnar Spjuth	S	Toyota Celica
3. Shekhar Mehta/Mike Doughty	EAK	Datsun Violet GT
4. Michel Mitri/Marcel Copetti	CI	Datsun 160J
5. Guy Frequelin/Jean Todt	F	Peugeot 504 Coupé V6

Lombard RAC Rally 22-25 November

1. Hannu Mikkola/Arne Hertz	SF/S	Audi Quattro
2. Ari Vatanen/David Richards	SF/GB	Ford Escort Rs
3. Stig Blomqvist/Björn Cederberg	S	Talbot Sunbeam Lotus
4. Pentti Airikkala/Phil Short	SF/GB	Ford Escort RS
5. Jean Ragnotti/Martin Holmes	F/GB	Renault 5 Turbo

1982 World Rally Championship Results

Monte Carlo Rally 16-22 January

1.	Walter Röhrl/Christian Geistdorfer	D	Opel Ascona 400
2.	Hannu Mikkola/Arne Hertz	SF/S	Audi Quattro
3.	Jean-Luc Therier/Michel Vial	F	Porsche 911SC
4.	Guy Frequelin/Jean-François Fauchille	F	Porsche 911 Sc
5.	Bruno Saby/Françoise Sappey	F	Renault 5 Turbo

Swedish Rally 12-14 February

1.	Stig Blomqvist/Björn Cederberg	S	Audi Quattro
2.	Ari Vatanen/Terry Harryman	SF/GB	Ford Escort Rs
3.	Walter Röhrl/Christian Geistdorfer	D	Opel Ascona 400
4.	Per Eklund/Ragnar Spjuth	S	Saab 99 Turbo
5.	Michele Mouton/Fabrizia Pons	F/I	Audi Quattro

Vinho do Porto Rallye de Portugal 3-6 March

1.	Michele Mouton/Fabrizia Pons	F/I	Audi Quattro
2.	Per Eklund/Ragnar Spjuth	S	Toyota Celica
3.	Franz Wittman/Peter Diekman	D	Audi Quattro
4.	Carlos Torres/Filipe Lopes	P	Ford Escort RS
5.	Alain Coppier/Josepha Laloz	F	Citroen Visa Trophee

Marlboro Safara Rally 8-12 April

1.	Shekhar Mehta/Mike Doughty	EAK	Nissan Violet GT
2.	Walter Röhrl/Christian Geistdorfer	D	Opel Ascona 400
3.	Mike Kirkland/Anton Levitan	EAK	Nissan Violet GTS
4.	Tony Pond/Terry Harryman	GB	Nissan Violet GTS
5.	Jayant Shah/Aslam Khan	EAK	Nissan 160J

Tour de Corse 6-8 May

1.	Jean Ragnotti/Jean-Marc Andrie	F	Renault 5 Turbo
2.	Jean-Claude Andruet/'Biche'	F	Ferrari 308GTB
3.	Bernard Beguin/Jean-Jacques Lenne	F	Porsche 911SC
4.	Walter Röhrl/Christian Geistdorfer	D	Opel Ascona 400
5.	Bruno Saby/Françoise Sappey	F	Renault 5 Turbo

Acropolis Rally 31 May-3 June

1.	Michele Mouton/Fabrizia Pons	F/I	Audi Quattro
2.	Walter Röhrl/Christian Geistdorfer	D	Opel Ascona 400
3.	Henri Toivonen/Fred Gallagher	SF/GB	Opel Ascona 400
4.	Shekhar Mehta/Yvonne Mehta	EAK	Nissan Violet GT
5.	George Moschous/Alexis Constantakatos	GR	Nissan Violet GTS

Motogard Rally of New Zealand 26-29 June

1.	Björn Waldegård/Hans Thorszelius	S	Toyota Celica
2.	Per Eklund/Ragnar Spjuth	S	Toyota Celica
3.	Walter Röhrl/Christian Geistdorfer	D	Opel Ascona 400
4.	Timo Salonen/Seppo Harjanne	SF	Nissan Violet GTS
5.	Rod Millen/John Bellefleur	NZ/CDN	Mazda RX7

Marlboro Rallye do Brasil 11-14 August

1.	Michele Mouton/Fabrizia Pons	F/I	Audi Quattro
2.	Walter Röhrl/Christian Geistdorfer	D	Opel Ascona 400
3.	Domingo De Vitta/Daniel Muzio	U	Ford Escort RS 1-cam
4.	Aparecido Rodriguez/Jose Joaquim Mattos	BR	VW Passat 1600

Rally of 1000 Lakes 27-29 August

1.	Hannu Mikkola/Arne Hertz	SF/S	Audi Quattro
2.	Stig Blomqvist/Björn Cederberg	S	Audi Quattro
3.	Pentti Airikkala/Juha Piironen	SF	Mitsubishi Lancer Turbo
4.	Timo Salonen/Seppo Harjanne	SF	Nissan Silvia Turbo
5.	Antero Laine/Risto Virtanen	SF	Talbot Sunbeam Lotus

Rallye San Remo 3-8 October

1.	Stig Blomqvist/Björn Cederberg	S	Audi Quattro
2.	Hannu Mikkola/Arne Hertz	SF/S	Audi Quattro
3.	Walter Röhrl/Christian Geistdorfer	D	Opel Ascona 400
4.	Michele Mouton/Fabrizia Pons	F/I	Audi Quattro
5.	Henri Toivonen/Fred Gallagher	SF/GB	Opel Ascona 400

Marlboro Rallye Cote d'Ivoire 27 October-1 November

1.	Walter Röhrl/Christian Geistdorfer	D	Opel Ascona 400
2.	Per Eklund/Ragnar Spjuth	S	Toyota Celica
3.	Björn Waldegård/Hans Thorszelius	S	Toyota Celica
4.	Bruno Saby/Daniel Le Saux	F	Renault 5 Turbo
5.	Alain Ambrosino/Jean-François Fauchille	F	Peugeot 505

Lombard RAC Rally 21-25 November

1.	Hannu Mikkola/Arne Hertz	SF/S	Autdi Quattro
2.	Michele Mouton/Fabrizia Pons	F/I	Audi Quattro
3.	Henri Toivonen/Fred Gallagher	SF/GB	Opel Ascona 400
4.	Markku Alèn/IlkkaKivimaki	SF	Lancia Rally
5.	Harald Demuth/John Daniels	D/GB	Audi Quattro

1983 World Rally Championship Results

Monte Carlo Rally 22-29 January

1.	Walter Röhrl/Christian Geistdorfer	D	Lancia Rally
2.	Markku Alèn/IlkkaKivimaki	SF	Lancia Rally
3.	Stig Blomqvist/Björn Cedeberg	S	Audi Quattro
4.	Hannu Mikkola/Arne Hertz	SF/S	Audi Quattro
5.	Ari Vatanen/Terry Harryman	SF/GB	Opel Ascona 400

Swedish Rally 11-13 February

1.	Hannu Mikkola/Arne Hertz	SF/S	Audi Quattro
2.	Stig Blomqvist/Björn Cederberg	S	Audi 80 Quattro
3.	Lasse Lampi/Pentti Kuukkala	SF	Audi Quattro
4.	Michele Mouton/Fabrizia Pons	F/I	Audi Quattro
5.	Kalle Grundel/Rolf Melleroth	S	VW Golf Gti

Vinho do Porto Rallye de Portugal 2-5 March

1.	Hannu Mikkola/Arne Hertz	SF/S	Audi Quattro
2.	Michele Mouton/Fabrizia Pons	F/I	Audi Quattro
3.	Walter Röhrl/Christian Geistdorfer	D	Lancia Rally
4.	Markku Alèn/IlkkaKivimaki	SF	Lancia Rally
5.	Adartico Vudafieri/Maurizio Perissinot	I	Lancia Rally

Marlboro Safari Rally 30 March-4 April

1.	Ari Vatanen/Terry Harryman	SF/GB	Opel Ascona 400
2.	Hannu Mikkola/Arne Hertz	SF/S	Audi Quattro
3.	Michele Mouton/Fabrizia Pons	F/I	Audi Quattro
4.	Jayant Shah/Aslam Khan	EAK	Nissan 240RS
5.	Yoshio Takaola/Shigeo Sunahara	J	Subaru 4WD Sedan

Tour de Corse 5-7 May

1.	Markku Alèn/Ilkka Kivimaki	SF	Lancia Rally
2.	Walter Röhrl/Christian Geistdorfer	D	Lancia Rally
3.	Adartico Vudafieri/Luigi Pirollo	I	Lancia Rally
4.	Attilio Bettega/Maurizio Perissinot	I	Lancia Rally
5.	Bruno Saby/Chris Williams	F/GB	Renault 5 Turbo

Acropolis Rally 30 May-2 June

1.	Walter Röhrl/Christian Geistdorfer	D	Lancia Rally
2.	Markku Alèn/IlkkaKivimaki	SF	Lancia Rally
3.	Stig Blomqvist/Björn Cedeberg	S	Audi Quattro
4.	Ari Vatanen/Terry Harryman	SF/GB	Opel Manta 400
5.	Attilio Bettega/Maurizio Perissinot	I	Lancia Rally

Sanyo Rally of New Zealand 25-28 June

1.	Walter Röhrl/Christian Geistdorfer	D	Lancia Rally
2.	Timo Salonen/Seppo Harjanne	SF	Nissan 240RS
3.	Attilio Bettega/Maurizio Perissinot	I	Lancia Rally
4.	Shekhar Mehta/Yvonne Mehta	EAK	Nissan 240RS
5.	Jim Donald/Chris Porter	NZ	Nissan Bluebird Turbo

Marlboro Rally Argentina San Carlos de Bariloche 2-6 August

1.	Hannu Mikkola/Arne Hertz	SF/S	Audi Quattro
2.	Stig Blomqvist/Björn Cederberg	S	Audi Quattro
3.	Michele Mouton/Fabrizia Pons	F/I	Audi Quattro
4.	Shekhar Mehta/Yvonne Mehta	EAK	Audi Quattro
5.	Markku Alèn/IlkkaKivimaki	SF	Lancia Rally

Rally of 1000 Lakes 26-28 August

1.	Hannu Mikkola/Arne Hertz	SF/S	Audi Quattro
2.	Stig Blomqvist/Björn Cederberg	S	Audi Quattro
3.	Markku Alèn/IlkkaKivimaki	SF	Lancia Rally
4.	Per Eklund/Ragnar Spjuth	S	Audi Quattro
5.	Pentti Airikkala/Juha Piironen	SF	Lancia Rally

Rallye San Remo 2-8 October

1.	Markku Alèn/IlkkaKivimaki	SF	Lancia Rally
2.	Walter Röhrl/Christian Geistdorfer	D	Lancia Rally
3.	Attilio Bettega/Maurizio Perissinot	I	Lancia Rally
4.	Henri Toivonen/Fred Gallagher	SF/GB	Opel Manta 400
5.	Massimo Biasion/Tiziano Siviero	I	Lancia Rally

Rallye Cote d'Ivoire 25-30 October

1.	Björn Waldegård/Hans Thorszelius	S	Toyota Celica Twincam Turbo
2.	Hannu Mikkola/Arne Hertz	SF/S	Audi Quattro
3.	Per Eklund/Ragnar Spjuth	S	Toyota Celica Twincam Turbo
4.	Samir Assef/Solange Barrault	CI	Toyota Celica
5.	Alain Ambrosino/Daniel Le Saux	CI	Peugeot 505

Lombard RAC Rally 19-23 November

1.	Stig Blomqvist/Björn Cedeberg	S	Audi Quattro
2.	Hannu Mikkola/Arne Hertz	SF/S	Audi Quattro
3.	Jimmy McRae/Ian Grindrod	GB	Opel Manta 400
4.	Lasse Lampi/Pentti Kuukkala	SF	Audi Quattro
5.	Russell Brookes/Mike Broad	GB	Vauxhall Chevette 2300HSR

1984 World Rally Championship Results

Monte Carlo Rally 21-27 January

1. Walter Röhrl/Christian Geistdorfer	D	Audi Quattro
2. Stig Blomqvist/Björn Cedeberg	S	Audi Quattro
3. Hannu Mikkola/Arne Hertz	SF/S	Audi Quattro
4. Jean-Luc Therier/Michel Vial	F	Renault 5 Turbo
5. Attilio Bettega/Maurizio Perissinot	I	Lancia Rally

Swedish Rally 10-12 February

1. Stig Blomqvist/Björn Cedeberg	S	Audi Quattro
2. Michele Mouton/Fabrizia Pons	F/I	Audi Quattro
3. Per Eklund/Dave Whittcok	S/GB	Audi Quattro
4. Mats Jonsson/Ake Gustavsson	S	Opel Ascona 400
5. Lars-Erik Torph/Jan Sandstrom	S	Opel Ascona

Vinho do Porto Rallye de Portugal 7-10 March

1. Hannu Mikkola/Arne Hertz	SF/S	Audi Quattro
2. Markku Alèn/IlkkaKivimaki	SF	Lancia Rally
3. Attilio Bettega/Maurizio Perissinot	I	Lancia Rally
4. Massimo Biasion/Tiziano Siviero	I	Lancia Rally
5. Jean Ragnotti/Pierre Thimonier	F	Renault 5 Turbo

Marlboro Safari Rally 19-23 April

1. Björn Waldegård/Hans Thorszelius	S	Toyota Celica Twincam Turbo
2. Rauno Aaltonen/Lofty Drews	SF/EAK	Opel Manta 400
3. Hannu Mikkola/Arne Hertz	SF/S	Audi Quattro
4. Markku Alèn/IlkkaKivimaki	SF	Lancia Rally
5. Shekhar Mehta/Bob Combes	EAK	Nissan 240RS

Tour de Corse 3-5 May

1. Markku Alèn/IlkkaKivimaki	SF	Lancia Rally
2. Massimo Biasion/Tiziano Siviero	I	Lancia Rally
3. Jean Ragnotti/Oierre Thominier	F	Renault 5 Turbo
4. Jean-Pierre Nicolas/Charley Pasquier	F	Peugeot 205 Turbo 16
5. Stig Blomqvist/Björn Cedeberg	S	Audi Quattro

Acropolis Rally 28-31 May

1. Stig Blomqvist/Björn Cedeberg	S	Audi Quattro
2. Hannu Mikkola/Arne Hertz	SF/S	Audi Quattro
3. Markku Alèn/IlkkaKimivaki	SF	Lancia Rally
4. Attilio Bettega/Sergio Cresto	I/USA	Lancia Rally
5. John Buffum/Fred Gallagher	USA/GB	Audi Quattro

Sanyo Rally of New Zealand 23-26 June

1. Stig Blomqvist/Björn Cedeberg	S	Audi Quattro
2. Markku Alèn/IlkkaKivimaki	SF	Lancia Rally
3. Hannu Mikkloa/Arne Hertz	SF/S	Audi Quattro
4. Timo Salonen/Seppo Harjanne	SF	Nissan 240Rs
5. Björn Waldegård/Hans Thorszelius	S	Toyota Celica Twincam Turbo

Marlboro Rally of Argentia YPF Cordoba 27 July-1 August

1. Stig Blomqvist/Björn Cedeberg	S	Audi Quattro
2. Hannu Mikkola/Arne Hertz	SF/S	Audi Quattro
3. Jorge Recalde/Jorge Del Buono	RA	Audi Quattro
4. Mario Stillo/Daniel Stillo	RA	Renault 12
5. Yasuhiro Iwase/Surinder Thatthi	EAK	Opel Ascona 400

Rally of 1000 Lakes 26-28 August

1. Ari Vatanen/Terry Harryman	SF/GB	Peugeot 205 Turbo 16
2. Markku Alèn/IlkkaKivimaki	SF	Lancia Rally
3. Henri Toivonen/Juha Piironen	SF	Lancia Rally
4. Stig Blomqvist/Björn Cedeberg	S	Audi Quattro
5. Juha Kankkunen/Fred Gallagher	SF/GB	Toyota Celica Twincam Turbo

Rallye San Remo 30 September-5 October

1. Ari Vatanen/Terry Harryman	SF/GB	Peugeot 205 Turbo 16
2. Attilio Bettega/Maurizio Perissinot	I	Lancia Rally
3. Massimo Biasion/Tiziano Siviero	I	Lancia Rally
4. Fabrizio Tabaton/Luciano Tedeschini	I	Lancia Rally
5. Jean-Pierre Nicola/Charley Pasquier	F	Peugeot 205 Turbo 16

Cote d'Ivoire Rally 31 October-4 November

1. Stig Blomqvist/Björn Cedeberg	S	Audi Sport Quattro
2. Hannu Mikkola/Arne Hertz	SF/S	Audi Quattro
3. Shekhar Mehta/Rob Combes	EAK	Nissan 240RS
4. Alain Ambrosino/Daniel Le Saux	CI	Opel Manta 400
5. Dave Horsoey/David Williamson	EAK	Peugeot 504 Pickup

Lombard RAC Rally 25-29 November

1. Ari Vatanen/Terry Harryman	SF/GB	Peugeot 205 Turbo 16
2. Hannu Mikkola/Arne Hertz	SF/S	Audi Quattro
3. Per Eklund/Dave Whittock	S/GB	Toyota Celica Twincam Turbo
4. Michele Mouton/Fabrizia Pons	F/I	Audi Sport Quattro
5. Russell Brookes/Mike Broad	GB	Opel Manta 400

1985 World Rally Championship Results

Monte Carlo Rally 26 January-1 February

1. Ari Vatanen/Terry Harryman	SF/GB	Peugeot 206 Turbo 16
2. Walter Röhrl/Christian Geistdorfer	D	Audi Sport Quattro
3. Timo Salonen/Seppo Harjanne	SF	Peugeot 205 Turbo 16
4. Stig Blomqvist/Björn Cedeberg	S	Audi Sport Quattro
5. Bruno Saby/Jean-François Fauchille	F	Peugeot 205 Turbo 16

Swedish Rally 15-17 February

1. Ari Vatanen/Terry Harryman	SF/GB	Peugeot 205 Turbo 16
2. Stig Blomqvist/Björn Cedeberg	S	Audi Sport Quattro
3. Timo Salonen/Seppo Harjanne	SF	Peugeot 205 Turbo 16
4. Hannu Mikkola/Arne Hertz	SF/S	Audi Sport Quattro
5. Per Eklund/Dave Whittock	S.GB	Audi Quattro

Vinho do Porto Rallye de Portugal 6-9 March

1. Timo Salonen/Seppo Harjanne	SF	Peugeot 205 Turbo 16
2. Massimo Biasion/Tiziano Siviero	I	Lancia Rally
3. Walter Röhrl/Christian Geistdorfer	D	Audo Sport Quattro
4. Stig Blomqvist/Björn Cedeberg	S	Audi Sport Quattro
5. Werner Grissmann/Jorg Pattermann	A	Audi Quattro

Marlboro Safari Rally 4-8 April

1. Juha Kankkunen/Fred Gallagher	SF/GB	Toyota Celica Twincam Turbo
2. Björn Waldegård/Hans Thorszelius	S	Toyota Celica Twincam Turbo
3. Mike Kirkland/Anton Levitan	EAK	Nissan 240RS
4. Rauno Aaltonen/Lofty Drews	SF/EAK	Opel Manta 400
5. Erwin Weber/Gunter Wanger	D	Opel Manta 400

Tour de Corse 2-4 May

1. Jean Ragnotti/Pierre Thimonier	F	Renault Maxi 5 Turbo
2. Bruno Saby/Jean-François Fauchille	F	Peugeot 205 Turbo 16 E2
3. Bernard Beguin/Jean-Jacques Lenne	F	Porsche 911SC RS
4. Billy Coleman/Ronan Morgan	IRL	Porsche 911SC RS
5. Yves Louber/Jean-Bernard Vieu	F	Alfa Romeo GTV6

Acropolis Rally 27-30 May

1. Timo Salonen/Seppo Harjanne	SF	Peugeot 205 Turbo 16
2. Stig Blomqvist/Björn Cedeberg	S	Audi Sport Quattro
3. Ingvar Carlsson/Benny Melander	S	Mazda RX7
4. Shekhar Mehta/Yvonne Mehta	EAK	Nissan 240RS
5. Saeed Al Hajri/John Spiller	Q/GB	Porsche 911SC RS

AWA Clarion Rally of New Zealand 29 June-2 July

1. Timo Salonen/Seppo Harjanne	SF	Peugeot 205 Turbo 16
2. Ari Vatanen/Terry Harryman	SF/GB	Peugeot 205 Turbo 16
3. Walter Röhrl/Christian Geistdorfer	D	Audi Sport Quattro
4. Stig Blomqvist/Björn Cedeberg	S	Audi Sport Quattro
5. Malcolm Stewart/Doug Parkhill	NZ	Audi Quattro

Rally of Argentina – Cordoba 30 July-3 August

1. Simo Salonen/Seppo Harjanne	SF	Peugeot 205 Turbo 16
2. Wilfried Wiedner/Franz Zehetner	A	Audi Quattro
2. Carlos Reutemann/Jean-François Fauchille	RA/F	Peugeot 205 Turbo 16
4. Shekhar Mehta/Yvonne Mehta	EAK	Nissan 240RS
5. Ernesto Soto/Martin Christie	RA	Renault 18GTX

Rally of 1000 Lakes 23-25 August

1. Simo Salonen/Seppo Harjanne	SF	Peugeot 205 Turbo 16 E2
2. Stig Blomqvist/Björn Cedeberg	S	Audi Sport Quattro E2
3. Markku Alèn/IlkkaKivimaki	SF	Lancia Rally
4. Henri Toivonen/Juha Piironen	SF	Lancia Rally
5. Kalle Grundel/Peter Dickmann	S/D	Peugeot 205 Turbo 16 E2

Rallye San Remo 29 September-4 October

1. Walter Röhrl/Christian Geistdorfer	D	Audi Sport Quattro E2
2. Timo Salonen/Seppo Harjanne	SF	Peugeot 205 Turbo 16 E2
3. Henri Toivonen/Juha Piironen	SF	Lancia Rally
4. Marrku Alèn/IlkkaKivimaki	SF	Lancia Rally
5. Dario Cerrato/Giuseppi Cerri	I	Lancia Rally

Cote d'Ivoire Rally 30 October-3 November

1. Juha Kankkunen/Fred Gallagher	SF/GB	Toyota Celica Twincam Turbo
2. Björn Waldegård/Hans Thorszelius	S	Toyota Celica Twincam Turbo
3. Alain Ambrosino/Daniel Le Saux	CI	Nissan 240RS
4. Mike Kirkland/Rob Combes	EAK	Nissan 240RS
5. Eugene Salim/Clement Konan	CI	Mitsubishi Lancer Turbo

Lombard RAC Rally 24-28 November

1. Henri Toivonen/Neil Wilson	SF/GB	Lancia Delta S4
2. Markku Alèn/IlkkaKivimaki	SF	Lancia Delta S4
3. Tony Pond/Rob Arthur	GB	MG Metro 6R4
4. Per Eklund/Björn Cedeberg	S	Audi Quattro
5. Juha Kankkunen/Fred Gallagher	SF/GB	Toyota Celica Twincam Turbo

1986 World Rally Championship Results

Monte Carlo Rally 18-24 January

1. Henri Toivonen/Sergio Cresto	SF/USA	Lancia Delta S4
2. Timo Salonen/Seppo Harjanne	SF	Peugeot 205 Turbo 16 E2
3. Hannu Mikkola/Arne Hertz	SF/S	Audi Sport Quattro E2
4. Walter Röhrl/Christian Geistdorfer	D	Audi Sport Quattro E2
5. Juha Kankkunen/Juha Piironen	SF	Peugeot 205 Turbo 16 E2

Swedish Rally 14-16 February

1. Juha Kankkunen/Juha Piironen	SF	Peugeot 205 Turbo 16 E2
2. Marrku Alèn/IlkkaKivimaki	SF	Lancia Delta S4
3. Kalle Grundel/Benny Melander	S	Ford RS200
4. Mikael Ericsson/Reinhard Michel	S/D	Audi 90 Quattro
5. Gunnar Pettersson/Arne Pettersson	S	Audi Coupé Quattro

Vinho do Porto Rallye de Portugal 5-8 March

1. Joaquim Moutinho/Edgar Fortes	P	Renault 5 Turbo
2. Carlos Bica/Candido Junior	P	Lancia Rally
3. Gionvanni Del Zoppo/Loris Roggia	I	Fiat Uno Turbo
4. Jorge Ortigao/Pedro Perez	P	Toyota Corolla GT 16v
5. 'Tchine'/Gilles Thimonier	MC/F	Opel Manta 400

Marlboro Safari Rally 29 March-2 April

1. Bjord Waldegård/Fred Gallagher	S/GB	Toyota Celica TCT
2. Lars-Erik Torph/Bo Thorszelius	S	Toyota Celica TCT
3. Markku Alèn/IlkkaKivimaki	SF	Lancia Rally
4. Erwin Weber/Gunter Wanger	D	Toyota Celica TCT
5. Juha Kankkunen/Juha Piironen	SF	Peugeot 205 Turbo 16 E2

Tour de Corse 1-3 May

1. Bruno Saby/Jean-François Fauchille	F	Peugeot 205 Turbo 16 E2
2. François Chatriot/Michel Perin	F	Renault Maxi 5 Turbo
3. Yves Loubet/Jean-Marc Andre	F	Alfa Romeo GTV6
4. Jean Ragnotti/Pierre Thimonier	F	Renault 11 Turbo
5. Jean-Claude Torre/Patrick Delafoata	F	Renault 5 Turbo

Acropolis Rally 2-4 June

1. Juha Kankkunen/Juha Piironen	SF	Peugeot 205 Turbo 16 E2
2. Massimo Biasion/Tiziano Siviero	I	Lancia Delta S4
3. Bruno Saby/Jean-François Fauchille	F	Peugeot 205 Turbo 16 E2
4. Saeed Al Hajri/John Spiller	Q/GB	Porsche 911SC RS
5. 'Stratissino'/Costas Fertakis	GR	Nissan 240RS

Rally of New Zealand 5-8 July

1. Juha Kankkunen/Juha Piironen	SF	Peugeot 205 Turbo 16 E2
2. Markku Alèn/IlkkaKivimaki	SF	Lancia Delta S4
3. Massimo Biasion/Tiziano Siviero	I	Lancia Delta S4
4. Mikael Ericsson/Claes Billstam	S	Lancia Delta S4
5. Timo Salonen/Seppo Harjanne	SF	Peugeot 205 Turbo 16 E2

Marlboro Rally of Argentina

1. Massimo Biasion/Tiziano Siviero	I	Lancia Delta S4
2. Markku Alèn/IlkkaKivimaki	SF	Lancia Delta S4
3. Stig Blomqvist/Bruno Berglund	S	Peugeot 205 Turbo 16 E2
4. Jorge Recalde/Jorge Del Buono	RA	Lancia Delta S4
5. Kenneth Eriksson/Peter Dickmann	S/D	VW Golf GTi

Rally of 1000 Lakes 5-7 September

1. Timo Salonen/Seppo Harjanne	SF	Peugeot 205 Turbo 16 E2
2. Juha Kankkunen/Juha Piironen	SF	Peugeot 205 Turbo 16 E21
3. Markku Alèn/IlkkaKivimaki	SF	Lancia Delta S4
4. Stig Blomqvist/Bruno Berglund	S	Peugeot 205 Turbo 16 E2
5. Mikael Ericsson/Claes Billstam	S	Lancia Delta S4

Cote d'Ivoire Rallye 24-27 September

1. Björn Waldegård/Fred Gallagher	S/GB	Toyota Celica TCT
2. Lars-Erik Torph/Bo Thorszelius	S	Toyota Celica TCT
3. Erwin Weber/Gunter Wanger	D	Toyota Celica TCT
4. Robin Ulyate/Ian Street	EAK	Toyota Celica TCT
5. Samir Assef/Christian Boy	RL/F	Opel Manta 400

Rallye San Remo 13-17 October

1. Markku Alèn/IlkkaKivimaki	SF	Lancia Delta S4
2. Dario Cerrato/Guiseppi Cerri	I	Lancia Delta S4
3. Massimo Biasion/Tiziano Siviero	I	Lancia Delta S4
4. Malcolm Wilson/Nigel Harris	GB	MG Metro 6R4
5. Kenneth Eriksson/Peter Dickmann	S/D	VW Golf Gti

Lombard RAC Rally 16-19 November

1. Timo Salonen/Seppo Harjanne	SF	Peugeot 205 Turbo 16 E2
2. Markku Alèn/IlkkaKivimaki	SF	Lancia Delta S4
3. Juha Kankkunen/Juha Piironen	SF	Peugeot 205 Turbo 16 E2
4. Mikael Sundstrom/Voitto Silander	SF	Peugeot 205 Turbo 16 E2
5. Kalle Grundel/Benny Melander	S	Ford RS200

Olympus Rally USA 4-7 December

1. Markku Alèn/IlkkaKivimaki	SF	Lancia Delta S4
2. Juha Kankkunen/Juha Piironen	SF	Peugeot 205 Turbo 16 E2
3. John Buffum/Neil Wilson	USA/GB	Audi Sport Quattro
4. Lars-Erik Torph/Bo Thorszelius	S	Toyota Celica Twincam Turbo
5. Björn Waldegård/Fred Gallagher	S/GB	Toyota Celica Twincam Turbo

1987 World Rally Championship Results

Monte Carlo Rally 17-22 January

1. Miki Biasion/Tiziano Siviero	I	Lancia Delta HF 4WD
2. Juha Kankkunen/Juha Piironen	SF	Lancia Delta HF 4WD
3. Walter Röhrl/Christian Geistdorfer	D	Audi 200 Quattre
4. Stig Blomqvist/Bruno Berglund	S	Ford Sierra XR4x4
5. Ingvar Carlsson/Per Carlsson	S	Mazda 323 4WD

Swedish Rally 13-14 February

1. Timo Salonen/Seppo Harjanne	SF	Mazda 323 4WD
2. Mikael Ericsson/Claes Billstam	S	Lancia Delta HF 4WD
3. Juha Kankkunen/Juha Piironen	SF	Lancia Delta HF 4WD
4. Ingvar Carlsson/Per Carlsson	S	Mazda 323 4WD
5. Markku Alèn/IlkkaKivimaki	SF	Lancia Delta HF 4WD

Vinho do Porto Rallye de Portugal 11-14 March

1. Markku Alèn/IlkkaKivimaki	SF	Lancia Delta HF 4WD
2. Jean Ragnotti/Pierre Thimonier	F	Renault 11 Turbo
3. Kenneth Eriksson/Peter Dickmann	S/D	VW Golf Gti 16v
4. Juha Kankkunen/Juha Piironen	SF	Lancia Delta HF 4WD
5. François Chatriot/Michel Perin	F	Renault 11 Turbo

Marlboro Safari Rally 16-20 April

1. Hannu Mikkol/Arne Hertz	SF/S	Audi 200 Quattro
2. Walter Röhrl/Christian Geistdorfer	D	Audi 200 Quattro
3. Lars-Erik Torph/Benny Melander	S	Toyota Supra 3.0i
4. Erwin Weber/Matthias Feltz	D	VW Golf Gti 16v
5. Per Eklund/Dave Whittock	S/GB	Subaru Coupé 4WD Turbo

Tour de Corse 7-9 May

1. Bernard Beguin/Jean-Jacques Lenne	F	BMW M3
2. Yves Loubet/Jean-Bernard Vieu	F	Lancia Delta HF 4WD
3. Miki Biasion/Tiziano Siviero	I	Lancia Delta HF 4WD
4. Jean Ragnotti/Pierre Thimonier	F	Renault 11 Turbo
5. François Chatriot/Michel Perin	F	Renault 11 Turbo

Acropolis Rally 31 May-3 June

1. Markku Alèn/IlkkaKivimaki	SF	Lancia Delta HF 4WD
2. Juha Kankkunen/Juha Piironen	SF	Lancia Delta HF 4WD
3. Hannu Mikkola/Arne Hertz	SF/S	Audi 200 Quattro
4. Jorge Recalde/Jorge Del Buono	RA	Audi Coupé Quattro
5. Jean Ragnotti/Pierre Thimonier	F	Renault 11 Turbo

Olympus Rally (USA) 26-29 June

1. Juha Kankkunen/Juha Piironen	SF	Lancia Delta HF 4WD
2. Miki Biasion/Tiziano Siviero	I	Lancia Delta HF 4WD
3. Markku Alèn/IlkkaKivimaki	SF	Lancia Delta HF 4WD
4. Rod Millen/John Bellefleur	NZ/CDN	Mazda 323 4WD
5. Paolo Alessandrini/Alessandro Alessandrini	I	Lanci Delta HF 4WD

Rally of New Zealand 11-14 July

1. Franz Wittmann/Jorg Pattermann	A	Lancia Delta HF 4WD
2. Kenneth Eriksson/Peter Dickmann	S/D	VW Golf Gti 16v
3. 'Possum' Bourne/Michael Eggleton	NZ	Subaru RX Turbo
4. Tony Teesdale/Greg Horne	NZ	Mazda 323 4WD
5. David Officer/Kate Officer	AUS	Mitsubishi Starion Turbo

Marlboro Rally of Argentina 4-8 August

1. Miki Biasion/Tiziano Siviero	I	Lancia Delta HF 4WD
2. Jorge Recalde/Jorge Del Buono	RA	Lancia Delta HF 4WD
3. Erwin Weber/Matthias Feltz	D	VW Golf Gti 16v
4. Kenneth Eriksson/Peter Dickmann	S/D	VW Golf Gti 16v
5. Gabriele Raies/Paul Campana	RA	Renault 18GTX

Rally of 1000 Lakes 27-30 August

1. Markku Alèn/IlkkaKivimaki	SF	Lancia Delta HF 4WD
2. Ari Vatanen/Terry Harryman	SF/GB	Ford Sierra RS Cosworth
3. Stig Blomqvist/Bruno Berglund	S	Ford Sierra RS Cosworth
4. Per Eklund/Dave Whittock	S/GB	Audi Coupé Quattro
5. Juha Kankkunen/Juha Piironen	SF	Lancia Delta HF 4WD

Cote d'Ivoire Rally 22-26 September

1. Kenneth Eriksson/Peter Dickmann	S/D	VW Golf Gti 16v
2. Shekhar Mehta/Rob Combes	EAK	Nissan 200SX
3. Erwin Weber/Matthias Feltz	D	VW Golf Gti 16v
4. Patrick Tauziac/Claude Papin	F	Mitsubishi Starion Turbo
5. Patrick Copetti/Jean-Michel Dionneau	F	Toyota Corolla 16v

Rallye San Remo 12-15 October

1. Miki Biasion/Tiziano Siviero	I	Lancia Delta HF 4WD
2. Bruno Saby/Jean-François Fauchille	F	Lancia Delta HF 4WD
3. Jean RAgnotti/Pierre Thimonier	F	Renault 11 Turbo
4. Didier Auriol/Bernard Occelli	F	Ford Sierra RS Cosworth
5. Fabrizio Tabaton/Luciano Tedeschini	I	Lancia Delta HF 4WD

Lombard RAC Rally 22-25 November

1. Juha Kankkunen/Juha Piironen	SF	Lancia Delta HF 4WD
2. Stig Blomqvist/Bruno Berglund	S	Ford Sierra RS Cosworth
3. Jimmy McRae/Ian Grindrod	GB	Ford Sierra RS Cosworth
4. Mikael Ericsson/Claes Billstam	S	Lancia Delta HF 4WD
5. Markku Alèn/IlkkaKivimaki	SF	Lancia Delta HF 4WD

1988 World Rally Championship Results

Monte Carlo Rally 16-21 January

1. Bruno Saby/Jean-François Fauchille	F	Lancia Delta HF 4WD
2. Alex Fiorio/Luigi Pirollo	I	Lancia Delta HF 4WD
3. Jean-Pierre Ballet/Maris-Christine Lallement	F	Peugeot 205GTI
4. Alain Oreille/Jean-Marc Andrie	F	Renault 11 Turbo
5. Timo Salonen/Seppo Harjanne	SF	Mazda 323 4WD

Swedish Rally 4-6 February

1. Markku Alèn/IlkkaKivimaki	SF	Lancia Delta HF 4WD
2. Stig Blomqvist/Benny Melander	S	Ford Sierra XR4x4
3. Lars-Erik Torph/Christina Thorner	S	Audi Coupé Quattro
4. Erik Johansson/Johnny Johansson	S	Audi Coupé Quattro
5. Hakan Eriksson/Jan Svanstrom	S	Opel Kadett Gsi

Vinho do Porto Rallye de Portugal 1-5 March

1. Miki Biasion/Carlo Cassina	I	Lancia Delta Integrale
2. Alex Fiorio/Luigi Pirollo	I	Lancia Delta Integrale
3. Yves Loubet/Jean-Bernard Vieu	F	Lancia Delta HF 4WD
4. Hannu Mikkola/Christian Geistdorfer	SF/D	Mazda 323 4WD
5. Stig Blomqvist/Benny Melander	S	Ford Sierra RS Cosworth

Marlboro Safari Rally 31 March-4 April

1. Miki Biasion/Tiziano Siviero	I	Lancia Delta Integrale
2. Mike Kirkland/Robin Nixon	EAK	Nissan 200SX
3. Per Eklund/Dave Whittock	S/GB	Nissan 200SX
4. Kenneth Eriksson/Peter Dickmann	S/D	Toyota Supra Turbo
5. Juha Kankkunen/Juha Piironen	SF	Toyota Supra Turbo

Tour de Course 3-6 May

1. Didier Auriol/Bernard Ocelli	F	Ford Sierra RS Cosworth
2. Yves Loubet/Jean-Bernard Vieu	I	Lancia Delta Integrale
3. Bruno Saby/Jean-François Fauchille	F	Lancia Delta Integrale
4. François Chatriot/Michel Perin	F	BMW M3
5. Carlos Sainz/Luis Rodriguez	E	Ford Sierra RS Cosworth

Acropolis Rally 29 May-1 June

1. Miki Biasion/Tiziano Siviero	I	Lancia Delta Integrale
2. Mikael Ericsson/Claes Billstam	S	Lancia Delta Integrale
3. Alex Fiorio/Luigi Pirollo	I	Lancia Delta Integrale
4. Markku Alèn/IlkkaKivimaki	SF	Lancia Delta Integrale
5. Rudolf stohl/Ernst Rohringer	A	Audi Coupé Quattro

Olympus Rally 23-26 June

1. Miki Biasion/Tiziano Siviero	I	Lancia Delta Integrale
2. Alex Fiorio/Luigi Pirollo	I	Lancia Delta Integrale
3. John Buffum/John Bellefleur	USA/CDN	Audi Coupé Quattro
4. Georg Fischer/Thomas Zeltner	A	Audi 200 Quattro
5. Giovanni Del Zoppo/Pierangelo Scalvini	I	Lancia Delta Integrale

Rothmans Rally of New Zealand 9-12 July

1. Josef Haider/Ferdinand Hinterleitner	A	Opel Kadett Gsi
2. Ray Wilson/Stuart Lewis	NZ	Mazda 323 4WD
3. Malcolm Stewart/John Kennard	NZ	Audi Coupé Quattro
4. David Officer/Kate Officer	AUS	Mitsubishi Starion Turbo
5. Ross Meekings/Steve March	NZ	Toyota Corolla 16v

Marlboro Rally of Argentina 2-6 August

1. Jorge Recalde/Jorge Del Buono	RA	Lancia Delta Integrale
2. Miki Biasion/Tiziano Siviero	I	Lancia Delta Integrale
3.Franz Wittmann/Jorg Pattermann	A	Lancia Delta Integrale
4. Rudolf Stohl/Ernst Rohringer	A	Audi 90 Quattro
5. Jose Celsi/Elvop Olave	RCH	Subaru RX Turbo

Rally of 1000 Lakes 26-28 August

1. Markku Alèn/IlkkaKivimaki	SF	Lancia Delta Integrale
2. Mikael Ericsson/Claes Billstam	S	Lancia Delta Integrale
3. Didier Auriol/Bernard Occelli	F	Ford Sierra RS Cosworth
4. Timo Salonen/Seppo Harjanne	SF	Mazda 323 4WD
5. Stig Blomqvist/Benny Melander	S	Ford Sierra RS Cosworth

Marlbo Cote d'Ivoire Rally 20-24 September

1. Alain Ambrosino/Daniel Le Saux	F	Nissan 200SX
2. Pascal Gaban/Willy Lux	B	Mazda 323 4WD
3. Patrick Tauziac/Claude Papin	F	Mitsubishi Starion Turbo
4. Alain Oudit/Patrice Lemarie	F	VW Golf Gti 16v
5. Adolphe Choteau/Jean-Pierre Claverie	F	Toyota Corolla 16v

Rallye San Remo 10-14 October

1. Miki Biasion/Tiziano Siviero	I	Lancia Delta Integrale
2. Alex Fiorio/Luigi Pirollo	I	Lancia Delta Integrale
3. Dario Cerrato/Guiseppi Cerri	I	Lancia Delta Integrale
4. Marrku Alèn/IlkkaKivimaki	SF	Lancia Delta Integrale
5. Carlos Sainz/Luis Rodriguez	E	Ford Sierra RS Cosworth

Lombard RAC Rally 20-24 November

1. Markku Alèn/IlkkaKivimaki	SF	Lancia Delta Integrale
2.Timo Salonen/Voitto Silander	SF	Mazda 323 4WD
3. Björn Waldegård/Fred Gallagher	S/GB	Toyota Celica 2000 GT4
4. Pentti Arikkala/Brian Murphy	SF/IRL	Lancia Delta Integrale
5. Armin Schwartz/Arne Hertz	D/S	Audi 200 Quattro

1989 World Rally Championship Results

Swedish Rallt 6-8 January

1. Ingvar Carlsson/Per Carlsson	S	Mazda 323 4WD
2. Per Eklund/Dave Whittock	S/GB	Lancia Delta Integrale
3. Kenneth Eriksson/Staffan Parmander	S	Toyota Celica GT-Four
4. Mikael Ericsson/Claes Billstam	S	Lancia Delta Integrale
5. Stig Blomqvist/Benny Melander	S	Audi 200 Quattro

Monte Carlo Rally 21-26 January

1. Miki Biasion/Tiziano Siviero	I	Lancia Delta Integrale
2. Didier Auriol/Bernard Occelli	F	Lancia Delta Integrale
3. Bruno Saby/Jean-François Fauchille	F	Lancia Delta Integrale
4. Hannu Mikkola/Christian Geistdorfer	SF/D	Mazda 323 4WD
5. Juha Kankkunen/Juha Pironen	SF	Toyota Celica GT-Four

Vinho do Porto Rallye de Portugal 28 February-4 March

1. Miki Biasion/Tiziano Siviero	I	Lancia Delta Integrale
2. Markku Alèn/IlkkaKivimaki	SF	Lancia Delta Integrale
3. Alex Fiorio/Luigi Pirollo	I	Lancia Delta Integrale
4. Georg Fischer/Thomas Zeltner	A	Audi 200 Quattro
5. Marc Duez/Alain Lopes	B	BMW M3

Marlboro Safari Rally 23-27 March

1. Miki Biasion/Tiziano Siviero	I	Lancia Delta Integrale
2. Mike Kirkland/Robin Nixon	EAK	Nissan 200SX
3. Stig Blomqvist/Björn Cedeberg	S	VW Golf 16v
4. Björn Waldegård/Fred Gallagher	S/GB	Toyota Supra Turbo
5. Ian Duncan/Ian Munro	EAK	Toyota Supra Turbo

Tour de Corse 23-26 April

1. Didier Auriol/Bernard Occelli	F	Lancia Delta Integrale
2. François Chatriot/Michel Perin	F	BMW M3
3. Juha Kankkunen/Juha Pironen	SF	Toyota Celica GT-Four
4. Yves Loubet.Jean-Marc Andrie	F	Lancia Delta Integrale
5. Bernard Beguin/Jean-Bernard Vieu	F	BMW M3

Acropolis Rally 27 May-1 June

1. Miki Biasion/Tiziano Siviero	I	Lancia Delta Integrale
2. Didier Auriol/Bernard Occelli	F	Lancia Delta Integrale
3. Alex Fiorio/Luigi Pirollo	I	Lancia Delta Integrale
4. Jimmy McRae/Rob Arthur	GB	Mitsubishi Galant VR-4
5. Jorge Recalde/Jorge Del Buono	RA	Lancia Delta Integrale

Rothmans Rally of New Zealand 15-18 July

1. Ingvar Carlsson/Per Carlsson	S	Mazda 323 4WD
2. Rod Millen/Tony Sircombe	NZ	Mazda 323 4WD
3. Malcolm Wilson/Ian Grindrod	GB	Vauxhall Astra GTE
4. Mats Jonsson/Lars Backman	S	Opel Kadett GSI
5. Colin McRae/Derek Ringer	GB	Ford Sierra RS Cosworth

Rally Argentina 1-5August

1. Mikael Ericsson/Claes Billstam	S	Lancia Delta Integrale
2. Alex Fiorio/Luigi Pirollo	I	Lancia Delta Integrale
3. Jorge Recalde/Jorge Del Buono	RA	Lancia Delta Integrale
4. Georg Fischer/Thomas Zeltner	A	Audi 200 Quattro
5. Ernesto Soto/Martin Christie	RA	Renault 18 GTX

Rally of 1000 Lakes 25-27 August

1. Mikael Ericsson/Claes Billstam	S	Mitsubishi Gallant VR-4
2. Timo Salonen/Voitto Silander	SF	Mazda 323 4WD
3. Carlos Sainz/Luis Moya	E	Toyota Celica GT-Four
4. Kenneth Eriksson/Staffan Parmander	S	Toyotal Celica GT-Four
5. Torbjorn Eding/Kent Nilsson	S	Mazda 323 4WD

Commonwealth Bank Australia Rally 14-17 September

1. Juha Kankkunen/Juha Pironen	SF	Toyota Celica GT-Four
2. Kenneth Eriksson/Staffan Parmander	S	Toyota Celica GT-Four
3. Markku Alèn/Ilkka Kivimaki	SF	Lancia Delta Integrale
4. Alex Fiorio/Luigi Pirollo	I	Lancia Delta Integrale
5. Rod Millen/Tony Sircombe	NZ	Mazda 323 4WD

Rallye San Remo 8-12 October

1. Miki Biasion/Tiziano Siviero	I	Lancia Delta Integrale 16v
2. Alex Fiorio/Luigi Pirollo	I	Lancia Delta Integrale
3. Carlos Sainz/Luis Moya	E	Toyota Celica GT-Four
4. Dario Cerrato/Guiseppi Cerri	I	Lancia Delta Integrale
5. Juha Kankkunen/Juha Pironen	SF	Toyota Celica GT-Four

Rallye Cote d'Ivoire 29 October-2 November

1. Alain Orielle/Gilles Thimonier	F	Renault 5 GT Turbo
2. Patrick Tauziac/Claude Papin	F	Mitsubishi Starion Turbo
3. Adolphe Choteau/Jean-Pierre Claverie	F	Toyota Corolla 16v
4. Andre Segolen/Yvan Aimon	F	Toyota Corolla 16v
5. Patrice Servant/David Charbonnel	F	Toyota Corolla 16v

Lombard RAC Rally 19-23 November

1. Pentti Airikkala/Ronan McNamee	SF/IRL	Mitsubishi Galant VR-4
2. Carlos Sainz/Luis Moya	E	Toyota Celica GT-Four
3. Juha Kankkunen/Juha Pironen	SF	Toyota Celica GT-Four
4. Kenneth Eriksson/Staffan Parmander	S	Toyota Celica GT-Four
5. Ari Vatanen/Bruno Berglund	SF/S	Mitsubishi Galant VR-4

1990 World Rally Championship Results

Monte Carlo Rally 19-25 January

1. Didier Auriol/Bernard Occelli	F	Lancia Delta Integrale
2. Carlos Sainz/Luis Moya	E	Toyota Celica GT-Four
3. Miki Biasion/Tiziano Siviero	I	Lancia Delta Integrale
4. Dario Cerrato/Guiseppi Cerri	I	Lancia Delta Integrale
5. Armin Schwartz/Klaus Wicha	D	Toyota Celica GT-Four

Vinho do Porto Rallye de Portugal 6-10 March

1. Miki Biasion/Tiziano Siviero	I	Lancia Delta Integrale
2. Didier Auriol/Bernard Occelli	F	Lancia Delta Integrale
3. Juha Kankkunen/Juha Pironen	SF	Lancia Delta Integrale
4. Dario Cerrato/Guiseppi Cerri	I	Lancia Delta Integrale
5. Carlos Bica/Fernando Prata	P	Lancia Delta Integrale

Marlboro Safari Rally 11-16 April

1. Björn Waldegård/Fred Gallagher	S/GB	Toyota Celica GT-Four
2. Juha Kankkunen/Juha Pironen	SD	Lancia Delta Integrale
3. Mikael Ericsson/Claes Billstam	S	Toyota Celica GT-Four
4. Carlos Sainz/Luis Moya	E	Toyota Celica GT-Four
5. Kenjiro Shinozuka/John Meadows	J/GB	Mitsubishi Galant VR-4

Tour de Corse 6-9 May

1. Didier Auriol/Bernard Occelli	F	Lancia Delta Integrale
2. Carlos Sainz/Luis Moya	E	Toyota Celica GT-Four
3. François Chatriot/Michel Perin	F	BMW M3
4. Bruno Saby/Daniel Grataloup	F	Lancia Delta Integrale
5. Raimund Baumschlager/Ruben Zeltner	A	VW Golf Gti

Acropolis Rally 3-6 June

1. Carlos Sainz/Luis Moya	E	Toyota Celica GT-Four
2. Juha Kankkunen/Juha Pironen	SF	Lancia Delta Integrale
3. Miki Biasion/Tiziano Siviero	I	Lancia Delta Integrale
4. Mikael Ericsson/Claes Billstam	S	Toyota Celica GT-Four
5. Alex Fiorio/Luigi Pirollo	I	Lancia Delta Integrale

Rothmans Rally of New Zealand 30 June-3 July

1. Carlos Sainz/Luis Moya	E	Toyota Celica GT-Four
2. Ingvar Carlsson/Per Carlsson	S	Mazda 323 4WD
3. Erwin Weber/Matthias Feltz	D	VW Rallye Golf G60
4. Ross Dunkerton/Fred Gocentas	AUS	Mitsubishi Galant VR-4
5. 'Possum' Bourne/Rodger Freeth	NZ	Subaru Legacy 4WD Turbo

Rally Argentina 24-28 July

1. Miki Biasion/Tiziano Siviero	I	Lancia Delta Integrale
2. Carlos Sainz/Luis Moya	E	Toyota Celica GT-Four
3. Didier Auriol/Bernard Occelli	F	Lancia Delta Integrale
4. Rudi Stohl/Reinhard Kaufmann	A	Audi 90 Quattro
5. Ernesto Soto/Jorge Del Buono	RA	Lancia Delta Integrale

Rally of 1000 Lakes 23-26 August

1. Carlos Sainz/Luis Moya	E	Toyota Celica GT-Four
2. Ari Vatanen/Bruno Berglund	SF/S	Mitsubishi Galant VR-4
3. Kenneth Eriksson/Staffan Parmander	S	Mitsubishi Galant VR-4
4. Markku Alèn/Ilkka Kivimaki	SF	Subaru Legacy 4WD Turbo
5. Juha Kankkunen/Juha Pironen	SF	Lancia Delta Integrale

Commonwealth Bank Rally Australia 20-23 September

1. Juha Kankkunen/Juha Pironen	SF	Lancia Delta Integrale
2. Carlos Sainz/Luis Moya	E	Toyota Celica GT-Four
3. Alex Fiorio/Luigi Pirollo	I	Lancia Delta Integrale
4. 'Possum' Bourne/Rodger Freeth	NZ	Subaru Legacy 4WD Turbo
5. Ingvar Carlsson/Per Carlson	S	Mazda 323 4WD

Rallye San Remo 14-18 October

1. Didier Auriol/Bernard Occelli	F	Lancia Delta Integrale
2. Juha Kankkunen/Juha Pironen	SF	Lancia Delta Integrale
3. Carlos Sainz/Luis Moya	E	Toyotal Celica GT-Four
4. Dario Cerrato/Guiseppi Cerri	I	Lancia Delta Integrale
5. Piero Liatti/Luciano Tedeschini	I	Lancia Delta Integrale

Rallye Cote d'Ivoire 28 October-1 November

1. Patrick Tauzia/Claude Papin	F	Mitsubishi Galant VR-4
2. Rudi Stohl/Ernst Rohringer	A	Audi 90 Quattro
3. Alan Oreille/Michel Roissard	F	Renault 5 GT Turbo
4. Alan Ambrosino/Daniel Le Saux	F	Nissan Super March Turbo
5. Patrice Servant/David Charbonnel	F	Toyota Corolla

Lombard RAC Rally 25-28 November

1. Carlos Sainz/Luis Moya	E	Toyota Celica GT-Four
2. Kenneth Eriksson/Staffan Parmander	S	Mitsubishi Galant VR-4
3. Miki Biasion/Tiziano Siviero	I	Lancia Delta Integrale
4. Mats Jonsson/Anders Olsson	S	Toyota Celica GT-Four
5. Didier Auriol/Bernard Occelli	F	Lancia Delta Integrale

1991 World Rally Championship Results

Monte Carlo Rally 24-30 January

1. Carlos Sainz/Luis Moya	E	Toyota Celica GT-Four
2. Miki Baision/Tiziano Siviero	I	Lancia Delta Integrale
3. François Delecour/Anne-Chantal Pauwels	F	Ford Sierra Cosworth 4x4
4. Armin Schwarz/Arne Hertz	D/S	Toyota Celica GT-Four
5. Juha Kankkunen/Juha Pironen	SF	Lancia Delta Integrale

Swedish Rally 16-18 February

1. Kenneth Eriksson/Staffan Parmander	S	Mitsubishi Galkant VR-4
2. Mats Jonsson/Lars Backman	S	Toyota Celica GT-Four
3. Markku Alèn/Ilkka Kivimaki	SF	Subaru Legacy 4WD Turbo
4. Ingvar Carlsson/Per Carlsson	S	Mazda 323 GTX
5. Lasse Lampi/Pentti Kuukkala	SF	Mitsubishi Galant VR-4

Vinho do Porto Rallye de Portugal 5-9 March

1. Carlos Sainz/Luis Moya	E	Toyota Celica GT-Four
2. Didier Auriol/Barnard Occelli	F	Lancia Delta Integrale
3. Miki Biasion/Tiziano Siviero	F	Lancia Delta Integrale
4. Juha Kankkunen/Juha Pironen	SF	Lancia Delta Integrale
5. Markku Alèn/Ilkka Kivimaki	SF	Subaru Legacy 4WD Turbo

Safari Rally 27 March-1 April

1. Juha Kankkunen/Juha Pironen	SF	Lancia Delta Integrale
2. Mikael Ericsson/Claes Billstam	S	Toyota Celica GT-Four
3. Jorge Recalde/Martin Chrstie	RA	Lancia Delta Integrale
4. Björn Waldegård/Fred Gallagher	S/GB	Toyota Celica GT-Four
5. Stig Blomqvist/Benny Melander	S	Nissan Pulsar GTI-R

Tour de Corse 28 April-1 May

1. Carlos Sainz/Luis Moya	E	Toyota Celica GT-Four
2. Didier Auriol/Bernard Occelli	F	Lancia Delta Integrale
3. Gianfranco Cunico/Stefani Evangelisti	I	Ford Sierra Coswroth 4x4
4. Marc Duez/Klaus Wicha	B/D	Toyota Celica GT-Four
5. Malcolm Wilson/Nicky Grist	GB	Ford Sierra Cosworth 4x4

Acropolis Rally 2-5 June

1. Juha Kankkunen/Juha Pironen	SF	Lancia Delta Integrale
2. Carlos Sainz/Luis Moya	E	Toyotal Celica GT-Four
3. Mikia Biasion/Tiziano Siviero	I	Lancia Delta Integrale
4. Didier Auriol/Bernard Occelli	F	Lancia Delta Integrale
5. Armin Schwarz/Arne Hertz	D/S	Toyota Celica GT-Four

Rothmans Rally of New Zealand 26-30 June

1. Carlos Sainz/Luis Moya	E	Toyota Celica GT-Four
2. Juha Kankkunen/Juha Pironen	SF	Lancia Delta Integrale
3. Didier Auriol/Bernard Occelli	F	Lancia Delta Integrale
4. Markku Alèn/Ilkka Kivimaki	SF	Subaru Legacy 4WD Turbo
5. Neil Allport/Jim Robb	NZ	Mazda 323 GTX

Rally YPF Argentina 'Elaion' 23-27 July

1. Carlos Sainz/Luis Moya	E	Toyota Celica GT-Four
2. Miki Biasion/Tiziano Siviero	I	Lancia Delta Integrale
3. Didier Auriol/Bernard Occelli	F	Lancia Delta Integrale
4. Juha Kankkunen/Juha Pironen	SF	Lancia Delta Integrale
5. Jorge Recalde/Martin Christie	RA	Lancia Delta Integrale

Rally of 1000 Lakes 22-25 August

1. Juha Kankkunen/Juha Pironen	SF	Lancia Delta Integrale
2. Didier Auriol/Bernard Occelli	F	Lancia Delta Integrale
2. Timo Salonen/Voitto Silander	SF	Mitsubishi Galant VR-4
3. Kenneth Eriksson/Staffan Parmander	S	Mitsubishi Galant VR-4
4. Carlos Sainz/Luis Moya	E	Toyota Celica GT-Four
5. Tommi Mäkinen/Seppo Harjanne	SF	Mazda 323 GTX

Commonwealth Bank Rally Australia 20-24 September

1. Juha Kankkunen/Juha Pironen	SF	Lancia Delta Integrale
2. Kenneth Eriksson/Staffan Parmander	S	Mitsubishi Galant VR-4
3. Armin Schwarz/Arne Hertz	D/S	Toyota Celica GT-Four
4. Markku Alèn/Ilkka Kivimaki	SF	Subaru Legacy 4WD Turbo
5. Timo Salonen/Voitto Silander	SF	Mitsubishi Galant VR-4E

Rallye San Remo 13-17 October

1. Didier Auriol/Bernard Occelli	F	Lancia Delta Integrale
2. Miki Biasion/Tiziano Siviero	I	Lancia Delta Integrale
3. Dario Cerrato/Guiseppi Cerri	I	Lancia Delta Integrale
4. François Delecour/Anne-C Pauwels	F	Ford Sierra Cosworth 4x4
5. Andrea Aghini/Sauro Farnocchia	I	Lancia Delta Integrale

Rallye Cote d'Ivoire-Bandama 27-31 October

1. Kenjiro Shinozuka/John Meadows	J/GB	Mitsubishi Galant VR-4E
2. Patrick Tauziac/Claude Papin	F	Mitsubishi Galant CR-4
3. Rudi Stohl/Reinhard Kaufmann	A	Audi 90 Quattro
4. Patrice Servant/Thierry Pansolin	F	Audi 90 Quattro
5. Adolphe Choteau/Jean-Pierre Claverie	CI/F	Toyota Corolla 16v

Rallye Espana-Catalunya Costa Brava 10-13 November

1. Armin Schwarz/Arne Hertz	D/S	Toyota Celica GT-Four
2. Juha Kankkunen/Juha Pironen	SF	Lancia Delta Integrale
3. François Delecour/Daniel Grataloup	F	Ford Sierra Cosworth 4x4
4. Jose-Maria Bardolet/Antonio Rodriguez	E	Ford Sierra Cosworth 4x4
5. Andrea Aghini/Sauro Farnocchia	I	Lancia Delta Integrale

Lombard RAC Rally 24-27 November

1. Juha Kankkunen/Juha Pironen	SF	Lancia Delta Integrale
2. Kenneth Eriksson/Staffan Parmander	S	Mitsubishi Galant VR-4E
3. Carlos Sainz/Luis Moya	E	Toyota Celica GT-Four
4. Timo Salonen/Voitto Silander	SF	Mitsubishi Galant VR-4E
5. Ari Vatanen/Bruno Berglund	SF/S	Subaru Legacy 4WD Turbo

1992 World Rally Championship Results

Monte Carlo Rally 23-28 January

1. Didier Auriol/Bernard Occelli	F	Lancia HF Integrale
2. Carlos Sainz/Luis Moya	E	Toyota Celica Turbo 4WD
3. Juha Kankkunen/Juha Pironen	SF	Lancia HF Integrale
4. François Delecour/Daniel Grataloup	F	Ford Sierra Cosworth 4x4
5. Philippe Bugalski/Denis Giraudet	F	Lancia HF Integrale

Swedish Rally 13-16 February

1. Mats Jonsson/Lars Backman	S	Toyota Celica GT-Four
2. Colin McRae/Derek Ringer	GB	Subaru Legacy 4WD Turbo
3. Stig Blomqvist/Benny Melander	S	Nissan Pulsar GTI-R
4. Markku Alèn/Ilkka Kivimaki	SF	Toyota Celica GT-Four
5. Leif Asterhag/Christina Thorner	S	Toyota Celica GT-Four

Vinho do Porto Rallye de Portugal 3-7 March

1. Juha Kankkunen/Juha Pironen	SF	Lancia HF Integrale
2. Miki Biasion/Tiziano Siviero	I	Ford Sierra Cosworth 4x4
3. Carlos Sainz/Luis Moya	E	Toyota Celica Turbo 4WD
4. Markku Alèn/Ilkka Kivimaki	SF	Toyota Celica Turbo 4WD
5. Timo Salonen/Voitto Silander	SF	Mitsubishi Galant VR-4E

Marlboro Safari Rally 27 March-1 April

1. Carlos Sainz/Luis Moya	E	Toyota Celica Turbo 4WD
2. Juha Kankkunen/Juha Pironen	SF	Lancia HF Integrale
3. Jorge Recalde/Martin Christie	RA	Lancia HF Integrale
4. Mikael Ericsson/Nicky Grist	S/GB	Toyota Celica Turbo 4WD
5. Markku Alèn/Ilkka Kivimaki	SF	Toyota Celica Turbo 4WD

Tour de Corse 3-6 May

1. Didier Auriol/Bernard Occelli	F	Lancia HF Integrale
2. François Delecour/Daniel Grataloup	F	Ford Sierra Cosworth 4x4
3. Philippe Bugalski/Denis Giraudet	F	Lancia HF Integrale
4. Carlos Sainz/Luis Moya	E	Toyota Celica Turbo 4WD
5. Armin Schwarz/Arne Hertz	D/S	Toyota Celica Turbo 4WD

Acropolis Rally 31 May-3 June

1. Didier Auriol/Bernard Occelli	F	Lancia HF Integrale
2. Juha Kankkunen/Juha Pironen	SF	Lancia HF Integrale
3. Miki Biasion/Tiziano Siviero	I	Ford Sierra Cosworth 4x4
4. Colin McRae/Derek Ringer	GB	Subaru Legacy 4WD Turbo
5. François Delecour/Daniel Grataloup	F	Ford Sierra Cosworth 4x4

Rothmans Rally of New Zealand 25-28 June

1. Carlos Sainz/Luis Moya	E	Toyota Celica Turbo 4WD
2. Piero Liatti/Luciano Tedeschini	I	Lancia HF Integrale
3. Ross Dunkerton/Fred Gocentas	AUS	Mitsubishi Galant VR-4
4. Mikael Sundstrom/Jakke Honkanen	SF	Lancia HF Integrale 16v
5. Ed Oordynski/Harry Mansson	AUS	Mitsubishi Galant VR-4

Rally YPF Argentina 22-25 July

1. Didier Auriol/Bernard Occelli	F	Lancia HF Integrale
2. Carlos Sainz/Luis Moya	E	Toyota Celica Turbo 4WD
3. Gustavo Trelles/Jorge Del Buono	U/RA	Lancia HF Integrale
4. Alex Fiorio/Vittorio Brambilla	I	Lancia HF Integrale
5. Rudi Stohl/Peter Dickmann	A/D	Audi 90 Quattro

Rally of 1000 Lakes 27-30 August

1. Didier Auriol/Bernard Occelli	F	Lancia HF Integrale
2. Juha Kankkunen/Juha Pironen	SF	Lancia HF Integrale
3. Markku Alèn/Ilkka Kivimaki	SF	Toyota Celica Turbo 4WD
4. Ari Vatanen/Bruno Berglund	SF/S	Subaru Legacy 4WD Turbo
5. Miki Biasion/Tiziano Siviero	I	Ford Sierra Cosworth 4x4

Telecom Rally Australia 19-22 September

1. Didier Auriol/Bernard Occelli	F	Lancia HF Integrale
2. Juha Kankkunen/Juha Pironen	SF	Lancia HF Integrale
3. Carlos Sainz/Luis Moya	E	Toyota Celica Turbo 4WD
4. Jorge Recalde/Martin Christie	RA	Lancia HF Integrale
5. Ross Dunkerton/Fred Gocentas	AUS	Mitsubishi Galant VR-4

Rallye San Remo 12-14 October

1. Andrea Ashini/Sauro Farnocchia	I	Lancia HF Integrale
2. Juha Kankkunen/Juha Pironen	SG	Lancia HF Integrale
3. François Delecour/Daniel Grataloup	F	Ford Sierra Cosworth 4x4
4. Miki Biasion/Tiziano Siviero	I	Ford Sierra Cosworth 4.4
5. Alex Fiorio/Vittorio Brambilla	I	Lancia HF Integrale

Rallye Cote d'Ivoire-Bandama 31 October-2 November

1. Kenjiro Shinozuka/John Meadows	J/GB	Mitsubishi Galant VR-4
2. Bruno Thiry/Stephane Prevot	B	Opel Kadett Gsi
3. Patrice Servant/Thierrey Brion	F	Audi 90 Quattro
4. Hiroshi Nishiyama/Hisashi Yamaguchi	J	Nissan Pulksar GTI-R
5. Samir Assef/Clement Konan	RL/CI	Toyota Celica GT-Four

Rallye Espana-Catalunya Costa Brava 9-11 November

1. Carlos Sainz/Luis Moya	E	Toyota Celica Turbo 4WD
2. Juha Kankkunen/Juha Pironen	SF	Lancia HF Integrale
3. Andrea Aghini/Sauro Farnocchia	I	Lancia HF Integrale
4. Alex Fiorio/Vittorio Brambilla	I	Lancia HF Integrale
5. Armin Schwarz/Arne Hertz	D/S	Toyota Celica Turbo 4WD

Lombard RAC Rally 22-25 November

1. Carlos Sainz/Luis Moya	E	Toyota Celica Turbo 4WD
2. Ari Vatanen/Bruno Berglund	SF/S	Subaru Legacy 4WD Turbo
3. Juha Kankkunen/Juha Pironen	SF	Lancia HF Integrale
4. Markku Alèn/Ilkka Kivimaki	SF	Toyota Celica Turbo 4WD
5. Miki Biasion/Tiziano Siviero	I	Ford Sierra Cosworth 4x4

1993 World Rally Championship Results

Monte Carlo Rally 21-27 January

1. Didier Auriol/Bernard Occelli	F	Toyota Celica Turbo 4WD
2. François Delecour/Daniel Grataloup	F	Ford Escort RS Cosworth
3. Miki Biasion/Tiziano Siviero	I	Ford Escort RS Cosworth
4. Kenneth Eriksson/Staffan Parmander	S	Mitsubishi Lancer Evolution
5. Juha Kankkunen/Juha Pironen	SF	Toyota Celica Turbo 4WD

Swedish Rally 12-14 February

1. Mats Jonsson/Lars Backman	S	Toyota Celica Turbo 4WD
2. Juha Kankkunen/Juha Pironen	SF	Toyota Celica Turbo 4WD
3. Colin McRae/Derek Ringer	GB	Subaru Legacy 4WD Turbo
4. Tommi Mäkinen/Seppo Harjanne	SF	Lancia HF Integrale
5. Björn Johansson/Anders Olsson	S	Mazda 323 GT-R

Vinho do Porto Rallye de Portugal 3-6 March

1. François Delecour/Daniel Grataloup	F	Ford Escort RS Cosworth
2. Miki Biasion/Tizano Siviero	I	Ford Escort RS Cosworth
3. Andrea Aghini/Sauro Farnocchia	I	Lancia HF Integrale
4. Markku Alèn/Ilkka Kivimaki	SF	Subaru Legacy 4WD Turbo
5. Kenneth Eriksson/Staffan Parmander	S	Mitsubishi Lancer Evolution

Trust Bank Safari Rally 8-12 April

1. Juha Kankkunen/Juha Pironen	SF	Toyota Celica Turbo 4WD
2. Markku Alèn/Ilkka Kivimaki	SF	Toyota Celica Turbo 4WD
3. Ian Duncan/Ian Munro	EAK	Toyota Celica Turbo 4WD
4. Yasuhiro Iwase/Sudhir Vinayak	J/EAK	Toyota Celica Turbo 4WD
5. Guy Jack/Des Page-Morris	EAK	Daihatsu Charade GTXX

Tour de Course 2-4 May

1. François Delecour/Daniel Grataloup — F — Ford Escort RS Cosworth
2. Didier Auriol/Bernard Occelli — F — Toyota Celica Turbo 4WD
3. François Chatriot/Denis Giraudet — F — Toyota Celica Turbo 4WD
4. Carlos Sainz/Luis Moya — E — Lancia HF Integrale
5. Colin McRae/Derek Ringer — GB — Subaru Legacy 4WD Turbo

Acropolis Rally 30 May-1 June

1. Miki Biasion/Tiziano Siviero — I — Ford Escort RS Cosworth
2. Carlos Sainz/Luis Moya — E — Lancia HF Integrale
3. Armin Schwarz/Nicky Grist — D/GB — Mitsubishi Lancer Evolution
4. Andrea Aghinis/Sauro Farnocchia — I — Lancia HF Integrale
5. Gustavo Trelles/Jorge Del Buono — U/RA — Lancia HF Integrale

Rally YPF Argentina 14-17 July

1. Juha Kankkunen/Nicky Grist — SF/GB — Toyota Celica Turbo 4WD
2. Miki Biasion/Tiziano Siviero — I — Ford Excort RS Cosworth
3. Didier Auriol/Bernard Occelli — F — Toyota Celica Turbo 4WD
4. Gustavo Trelles/Jorge Del Buono — U/RA — Lancia HF Integrale
5. Carlos Menem Jnr/Victor Zucchini — RA — Ford Escort RS Cosworth

Rothmans Rally of New Zealand 5-8 August

1. Colin McRae/Derek Ringer — GB — Subaru Legacy 4WD Turbo
2. François Delecour/Daniel Grataloup — F — Ford Escort RS Cosworth
3. Didier Auriol/Bernard Occelli — F — Toyota Celica Turbo 4WD
4. Carlos Sainz/Luis Moya — E — Lancia HF Integrale
5. Juha Kankkunen/Nicky Grist — SF/GB — Subaru Legacy 4WD Turbo

Rally of 1000 Lakes 27-29 August

1. Juha Kankkunen/Denis Giraudet — SF/F — Toyota Celica Turbo 4WD
2. Ari Vatanen/Bruno Berglund — SF/S — Subaru Impreza 555
3. Didier Auriol/Barnd Occelli — F — Toyota Celica Turbo 4WD
4. Tommi Mäkinen/Seppo Harjanne — SF — Lancia HF Integrale
5. Kenneth Eriksson/Staffan Parmander — SF — Mitsubishi Lancer Evolution

Telecom Rally Australia 18-21 September

1. Juha Kankkunen/Nicky Grist — SF/GB — Toyota Celica Turbo 4WD
2. Ari Vatanen/Bruno Berglund — SF/S — Subaru Impreza 4WD Turbo
3. François Delecour/Daniel Grataloup — F — Ford Escort RS Cosworth
4. Ross Dunkerton/Fred Gocentas — AUS — Mitsubishi Lancer Evolution
5. Sepp Haider/Klaus Wendel — A/D — Audi Coupé S2

Rallye San Remo 11-13 October

1. Gianfranco Cunico/Stefano Evangelisti — I — Ford Escort RS Cosworth
2. Carlos Sainz/Luis Moya — E — Lancia HF Integrale
3. Patrick Snyers/Dany Colebunders — B — Ford Escort RS Cosworth
4. Gilberto Pianezzola/Loris Roggia — I — Lancia HF Integrale
5. Piero Liatti/Alessandro Alessandrini — I — Subaru Legacy 4WD Turbo

Rallye Catalunya-Costa Brava 2-4 November

1. François Delecour/Daniel Grataloup — F — Ford Escort RS Cosworth
2. Didier Auriol/Bernard Occelli — I — Toyota Celica Turbo 4WD
3. Juha Kankkunen/Nicky Grist — SF/GB — Toyota Celica Turbo 4WD
4. Miki Biasion/Tiziano Siviero — I — Ford Escort RS Cosworth
5. Alex Fiorio/Vittorio Brambilla — I — Lancia HF Integrale

Network Q RAC Rally

1. Juha Kankkunen/Nicky Grist — SF/GB — Toyota Celica Turbo 4WD
2. Kenneth Eriksson/Staffan Parmander — S — Mitsubishi Lancer Evolution
3. Malcolm Wilson/Bryan Thomas — GB — Ford Escort RS Cosworth
4. François Delecour/Daniel Grataloup — F — Ford Escort RS Cosworth
5. Ari Vatanen/Bruno Berglund — SF/S — Subaru Impreza 555

1994 World Rally Championship Results

Monte Carlo Rally 22-27 January

1. François Delecour/Daniel Grataloup — F — Ford Escort Cosworth
2. Juha Kankkunen/Nicky Grist — SF/GB — Toyota Celica Turbo 4WD
3. Carlos Sainz/Luis Moya — E — Subaru Impreza 555
4. Miki Biasion/Tizano Siviero — I — Ford Escort Cosworth
5. Kenneth Eriksson/Staffan Parmander — S — Mitsubishi Lancer RS-E

TAP Rallye de Portugal 1-4 March

1. Juha Kankkunen/Nicky Grist — SF/GB — Toyota Celica Turbo 4WD
2. Didier Auriol/Bernard Occelli — I — Toyota Celica Turbo 4WD
3. Miki Biasion/Tiziano Siviero — I — Ford Escort Cosworth
4. Carlos Sainz/Luis Moya — E — Subaru Impreza 555
5. Fernando Peres/Ricardo Caldeira — P — Ford Escort Cosworth

Trust Bank Safari Rally 31 March-3 April

1. Ian Duncan/David Williamson — EAK — Toyota Celica Turbo 4WD
2. Kenjiro Shinozuka/Pentii Kuukkala — J/SF — Mitsubishi Lancer RS-E
3. Didier Auriol/Bernard Occelli — I — Toyota Celica Turbo 4WD
4. Patrick Njiru/Abdul Sidi — Subaru Impreza WRX-RA
5. Richard Burns/Robert Reid — Subaru Impreza WRX-RA

Tour de Corse 5-7 May

1. Didier Auriol/Bernard Occelli — I — Toyota Celica Turbo 4WD
2. Carlos Sainz/Luis Moya — E — Subaru Impreza 555
3. Andrea Aghini/Sauro Farnocchia — I — Toyota Celica Turbo 4WD
4. Juha Kankkunen/Nicky Grist — SF/GB — Toyota Celica Turbo 4WD
5. Miki Biasion/Tiziano Siviero — I — Ford Escort Cosworth

Acropolis Rally 28 May-1 June

1. Carlos Sainz/Luis Moya — E — Subaru Impreza 555
2. Armin Schwarz/Klaus Wicha — D — Mitsubishi Lancer RS-E2
3. Juha Kankkunen/Nicky Grist — SF/GB — Toyota Celica Turbo 4WD
4. Alex Fiorio/Vittoriop Brambilla — I — Lancia Delta HF Integrale
5. Ari Vatanen/Fabrizia Pons — SF/I — Ford Escort Cosworth

Rally YPF Argentina 30 June-2 July

1. Didier Auriol/Bernard Occelli — I — Toyota Celica Turbo 4WD
2. Carlos Sainz/Luis Moya — E — Subaru Impreza 555
3. Ari Vatanen/Fabrizia Pons — SF/I — Ford Escort Cosworth
4. Bruno Thiry/Stephane Prevot — B — Ford Escort Cosworth
5. Jorge Recalde/Martin Christie — RA — Mitsubishi Lancer RS-E

Rothmans Rally of New Zealand 29-31 July

1. Colin McRae/Derek Ringer — GB — Subaru Impreza 555
2. Juha Kankkunen/Nicky Grist — SF/GB — Toyota Celica Turbo 4WD
3. Armin Schwarz/Klaus Wicha — D — Mitsubishi Lancer RS-E2
4. Kenneth Eriksson/Staffan Parmander — S — Mitsubishi Lancer RS-E2
5. Didier Auriol/Bernard Occelli — I — Toyota Celica Turbo 4WD

Rally of 1000 Lakes 26-28 August

1. Tommi Mäkinen/Seppo Harjanne — SF — Ford Escort Cosworth
2. Didier Auriol/Bernard Occelli — I — Toyota Celica Turbo 4WD
3. Carlos Sainz/Luis Moya — E — Subaru Impreza 555
4. François Delecour/Daniel Grataloup — F — Ford Escort Cosworth
5. Marcus Gronholm/Voitto Silander — SF — Toyota Celica Turbo 4WD

Rallye San Remo 10-12 October

1. Didier Auriol/Bernard Occelli — I — Toyota Celica Turbo 4WD
2. Carlos Sainz/Luis Moya — E — Subaru Impreza 555
3. Miki Biasion/Tiziano Siviero — I — Ford Escort Cosworth
4. Bruno Thiry/Stephane Prevot — B — Ford Escort Cosworth
5. Colin McRae/Derek Ringer — GB — Subaru Impreza 555

Network Q RAC Rally 20-23 November

1. Colin McRae/Derek Ringer — GB — Subaru Impreza 555
2. Juha Kankkunen/Nicky Grist — SF/GB — Toyota Celica GT4
3. Bruno Thiry/Stephane Prevot — B — Ford Escort Cosworth
4. Stig Blomqvist/Benny Melander — S — Ford Escort Cosworth
5. Ari Vatanen/Fabrizia Pons — SF/I — Ford Escort Cosworth